T0329255

INCREASING RETURN

INCREASING RETURN

A STUDY OF THE RELATION BETWEEN THE
SIZE AND EFFICIENCY OF INDUSTRIES
WITH SPECIAL REFERENCE TO
THE HISTORY OF SELECTED
BRITISH & AMERICAN
INDUSTRIES
1850–1910

BY THE LATE

G. T. JONES

Edited by

COLIN CLARK

*Lecturer in Statistics in the
University of Cambridge*

CAMBRIDGE
AT THE UNIVERSITY PRESS
1933

CAMBRIDGE
UNIVERSITY PRESS

University Printing House, Cambridge CB2 8BS, United Kingdom

Cambridge University Press is part of the University of Cambridge.

It furthers the University's mission by disseminating knowledge in the pursuit of
education, learning and research at the highest international levels of excellence.

www.cambridge.org
Information on this title: www.cambridge.org/9781316509562

© Cambridge University Press 1933

First published 1933
First paperback edition 2015

A catalogue record for this publication is available from the British Library

ISBN 978-1-316-50956-2 Paperback

ANALYTICAL TABLE OF CONTENTS

PART III

THE LANCASHIRE COTTON INDUSTRY
1845–1913

PART IV

THE CLEVELAND PIG IRON INDUSTRY
1883–1925

PART V

THE MASSACHUSETTS COTTON INDUSTRY
1845–1920

PREFACE

IT is clear, other things being equal, that improvements in industrial efficiency whereby the physical quantity of productive resources consumed in the production of a unit of a particular commodity is reduced will increase economic welfare. It is the purpose of this study to enquire how far this economy of means toward ends progressed in certain industries during the period 1850–1910, and to what extent these changes were due to the expansion of the industries concerned.

Part I discusses the theory of Increasing Return and develops an original method of deriving a measure of changes in the real cost of particular commodities from selling price index numbers.

In Parts II–VI the method described in Part I is applied to obtain index numbers measuring changes in the real cost of (a) constructing and repairing buildings in London 1850–1910, (b) manufacturing unbleached cotton cloth in Lancashire and in Massachusetts 1850–1910, (c) smelting iron on the north-east coast of England (i.e. the Cleveland district) and in the United States 1883–1913.

Part VII discusses the general significance of the results obtained in Parts II–VI; first in their historical aspects (as a measure of industrial progress); second, as measures of the elasticities of return in particular industries during certain intervals of time, which is the coefficient chosen to indicate the relation between the size and the efficiency of an industry. The results, together with the original data, are presented in tabular form in the statistical appendices.

The entire thesis is original in conception and execution. The bulk of the statistical material has been taken from official documents and standard trade journals. A large part of it has not been available hitherto in a form convenient for the economist. My intellectual debts to Dr Marshall and Professor Pigou will be obvious even to a cursory reader.

G. T. J.

FOREWORD

G. T. JONES was born at Tunstall, Stoke-on-Trent, and lived there or in the immediate neighbourhood of the Potteries until his University days. He passed from the Newcastle-under-Lyme Grammar School to Emmanuel College in 1921. His was an able and dynamic personality, and his early environment, working on an already combative disposition, produced an individualistic outlook which was never materially modified, and afterwards influenced his Economic thinking more than he was prepared to admit.

It was almost a matter of accident that Economics became his main interest. He intended at first to follow a business career in the Pottery Industry in his own town. In view of this he decided to study for Part I of the Natural Sciences Tripos and to spend his third year "dabbling" in Economics. But "dabbling" was incompatible with his temperament. He was thorough and enthusiastic over most things that he took up; indeed his almost passionate concentration to see an undertaking through was reminiscent of the Ancient Mariner in its intensity and disregard for the exigencies of domestic organisation. This, together with a strong sense of responsibility, usually impelled him to take a leading part. His sympathies did not therefore run in narrow channels. He had energy to spare for wide interests both theoretical and practical, while his genius for friendships gathered together a large and most interesting circle of friends of very different types. Into these friendships, as into most things, he plunged with a suddenness sometimes disconcerting to such as lay store by the art of preliminary skirmishing.

Always susceptible to the attraction of strong personalities, he was lastingly indebted to the influence and friendship of his first tutor, Alex. Wood, and to all that he stands for in University life.

At the end of his second year he gained a first class in the Natural Sciences Tripos and in the next year attended lectures in Part II Economics. This course proved so attractive that he was persuaded to stay at Cambridge for a fourth year in order to complete it. Again he was placed in the first class at the final examination and attributed much of his success to the unobtrusive help and inspiration of his Director of Studies, the late Mr Lavington.

The Adelaide Stoll Scholarship, awarded by Christ's College, gave him a fifth year at Cambridge and an opportunity for research upon the problem of the statistical measurement of increasing returns in industry. By the end of the year he had worked out the method and applied it to three typical industries in Great Britain, namely, the Cotton, Pig Iron and Building trades—the latter presenting a formidable complex for statistical treatment. His work completed to this point received the Adam Smith Prize for 1926.

He was given the further opportunity of making an interesting though limited comparison between the rates of increasing returns in Great Britain and the United States, when he was awarded a Laura Spelman Rockefeller Fellowship tenable for two years in the United States. That summer he married and in the autumn sailed with his wife to America.

The first year was spent mainly at Harvard University attending lectures and collecting statistics. With regard to the latter he found it necessary to confine his attention to the Pig Iron and Cotton Industries, since the product of the American Building Industry is so different from that of Great Britain, that it defies statistical comparison. This work and all subsequent investigations throughout the States were made possible only by the extraordinary hospitality and practical friendship with which foreign students are welcomed. Among many others, Professor Taussig and the late Professor Allyn Young freely gave their time and the benefit of their advice and criticism.

The second year of this Fellowship was colourful and occasionally highly adventurous. He accomplished a tour of the States by car and train, courting many fruitful experiences by helping the seasonal immigration of labour from North to South. He punctuated his travel with concentrated bursts of writing, visits to important Universities en route and a prodigious number of interviews with business leaders of all types. Most of these interviews were naturally directed to throw light on the central problem of this book and form an interesting background to the statistical outline.

The thesis took final shape at Stanford University, California, and on his return to England he presented it at Cambridge and was awarded the Ph.D. degree in the autumn of 1928.

In the conclusion of this thesis one point emerges in connection with the relation between the size and efficiency of an industry, namely the importance of the part played by inventive ability responsible for the introduction of minor improvements in technique and organisation as opposed to those effected by great technical discoveries. To consider this more fully and to gain knowledge of the language and economic conditions of the country, G. T. Jones applied for a year's extension of his Fellowship for the purpose of travelling in Germany, where the extensive development of large scale industry along characteristic lines offers an interesting field for investigation. This extension was granted and he settled in Berlin for the winter to acquire a good working knowledge of German, and planned a tour of the chief industrial areas for the following spring and summer.

During the previous year he had decided, at the expiration of his travelling Fellowship, to accept a post offered him by the Gramophone Co., at Hayes, Middlesex. He was to have been an assistant to the General Manager and to have specialised in market research to discover whether the needs of actual and potential markets were being adequately met and also to estimate the probable demand for entirely new products. His qualifications in Science and Economics as well as his experience abroad were valuable assets for such work. It would, in addition, have afforded scope for the constructive imagination and power of leadership which he possessed in combination with keen analytical and critical powers. He ventured to hope too, that by supplementing his academic knowledge with business experience he might qualify himself to take part in some capacity in the considered solution of economic problems.

But before his Fellowship expired he was killed at the age of twenty-six in a motor accident in Rouen. He leaves two children, a daughter and a son.

Those who are particularly concerned that his work should be published, wish to express their thanks to Emmanuel College, and to the Rockefeller Foundation for the generosity that made it possible. Particularly are they indebted to Dr Alex. Wood who was mainly responsible for conducting negotiations to that end, and to Professor Pigou, Mr Dennis Robertson and Mr Colin Clark for their revision of the manuscript.

EDITH JONES

1933

PART I

INTRODUCTION

§1. DEFINITION

I

"INCREASING return is a relation between a quantity of effort and sacrifice on the one hand and a quantity of product on the other."[1] The theory discusses changes in industrial efficiency in relation to expanding industries and growing business units. It is therefore a part of the larger problem of social progress; the sketch which the discerning artist may clothe with colour.

The direct measurement of social progress is impossible, for it involves judgment of the relative values of different modes of living. Fortunately men differ widely in their appreciation of various states of consciousness and cannot therefore be persuaded to agree, for long, upon a direct measure of social welfare. The economist is more fortunate than the sociologist, for the measuring rod of money enables him, with care, to estimate the relative strength (at the margin) of heterogeneous motives. But with lapse of time or change of place the subjective value of money is liable to change in consequence of changes in the character of the subject, in the distribution of wealth, in the size of the national dividend, or in the efficiency of money as a medium of exchange. These changes in the measure itself are often so very important and difficult to correct that it is hazardous to draw any conclusions concerning economic progress or the economic welfare of different countries from statistics of national income. There is general agreement that, other things being equal, changes in the *per capita* output of concrete goods and services indicate economic progress. But the measurement of the physical growth of the national dividend is obstructed by changes in its composition: dividends which differ only in the proportions of

---

[1] Marshall, *Principles*, p. 319.

their constituents may be compared by index numbers; but qualitative changes elude measurement except by the device of chain index numbers. Large changes in the composition of the national dividend, whether of the quantitative or of the qualitative type, defy the technique of index numbers and the attempt to measure general economic progress therefore fails; but certain factors in the general process lend themselves more readily to statistical treatment and serve as a guide in speculation about the growth of economic welfare. In particular it is clear, other things being equal, that improvements in industrial efficiency, whereby the physical quantity of productive resources consumed in the production of a unit of a particular commodity is reduced, will increase economic welfare by enabling people to satisfy more wants with a given effort. It is my purpose in this investigation to enquire how far this economy of means towards ends progressed in certain industries during the closing decades of the nineteenth and the first decade of the twentieth century, and to what extent the changes were due to the expansion of the industries.

Throughout this enquiry that view of the production, value, and distribution of wealth which Dr Marshall has developed is assumed. "Fragmentary statical hypotheses are used as temporary auxiliaries to dynamical, or rather biological, conceptions." I have attempted to take up the concept of a negatively (or positively) inclined normal supply curve and adapt it to the phenomenon of industrial expansion as we know it in the Western world. Though the substance of my remarks comes from Marshall's fertile brain, their form has very largely been determined by Professor Pigou's writings. The National Dividend is central and it is considered in relation to the scale upon which industries and firms operate and to industrial forms. My object is twofold: to trace the influence of these factors upon production in the past and thence to learn what are the important questions in the study of present and future industrial development. It will save much vain labour if I may be allowed to refer to the *Economics of Welfare* (second edition), Part I and Part II, chapters i–x, for the background of my picture.

Some modern writers have formulated "abstract laws" calculated to bring into prominence one or other of the many causes which combine to produce those changes in the efficiency of production which are here designated "increasing" or "diminishing return". These variant terminologies are sometimes useful in analytical discussions, but many of them emphasise points which are obvious to anyone familiar with business practice. In the present essay I shall endeavour to measure the resultant effect of the expansion of particular industries upon their efficiency considered as instruments in the service of society, and shall define increasing return in accordance with my purpose. The interpretation of the results of the statistical enquiry is a study in organic growth, and in this connection I shall resort from time to time to one or other of the special meanings of the term, relying upon qualifying phrases together with the context to make my meaning clear. It is as if one sought to understand why an Irishman weighing twenty stones is able to put the shot more than twice as far as a Welshman weighing only ten stones: one has to consider advantages of height, reach, girth, biceps and calf measurements, in order to give a "scientific" explanation; yet, if the two be in proper training, it is sufficient to state that the one is twice as big as the other and can throw more than twice as far. So when we speak of increasing return to resources invested in industry, our attention is at once directed to the significant result of a complex process which is familiar, at least to economists.

In arriving at a convenient definition of the terms "increasing" and "diminishing returns" I shall follow Dr Marshall and Professor Pigou in conceiving economic activity to consist in the continuous flow of resources—land, labour, capital, business ability, supplied by the bounty of Nature or the effort of mankind—into the various industries, whence there flows a stream of goods and services which satisfy directly the needs and desires of men or facilitate the production of a larger stream of commodities. This point of view brings us into close touch with life and avoids certain difficulties inherent in the cruder static analyses.[1] It is necessary to make the further assumption that the rate of flow of resources, though subject periodically to temporary checks, does not fall off permanently in any of the

[1] Cf. Marshall, *Principles*, p. 808, n. 2.

industries under consideration. A study of decaying industries might be carried through by statistical methods similar to those here employed, but the interpretation of the results would be different. When population is expanding and industries are growing one may assume that resources will quickly distribute themselves so that each factor is remunerated at approximately the same rate in every employment in the country; but when industries are decaying the process of adjustment may take many years; the immobility of fixed capital, skilled labourers, and highly specialised business men dominate the situation. Moreover the technique developed during prosperous times may enable an industry to contract its output and establish itself on a smaller scale without losing some of the more important economies that accompanied its expansion; indeed the cost of production of an industry that showed markedly increasing returns may actually fall with the output.[1] We are concerned, therefore, with industries which are all expanding, though at different rates.[2]

II

To the modern economist it is clear that the satisfaction obtained from a given effort will be greatest when industry is so organised that a small increase in the effort put into each of several industries produces the same increase in aggregate satisfaction, i.e. makes the same addition to social welfare, in each industry, for if any other distribution existed, aggregate satisfaction could be increased by a transfer of resources from those occupations where their marginal contribution to satisfaction is relatively small to those where it is relatively large. In technical terms we may say that social welfare will be maximised by so distributing the efforts of a community that the marginal net product in satisfaction of a unit of effort is the same in all uses. Whether our object be to maximise average or total welfare, marginal and not average net products should be equated. Unfortunately the conception of increasing return as a relation between effort and

---

[1] Cf. C. J. Bullock, *Quarterly Journ. of Economics*, August 1902, pp. 505–9.

[2] A tax or bounty should therefore be conceived as checking or encouraging the expansion of the industry upon which it falls, but in no case producing an actual diminution of its output.

satisfaction to which this argument naturally leads, is valueless as a guide to industrial policy in the absence of some measure of changes in effort and satisfaction. Dr Marshall warns us that "to measure outlay and output in terms of money is a tempting but a dangerous resource", but the transition must needs be made.

The expansion of a particular industry may confer special benefit upon the rich or upon the poor, or it may throw a burden of smoke upon people who cannot obtain damages from the prosperous manufacturer; the very tastes and customs of the people may be changed.[1] These and other questions must be considered in each case; they exhibit no measurable tendency which can be embodied in a manageable definition of increasing return. Industrial development may, however, lead to changes which are more significant, from the present point of view. The physical volume of resources required to produce a physical unit of the product may increase or decrease as a result of expansion, and where this occurs it is probable that the industry is yielding a diminishing or increasing return in satisfaction as greater effort is devoted to it. *When, time being allowed for appropriate reorganisation, an increase in the quantity of resources invested in an industry causes a more than proportionate increase in the physical volume of the product, the industry is subject to Increasing Return. Diminishing Return is correspondingly defined.*[2]

The term "quantity of resources" presents certain difficulties. The unit is complex, comprising labour, materials, the use of buildings, machines and land, the services of management, etc.,

[1] Pigou, *Economics of Welfare*, Pt II, chap. viii.

[2] Cf. Edgeworth's definition (*Economic Journ.* September 1911, pp. 350–9: reprinted in *Collected Papers*, vol. I, pp. 71 seq.).

My definition corresponds to Edgeworth's secondary definition and it is the primary which is important for welfare theory. Since, in competitive conditions, price tends always to equal average rather than marginal cost (in terms of resources) statistical studies based on selling price reveal directly the presence of increasing or diminishing return according to the secondary definition. It is true that an aggregate cost schedule might be computed from the list of average costs and the corresponding output and the marginal cost function required for the primary definition might be deduced, but this is hardly worth while so far as the present enquiry is concerned, for all the industries studied show constant or continuously increasing return so that the all flowing into production in a bewildering variety of qualities and combinations. How can one determine the relative importance of the several factors? Up to a point I follow Professor Pigou: "A unit, or if we prefer the term, a dose of resources, may be taken to mean the use for a unit of time of a pound's worth of resources, so that two units or doses are equal, whatever their internal constitution, provided only that the aggregate market values of the constituents of each of them make up £1".[1] In short the different factors are to be "weighted" according to their relative prices. So long as the supply prices of the different kinds of resources remain stable this method suffices, but when the prices of the factors vary there may be changes in the money value of the resources employed in an industry without any changes in the physical quantities. This difficulty cannot be surmounted entirely[2] but, provided that the comparative prices of the factors do not change greatly during the period under investigation, valuable practical results can be obtained by assigning weights in accordance with the prices at a given time (the base year) and *keeping them constant* throughout the period studied. This is the

difference between the two definitions is one of degree only. Moreover, the schedule of average real costs shows more clearly the origin of the data and is useful for other purposes than the present. The inclusion of a law of diminishing returns co-ordinate with my law of increasing returns appears at first sight an idle formality; but I suspect that some of the forces tending to raise the real cost of production as industry expands may be as powerful as those which make for economy. Apart from the consideration that scarcity of natural resources may shift the intensive margin and compel the adoption of a less efficient proportionate combination of the factors as production increases, there is the fact that the work of co-ordinating the several parts necessarily increases the growth of the economic organism. The social costs of industrial expansion are not commonly recognised simply because they do not fall directly upon the expanding enterprises but are disseminated like external economies, through the community, and return after many days in the form of municipal taxes, collective bargaining machinery, etc. Yet the reality of these external diseconomies is clear when one compares, say, the iron industry of Pittsburgh, Pa., with that of Birmingham, Ala.; or the manufacture of cotton textiles in New England with the corresponding industry in North and South Carolina. Cf. pp. 25–6.

Just as individual enterprise cannot appropriate external economies, it cannot avoid these diseconomies of expansion or, in practice, be compelled to bear their full cost. It is incorrect to suppose therefore that, the supply prices of the factors being constant, the expansion of an industry will never entail increasing unit costs. Cf. Pigou, *Economic Journ.* June 1927, p. 197.

[1] *Economics of Welfare*, p. 113.
[2] Marshall, *Principles*, p. 171.

policy here adopted. Changes in "real costs" (so defined) will reflect changes that have taken place in the rate of return to labour and sacrifice more closely, the smaller the changes that have taken place in relative prices during the period. In the statistical work which follows, I have taken as base a year near the end of the period studied (*circa* 1850–1910) in which the prices of the factors appear to have been fairly normal. My index numbers therefore reflect changes in the "real cost" of production from the point of view of the residents of the countries concerned, in the years immediately preceding the Great War.

At the suggestion of Professor Sraffa, Professor Pigou has recently restricted his discussion of variations in real costs with the size of industries to "commodities which individually employ so small a proportion of each of the several factors of production that no practicable changes in the scale of their output could sensibly affect the relative values of these factors".[1] This is an unworkable conception, for it is doubtful if any commodity satisfies this condition if productive resources are classified into homogeneous factors. The various kinds of land, labour and capital have their special aptitudes and earn special rents when those industries expand which they are particularly well suited to serve. Changes in the expenses of production due to these special rents do not represent changes in real cost in any sense of the term, for, *ex hypothesi*, they could not be earned in other opportunities; they are simply transfers from consumers to producers. The difficulty cannot be avoided by assuming that the several homogeneous factors have definite supply prices towards which their values will always tend, for the various kinds of land and types of men are jointly supplied by Nature and we have little if any control over the proportions.

In all discussions of real cost functions it is sufficient to treat these special rents as simple transfers without influence upon real costs. Those changes, however, in the prices of the factors which react upon the costs of other industries cannot be neglected, nor can the discussion be confined in practice to industries so small that sensible price changes of this kind do not occur as

[1] *Economic Journ.* June 1927, p. 192.

a consequence of changes in the size of individual industries; for the greater specialisation of labour, machinery and managing ability which make possible a larger output at a lower average cost are associated with the growth of large industries or groups of allied industries, while those investments in technical development which are coming to play an important rôle in industrial growth are profitable or unprofitable according to the aggregate size of all the industries which can make use of the inventions. It is true, as Professor Pigou points out, that a hypothetical cost function can, in imagination, be constructed to show the causal relation between these economies and the output of any particular commodity; but why try? The interdependence of the demand functions and of the supply functions of various commodities is not a serious obstacle to the mathematical economist who wishes to formulate in the abstract an equilibrium theory of value, nor yet to the realistic economist who would explain the process by which the prices of commodities are caused to approximate to their equilibrium values. The choice between the monopolistic and the competitive approach to the latter problem must be decided by the attitude of the entrepreneur; if it is the general policy of the directors of industrial enterprises to push their production up to the margin where cost equals price in the manner outlined in Appendix III, the competitive analysis is appropriate; if, on the contrary, the directors of industry endeavour to set a price which will maximise their monopoly revenues, then the pricing process should be described in the manner indicated by Professor Sraffa[1] and worked out in detail by Mr E. H. Chamberlain.[2] Upon the whole I think it safe to assume that the competitive policy prevails in manufacturing industry generally, although there are undoubtedly situations in which producers exercise their (temporary) monopoly power. The growth of producers' associations and a more intelligent appreciation of the inter-relation of markets have encouraged the monopolistic policy, but these tendencies have been checked by the corporate organisation of industry which

[1] *Economic Journ.* December 1926, pp. 535–50.
[2] *Monopolistic Competition*, a thesis presented for the degree of Ph.D. at Harvard University, 1927.

has placed expansion on a par with profit as a measure of business success.

The normal (long period) supply schedule simply summarises the results of the competitive process of price-making for the commodity (or group of commodities) to which it refers. The several supply prices represent the normal full expenses per unit of the corresponding outputs. Since changes which originate in other industries are excluded, the normal supply curve can only be drawn by the aid of speculation concerning the consequences of changes in the normal volume of production in the industry considered; but all changes in the expenses of production which may be expected to result from the expansion of the industry must be included, whether they occur directly or through the reaction of other industries to the growth of the one. If sufficient data were available it might be possible, by partial correlation, to estimate the causal relationship between past changes in cost and the output of particular commodities although the logic of the process would be suspicious. Looking forward to the future we cannot make even an intelligent guess about the normal supply schedule unless we treat as units industries which are intimately connected by technological and geographical ties. "That is to say, the economies of large scale production can seldom be allocated exactly to any one industry: they are in great measure attached to groups, often large groups, of correlated industries."[1] There is no reason to despair because of this limitation, for the concept of a normal (long period) supply schedule is a tool for the analysis of economic progress (past and future), and for this purpose the restriction, though inconvenient, is not an insuperable obstacle. Indeed those industrial units which are most convenient for the analysis of the economies of production on a large scale are often also the most convenient units for statistical treatment, e.g. the manufacture of cotton textiles, the building trades, the milling industry. It is true that there are a few large industries, e.g. the chemical group, the heavy iron and steel industry and the engineering trades, which embrace such a heterogeneous mass of products and processes that they defy our present

[1] Marshall, *Industry and Trade*, p. 188.

statistical technique, and are yet integers so far as the processes of reorganisation which make for increasing return are concerned.

For the purposes of this enquiry, therefore, the boundaries between industries must be determined by technological considerations rather than the convenience of the theory of value. The product of an industry will usually be complex, and changes in the size of a single industry may be expected to cause sensible changes in the supply prices of the factors of production. Further difficulties arise from the fact that industrial expansion often results in the employment of new kinds of labour and materials and the production of new qualities of goods and services; but it will be convenient to postpone consideration of these difficulties until the next chapter, and to assume for the present that the product of an industry is a composite commodity of uniform quality and that the same factors are used in its production throughout the period, though in varying proportions. We shall see later that these assumptions might be removed without altering our conclusions, but the discussion would become exceedingly clumsy. A schedule may now be constructed showing the prices that will be necessary to call forth the regular production of different amounts of the product as an industry expands (for the normal supply curve is not reversible), assuming that no changes take place which are not causally related to the expansion of the industry. The problem is to deduce from the normal supply schedule the cost function which will indicate what changes in the rate of return society may expect from the industry as it expands. In competitive conditions normal price is equal to the average full expenses of production of the corresponding output, and it is clear that changes in the expenses of production are the resultant of changes in the quantities of the several factors employed per unit of product and changes in their prices. *Prima facie* it appears that all changes in the prices of the factors of production should be regarded as transfers and eliminated, so that the cost function would be derived from the expense function by simply correcting for changes in the prices of the factors. This I believe to be the practical solution of the problem, but there are difficulties. A rise in the prices of specialised factors may be expected to call forth a larger supply but only at a greater subjective cost, that is to say, the marginal disutility of supplying specialised factors increases considerably with the supply. This applies not only to the services of workers, managers, etc., who by reason of their natural aptitudes or immobility seek employment in the particular industry; but also to materials (e.g. cotton and iron ore) which are specially suited to the industry but limited in supply, for the producers of such materials will encounter a diminishing return to their efforts as they endeavour to force larger supplies from limited sources. A slight shifting of the intensive margin occurs of course in respect of the supply of all factors of production whenever an industry expands, but the movement will generally be negligible in the case of non-specialised factors. Even in the case of specialised factors the *average* disutility per unit supplied is not likely to change appreciably with practicable variations in the amounts supplied. Changes in the prices of specialised factors may therefore be regarded simply as transfers without serious error. There remains the question how to weight the different items in the complex unit of resources. So far as specialised factors are concerned it is a matter of practical indifference whether the relative values which prevailed when the old output was being produced or those which prevail when the industry is established upon the new scale are chosen. But those changes in the relative values of the factors which react upon the costs of other industries cannot be neglected without serious error. For an apparent increase in the rate of return to resources invested in one industry may have been secured by depriving other industries of the co-operation of Nature or of the assistance of skilled labour. In these circumstances it is impossible to devise a precise measure of changes in the quantity of resources employed per unit of product, although, by weighting first according to the old and then the new relative values, limits may be defined within which the change must lie. If these limits be close together the upper or the lower or any intermediate value such as the arithmetic mean may be used indifferently when constructing the cost function. If the range of indeterminateness is wide the task must not be attempted. This is ambiguous and unsatisfactory in point of logic, but the tool should not be discarded because its usefulness is limited. As a matter of fact, the range of indeterminateness of real costs is likely in practice to be very small, even for large industries. The statistical work which follows refers to past developments, and no distinction is made between those changes in the relative values of the factors which were and those which were not the result of the expansion of the particular industry. In the index numbers of real costs the various factors of production are weighted according to their relative values at the end of the period studied (1910). As a check I recalculated the index numbers for Massachusetts Cotton Textiles, assigning weights according to the relative values of the factors in 1860. This industry was chosen as a check and the year 1860 as a secondary base because it appeared that the discrepancy between the two measures of real costs would be larger than would be revealed by any other choice from the data under investigation. Yet the two curves showing changes in the real cost of cotton manufacture in Massachusetts between 1850 and 1910 are so similar in shape that the difference is negligible; while the ratio between the real cost of cotton manufacture in Massachusetts in 1850 and 1910 was $\frac{185}{101}$ according to the base 1910 and $\frac{162}{100}$ according to the base 1860. Thus the two measures are as $1 : 1 \cdot 14$ and the range of indeterminateness in this extreme case is less than 15 % of the change to be measured.

A second difficulty arises from the inclusion of land as a productive resource valued in the "real costs of production" at its rental in the base year.[1] From the social point of view, rent is not the reward of effort and does not, therefore, represent a real cost of production in the accepted sense of the term. But

[1] Sir William Petty writing in 1691 appears to have been among the first to reckon the use of land a real cost of production (*vide Political Anatomy of Ireland*, pp. 63–7, i.e. pp. 180–2 in C. H. Hull's collected works of Petty). He values all the factors of production in terms of the day's food—a biological utility—and imputes a specific product to Land and to Art as well as Simple Labour. Petty's argument is thus far lucid, but he becomes confused when attempting to explain scarcity value by the equation of Art and Opinion.

the maximisation of the national dividend requires that the marginal net product of land shall be equal in all uses, just as the marginal net products of labour, or capital, while there are elements of surplus in the return to labour and capital. The normal rates of wages and interest measure on the one hand the marginal disutility of supply, and on the other the marginal contribution of capital or labour to the product, so the additional outlay on rent in an expanding industry measures on the one hand the dissatisfaction involved in diverting the land to the new employment, i.e. the measure of the loss of Nature's co-operation in the industries from which it is withdrawn, on the other hand its marginal utility to the new tenant. Thus, when considering small transfers of resources from industry to industry, we are close to a measure of the changes of effort and satisfaction involved if we weight the various items at their money values, including the use of land as a productive resource and an item in real costs.[1]

Thirdly, the amount of resources required per unit of the product produced is to be estimated when the industry has fully adapted itself to the normal production of the output in question. Thus the problem is essentially long period.[2] The potency of that principle of substitution, whose working in a competitive regime Dr Marshall has made familiar, is assumed and time allowed for it to bring about the most economical distribution of resources among their different uses which is possible in the prevailing state of knowledge and business technique. Professor Edgeworth has discussed this process of adjustment from the standpoint of increasing returns to further investment in a single

[1] It is perhaps worth while to point out that the rent element appears mostly in the cost of raw materials when the subject under investigation is a manufacturing or distributing industry. My method would be difficult to apply to extractive industries because location rather than "fertility" dominates the rentals of agricultural land, mines and quarries so that it would be exceedingly difficult to compile an index of changes in the price of land of a given quality.

[2] But not too long! There are some applications of the theory of increasing return in which it is proper to permit a generation to elapse before appraising the results of industrial expansion (e.g. the protection of infant industries) but it is sufficient in the present study if time is allowed for workmen to be trained to new duties, for new factories to be erected, and for machines adapted to the new scale of production to be designed and installed.

concern.[1] He shows how business psychology and technical difficulties (e.g. the finite and varying size of the units of the factors of production, shortage of capital and lack of borrowing power) may modify the path by which the entrepreneur proceeds towards that combination of resources which yields him the greatest profit, but cannot substantially affect the ultimate result of the process.

Lastly, my definition must not be taken to imply a search for historical laws. Knowledge of the changes which have taken place in industrial efficiency is not without interest to the economic historian, but the propositions which I am anxious to apply to the industries I study are concerned with the relation between such changes in the real cost of production and the magnitude first of the undertaking, second of the industry of which it is a part. It is an easy matter to distinguish in theory between those changes in efficiency which are and those which are not the result of the expansion of an industry, but only a very rough delimitation of the two classes is possible in practice. All changes in technique—inventions, division of labour, differentiation and integration of business units, etc., etc.—which result from the employment of a larger volume of resources in an industry are elements in the social net product of the additional investment, while such changes as would have occurred independently of the expansion must be excluded from our consideration.[2] Both kinds of industrial progress take place concurrently, and it is therefore impossible to obtain a precise measure of the strength of the tendency to increasing return by analysis of the trend of real costs in an industry. Few would deny, however, that external forces operated to lower real costs almost continuously in the manufacturing industries of the Western world during the period 1850–1910; and this statement may be expected to hold generally except in time of war or other violent political disturbance. Correlation of changes in the real cost of production with the expansion of manufacturing industries therefore fixes an upper limit to the tendency to in-

---

[1] "Contributions to the Theory of Railway Rates". Section 1 is highly relevant; see especially *Economic Journ.* 1911, pp. 366, 367.

[2] Cf. Marshall, *Principles*, pp. 460–1.

creasing return in each industry; that is to say, it gives limiting values for the elasticities of return in the several industries.[1] No general rule can be given for estimating by how much the actual value of the elasticity of return differs from the limiting value obtained by statistical investigation. It is sometimes possible, as with the introduction of machine-made woodwork in the London building trade during the 'seventies and 'eighties, to correct specifically for the major external influences, but these cases are rare. It is usually necessary to confine one's investigations to periods of tranquillity when the industry in question is progressing steadily by the application of known mechanical principles rather than by revolutionary changes in technique, e.g. the principles of modern cotton manufacturing machinery (with the exception of the automatic loom which was the calculated result of experimentation) were widely known in both America and England before 1850, the beginning of my statistical enquiry. In these circumstances correlation of the trend of real costs with the expansion of an industry is a useful indication of the strength of the tendency to increasing return in that industry. A rough allowance may be made when interpreting the results for external influences, but for many purposes the limiting value obtained by statistical enquiry may be used as a measure of the elasticity of return without serious error. External influences upon the efficiency of an industry may take the form of labour agitation or legal restrictions, but the prototype is invention.

There are epoch-making discoveries (e.g. the steam engine, the electric motor, the internal combustion engine) which, as we look backward, may appear to have been the inevitable consequence of the social developments preceding them, but which one could not possibly have anticipated however intimately one knew the environment from whence they sprang. Such discoveries are the creators of new industries rather than economies reaped from the growth of old. But the *application* of known mechanical principles to particular industries bears a closer relation to their growth; one may reasonably expect that the development of commercial flying will bring with it numerous inventions which

---

[1] Elasticity of return is the ratio between the rate of expansion of the industry and the rate of fall of real costs.

are in a very real sense "called forth" by the expansion of the industry. Moreover the entrepreneur who is considering a venture in commercial aviation will expect to reap large gains from such technical progress; these economies must therefore be reckoned in the long period supply price of aerial transport.[1]

But there is need for caution in drawing this distinction. Scientific interest, sheer curiosity, mere accident play a large part in discovery; commercial interest may only have hastened inventions which would have happened sooner or later in any case. This consideration is especially important when we are comparing the relative strength of the tendencies to increasing return in the industries of different countries. Allowances must be made for differences in the natural inventiveness of the people in the two countries, and at different times in the same country. The matter needs careful consideration in each concrete case, but sufficient has perhaps been said to indicate the solution in broad outline. All those changes in technique which might reasonably be expected to follow from, or to be hastened by, the expansion of an industry, are part of the social net product of the additional investment and are elements in the tendency to increasing return.

This conception of increasing return facilitates analysis of certain divergences between the social and the private interest in a competitive regime. The essence of the matter is that the principle of substitution operates to secure the most efficient proportionate combination of the factors of production in each industry, but fails to effect the optimum distribution of resources among the various industries because the rate of return to each unit of resources must be the same.[2] "The key fact", says Professor Pigou, "is that, under conditions of simple competition the gain due to the economies that make increasing return possible—it does not matter whether they are internal or external—cannot stay with the producers, for if it did these producers would be obtaining an exceptional profit and new resources would be tempted into the industry."[3] Under competitive con-

---

[1] Cf. Marshall, *Principles*, p. 460.
[2] Cf. Professor Pigou, "The Laws of Diminishing and Increasing Cost", *Economic Journ.* June 1927, p. 197.
[3] *Economics of Welfare*, 2nd ed., p. 193.

ditions, therefore, while the value of the marginal private net products of resources will, in equilibrium, be the same in all industries, there will be a tendency for the marginal social net product of resources to be high in industries showing an increasing return and low in diminishing returns industries. A *prima facie* case is thus established for a bounty upon the former and a tax upon the latter group, or for such state interference as will bring about the same result. If "elasticity of return" be defined as the ratio of the rate of the expansion of the industry (measured in output) to the proportionate fall in the "real cost" of production (measured in resources) then the *ad valorem* rate of bounty or tax called for will vary directly as the difference between the reciprocals of the elasticities of demand and return. (In the case of diminishing return the elasticity of return is negative and the numerical quantities are therefore added.)[1]

This simple statement of "the case against *laissez faire*" can only be made if we adhere rigidly to the definition of increasing return as a relation between a quantity of resources and a physical product. "Changes in the prices of the product and of resources are of the very essence of the situation. Increased prices for the use of land and of the other factors in production do not represent an increased using up of resources in the work of production. They merely represent transfers of purchasing power."[2] In his early treatment of this problem, Professor Pigou brushed aside these price changes as negligible; in the second edition of the *Economics of Welfare*, the importance of changes in the rent of land consequent upon the growth of particular industries is admitted. But it is clear that appreciable changes in the supply price of other factors of production may result from the expansion of particular industries and may continue long enough to command notice in the present analysis.[3] The contention that

---

[1] This result holds only for conditions in which the whole of the bounty goes to the entrepreneur, i.e. there is no rise in the supply prices of the factors of production upon expansion of the industry.

[2] Allyn Young, *Quarterly Journ. of Economics*, 1913, p. 683.

[3] H. S. Jevons in the *British Coal Trade* (pp. 103–5) lays stress upon the fact that high wages had to be paid to secure an adequate supply of labour in the South Wales coal fields during the period 1840–70. Collieries in the new districts had to pay higher wages than the correct rates in the older neighbouring districts in order to attract labour, "although the description of work

the changes in the supply prices of capital and labour, consequent upon the expansion of particular industries will be negligible, rests upon the assumption that the increase in demand for any factor will be but a small proportion of the available supply of the factor. If all labour or all capital were homogeneous this assumption would be justifiable. Account must, however, be taken of the fact that these terms are but generic names for innumerable species differing according as the worker is required to display qualities of physical or mental strength, patience and imitation or independence and assertiveness; or the lender is asked to combine with the service of waiting a large or a small amount of risk bearing or management. When it is considered that there is a large element of jointness in the supply of the different qualities and kinds of labour or of capital, it appears that the expansion of particular industries will frequently modify the supply prices of the factors of production, other than land, engaged therein. Such changes will, in general, be negligible only when infinitesimal changes in the scale of production are under consideration. For practical purposes finite changes must be considered, and changes in the supply prices of the factors of

and the seams in which that work was to be done were identical in every respect". The grounds upon which the higher rates of pay were claimed by the men were often sound at the time: such as lack of housing accommodation near the new pits which caused the men to walk several miles to and from work, or the distance of meat and vegetable markets from such dwelling places as were available near to work. In later times employers erected ample dwelling accommodation—villages sprang up, markets were established, and all the advantages, including regularity of employment, which the workmen possessed in the older districts were available in the new, but the difference in wage rates continued. Jevons quotes from Alexander Dalziel who wrote in 1872: "The owners of every new colliery acting upon this principle of offering inducements to obtain labour, several anomalies in the rates of wages were created, and they have not since been reconciled". It is estimated (1872) that the scales of wages at pits belonging to the colliery owners in the Aberdare Valley are 15 % higher than at the pits of the iron-masters in the Merthyr Valley, while wage rates in the Rhondda Valley are 10 % higher still. It appears that long continued changes of wages amounting to 15–25 % were in this instance directly caused by the expansion of the coal industry in South Wales. In a recent study of *Wages in the Coal Industry* (p. 86) J. W. F. Rowe finds startling anomalies which are in some cases correlated with the expansion of the local industry, but "the generalisation that the increase (in wages) is connected with the rate of expansion will not hold good". On the other hand the great differences that he finds in the relative movements between the wages of skilled and unskilled workers in the different districts suggests a high degree of immobility as between districts.

production specifically eliminated before the elasticity of return is discussed. In short, elasticity of return and elasticity of supply are only equal when the prices of the factors of production are unaltered by the industrial expansion under discussion.

In the current version of his argument[1] Professor Pigou appears to define increasing and diminishing return in terms of resources: "We are here thinking forward and considering whether an increase in the scale of production in an industry...would, taken by itself, *cause* the *real* cost of production per unit to be greater or less" (section 3). (I have taken the liberty of italicising "real".) Yet in the next section (4) he makes rising or falling *costs to purchasers* the criterion of increasing or diminishing return. If the conception of varying real costs (in terms of resources) be retained, the argument of section 3 may be extended to cover diminishing returns, while that of section 6 (which modifies section 3) may be omitted. On the other hand the conception of varying cost to the consumer as output is varied in a competitive market, is convenient in certain problems of normal value and is in general use. Perhaps it is best to separate the two, reserving increasing and diminishing *returns* for the notion of varying real costs in terms of resources, and decreasing and increasing expenses to describe a relation between normal supply price and output. Had this distinction been emphasised in our terminology many mistakes might have been avoided. In the next section of the present essay some reference is made to the long period relation between increasing return and price; the difficult short period problem is touched upon in Appendix II. Apart altogether from matters of exposition it seems necessary to distinguish between economies which are, at first, internal to the firm making the investment and those which are external to it: to revive that distinction between the direct and indirect product of an additional unit of resources which was well made in the first edition of the *Economics of Welfare* (Pt II, chap. viii, section 2).

If competition is effective the investor will doubtless be compelled ultimately to transfer any excess of the direct product above the normal return to his investment either to the con-

---

[1] *Economics of Welfare*, 2nd ed., Pt II, chap. x.

sumers in the form of lower prices or to the whole body of
producers in higher wages for labour, prices for raw materials,
or interest upon capital. But he may be left in possession of the
direct fruits of his enterprise for so long that the distant prospect
of being compelled to share with others is no deterrent to his
present investment; so far as this is the case there is no divergence between the private and the social interest where increasing return is due to internal economies—there remains only
the difference measured by the indirect product. The importance
of this consideration will of course vary with the relative importance of external and internal economy and the time required
for adaptation to a new scale of production—each case demands
separate investigation but some broad generalisations seem
possible. First, there is a correlation between the importance of
internal economies and the time allowed for the investor to enjoy
the fruits of his enterprise or good fortune. For example, the
iron and steel manufacturer who decides to install a large plant
and to spend a large sum upon experiments with a new furnace
design, electrical charging, mechanical casting, or rolling stock
transferring the metal matter from stage to stage of its manufacture, may reasonably expect that the long life of this plant
and the very magnitude of the undertaking will deter rivals from
following his example for several years—he expects important
internal economies and time to reap the fruits. Mr Henry Ford
forges ahead with ambitious schemes for internal economies,
and his own achievements constitute a formidable protective
barrier against the competition of rivals. Second, the patent
laws enable inventors to retain the advantage of their discoveries
for many years if they wish. Now it is not generally possible to
protect fundamental discoveries such as the thermionic valve
effectively, but these are rarely the anticipated product of commercial enterprise. Moreover the successful business concern
wins its high profits not by guarding secrets jealously, but by
keeping just a little ahead of its rivals, adopting new processes a
little earlier, and continually improving its organisation—a quite
small differential advantage constantly flying before them seems
to suffice to tempt business men to a prodigious expenditure of
effort. Third, the average life of firms engaged in an industry

will be an important factor in the situation. In the days of the private business or partnership, the entrepreneur rarely enjoyed the fruits of his ingenuity or daring for long, "for the full life of a large concern rarely extends over more than eight or ten years"; on the other hand, the business man of that day probably did not look so far ahead as his modern successors. The modern corporation, immortal in law, may build up strong business connections which give it a touch of monopoly power and enable it to retain the fruits of internal economies for many years, although the conditions are competitive in the broad sense required for long period problems; but it also lays its plans in a more far-sighted fashion so that the differential gains may be necessary to call forth the supply.

It appears, therefore, that the investor is likely to enjoy the whole direct product of his enterprise for so long a time that there is no appreciable difference between the private and social interest so far as internal economies are concerned. The original analysis in the text of the first edition of the *Economics of Welfare* (Pt II, chap. viii) therefore stands substantially correct, the difference between the private and social net product of additional investment is measured by the indirect product, and the distinction between internal and external economies, or diseconomies, of expansion becomes all important.[1]

Dr Marshall[2] reached conclusions similar to those of Professor Pigou in this matter by an analysis of the effect of a tax or bounty upon industries obeying the laws of decreasing and increasing cost, and on the consumers' surplus. The method has attractions but it is difficult to adapt satisfactorily to the concrete problem

---

[1] The benefits of external economies are of course often enjoyed for a considerable period by the entrepreneurs who happen to be entrenched when the economies become available but these returns are in the nature of windfalls, they are not the anticipated product of investment. It is clear from the discussion in the text that there would be a historical decline in the real costs of manufacture without industrial expansion and these developments must be included among the economies which individual firms entering an industry may expect to accrue to them as they grow, i.e. they are internal economies; but they are not part of the tendency to increasing return in the sense in which it is employed in the text. External economies, on the other hand, wait upon the expansion of markets and are the technological expression of the tendency to increasing return.

[2] *Principles*, Bk v, chap. xiii.

of the private versus the social interest in the development of industry. In a series of brilliant footnotes (esp. p. 469 n. 2 and 473 n.) and in Appendix H Marshall gives specific warnings of the difficulties on the side of supply; but he also assumes that the demand curve represents the utility curve and is stable throughout. This seems to me to do violence to the facts and to be unnecessary to the argument. The benefit accruing to the community from the development of industries which obey the law of increasing returns lies in the larger flow of goods and services from a given effort. Money need only be introduced as a common measure of the different factors of production and the various kinds of product; the key fact remains true if we reject the notion of consumers' surplus—the appropriable return to resources invested in industries which yield an increasing return is less than the full net product of the investment, whereas in diminishing returns industries it may be greater.[1] Society has, therefore, a direct economic interest in the way a man spends his income: "For in so far as he spends it on things which obey the law of diminishing return, he makes those things more difficult to be obtained by his neighbours, and thus lessens the real purchasing power of their incomes; while in so far as he spends it on things which obey the law of increasing return, he makes those things more easy of attainment to others, and thus increases the real purchasing power of their incomes".[2]

So far it has been implicitly assumed that the real cost of production is an almost continuously increasing or decreasing function of the quantity produced: no account has been taken of the fact that the factors of production are not continuously variable and that we must consider finite increments of output, the addition of new *processes* of production; but these considerations do not affect the long period problem very much. There remains, however, another type of argument for state interference: the bounty will encourage private enterprise to press forward and reap those economies which result from the

---

[1] The fact remains true but we could not make use of it without the philosophical concept of consumers' surplus (i.e. of diminishing utility), for without it our welfare theory would be untenable.

[2] Marshall, *Principles*, p. 470.

natural development of the existing organisation: the more minute division of labour and specialisation of machines and businesses upon narrower ranges of work, etc.—such results will be effected by the principle of substitution. But it is possible that very great economies might be reaped and an industry re-established upon a more efficient basis by a change in the character of its organisation. Such reorganisation would generally involve a much larger output at much lower cost and may, therefore, be considered under the head of increasing return. It may happen that a business genius sees how these economies could be effected, and devotes his energies to their achievement by forming a combine to control the industry or by the peaceful persuasion of his associates; but the legal and financial difficulties besetting the former path and the persistence called for in the face of stupid opposition to the latter, make it improbable that such developments will take place quickly unless society interferes on its own behalf. "More advantageous systems are approached only through fundamental reconstructions and then realised in detail by the operation of the law of substitution."[1] The type of interference called for in this connection is, I think, best distinguished from the "bounty" by the name "specific".[2] For example, one might have specific interference designed to standardise the essential parts of the motor or aeroplane by a national or international agreement; to establish a produce market for iron and steel goods at various stages of manufacture so that the system of contracting with particular firms might be superseded by the method of purchase by description in the open market, as in the Manchester Cotton Exchange, thus enabling firms to specialise on narrower ranges of production, confident that they can get their share of the orders coming into the market whatever their source; to cause producers to pool information which is of common interest, e.g. by establishing central research institutes. I suspect that enquiry would show that society would benefit greatly if governments adopted a policy of specific interference designed to secure the

[1] Chapman, *Economic Journ.* March 1908, p. 55 n.
[2] Mr Herbert Hoover's work as United States' Secretary of Commerce is an outstanding example of specific interference; *vide* recent annual reports of the United States Department of Commerce.

advantages of production on a great scale largely as external economies instead of allowing great combines to grow up and then seeking in vain to control them. I shall return to the point later, but it may be observed here that the same result may finally be achieved by the disintegration of large combinations into a group of departments which are in effective competition for the most part, but have a common policy in, say, finance and marketing. It seems likely, however, that such a loose combination, though highly efficient internally, will exercise monopoly power to the social hurt in a way not open to specialised independent firms integrated by a well-organised produce market.

Notice that interference of the first type fails to achieve its object if the required revenue be derived from the producers who are to receive the bounty; but the cost of specific interference may be defrayed by a tax upon the industry without affecting the result. Of course the arguments put forward only suggest lines of thought for the statesman, for chambers of commerce and the like; a host of economic considerations would need to be taken into account in fashioning a practical policy.

III

Statistical convenience combined with the reasons suggested above have led to the following definitions:

If, time being allowed for appropriate reorganisation, an increase in the size of an industry causes a fall in the average real costs (measured in resources and including the use of land) per physical unit of product, the industry is subject to increasing returns, if to a rise in real costs to diminishing returns.

The strength of the tendency to increasing returns is to be measured by the ratio between the proportionate fall in real costs and the proportionate increase in the physical volume of production, i.e. the reciprocal of the elasticity of return.

The elasticity of return is a measure of the relation between the efficiency and size of an industry. It can be applied to each stage of production if desired, i.e. the industry may be taken to extend from land to the consumer, or it may be confined to a single stage, provided the measures of resources invested and product obtained are appropriate. The choice of boundaries between industries for statistical investigation is determined very largely by the facilities available for computing a measure of resources and product at the transitions from stage to stage of production; but there is the further consideration that enterprises which are intimately related by technological and geographical ties should be embraced by the same industry in order that it may be feasible to interpret the statistical results. Even when the task of delimitation of industries has been well done, it is often impossible to say how far the decline in real costs revealed by statistical enquiry was caused by the expansion of the market and how far by other (so-called "external") influences. It appears that many of those inventions which are the anticipated result of investment would probably occur without industrial expansion, and the same may probably be said of new discoveries. The subdivision of labour (including the work of management) is the chief economy of industrial expansion, although an increase in the size of the market will generally make a more "roundabout" process of production economical. The former tendency is seen in the progressive specialisation of all the factors of production as the market expands, the latter in the increase in the quantity of capital employed relative to other factors, with given comparative prices for the factors.[1] Opposed to these economies are two kinds of diseconomy which generally accompany industrial expansion. First, the greater specialisation of the factors increases the work of co-ordinating the several parts of the economic organism. ("The development of the organism whether social or physical involves an increasing subdivision of functions between its separate parts on the one hand,

---

[1] Cf. Marshall, *Principles*, p. 255. "It is the largeness of markets, the increased demand for great numbers of things of the same kind, and in some cases of things made with great accuracy that leads to the subdivision of labour; the chief effect of the improvement of machinery is to cheapen the work which would anyhow have been subdivided."

The key to the success of many large corporations in American industry is, I believe, the fact that the size of the markets makes economical minute subdivision of the work of management so that the activities of the several departments and the policy of the corporation as a whole are directed by specialists. The scarcity of business ability in relation to the opportunities in the United States has hastened this development.

and on the other, a more intimate connection between them."[1]) Industrial growth necessitates the adoption of more elaborate (and costly) machinery for the regulation of the wage contract; while "the newer methods of production, in general, lessen the scope of the labourer's own discretion, and call for more management. The labourer is rather more like a machine and rather less like a manager than he was in 1850".[2] The increase in the size of the business unit makes it more difficult to co-ordinate the departments and may call for a more than proportionate increase in the resources devoted to organisation; while the larger market and greater number of producers provide more work for produce exchanges, employers' associations and trade journals.[3] The second class of diseconomy of industrial expansion arises from the relative scarcity of some of the factors of production (e.g. land and mineral products), which compels the adoption of a different proportionate combination of the factors of production which may increase the real cost of production.[4] For the purposes of pure theory it would be convenient if this phenomenon did not occur or could be impounded in *ceteris paribus*. The normal supply schedule would then be described by one of a series of cost functions constructed with different sets of relative supply prices for the factors of production. Functions of this type would be extremely useful to one attempting to predict, say, the future of cotton manufacture in India from the history of cotton manufacture in England and America, but unfortunately the statistical records will not take the shape of these convenient functions. Changes in the comparative prices of the factors of production do occur with industrial expansion and make it impossible to measure changes in real costs precisely, but their influence upon the efficiency of production is of the second order of small quantities while the changes them-

---

[1] Marshall, *Principles*, p. 241.

[2] Allyn A. Young, Private communication, December 1926.

[3] This reorganisation is effected through the medium of changes in the relative prices of the factors of production and those factors which are limited in supply earn rents which harmonise the private and the social interest. But many of the diseconomies of co-ordination are external so that the marginal private net product might be greater than the marginal social net product of investment in an industry dominated by this phenomenon.

[4] Cf. p. 5, n. 2.

selves are small in single manufacturing industries compared with the economies of expansion.

My statistical investigations have been confined to manufacturing industries and all show a tendency for returns to increase, but this is not necessarily the case. The ratio between the decline of real costs and the expansion of an industry probably overestimates the net economies of expansion owing to external influences, yet the London building industry, for example, showed a very slowly increasing return (elasticity of return varying between 3 and 8) during the second half of the nineteenth century. It is probable that many extractive industries operate under diminishing returns, but there are great technical obstacles to statistical enquiry into the course of real costs in extractive industries.

§ 2. METHOD

I

The main purpose of the present enquiry is to estimate the strength of the tendency to increasing return in certain industries during the half century immediately preceding the recent war. The first step is the measurement of the changes which occurred during this period in the real cost of production in the several industries. It appears at first sight that the trend of real costs in an industry could be ascertained from the accounts of a number of firms for successive years; but this is not the case. If it were possible to assess correctly the relative values of different managers and operatives and the varying natural facilities at the disposal of the several enterprises, there would remain the difficulty that external economies are often realised through a process of proliferation so that the representative firm of one period is succeeded by a number of more highly specialised enterprises which divide its functions. The only feasible plan is to assume that the principle of substitution works effectively, so that the returns enjoyed by the several factors are proportionate to their efficiencies as agents of production, an assumption which is approximately true for industries which are expanding under competitive conditions. Value then tends to equal cost of production with normal profit to the entrepreneur. Varying demand combined with the intractability of Nature and our imperfect anticipation of events will cause prices to fluctuate from day to day and year to year; while monopolists may exert a powerful influence upon prices for short periods. It seems reasonable, however, to presume that the *trend* of selling prices in an established industry is closely paralleled by changes in the money costs of production with normal profit. That is to say, that the normal price of a commodity is equal to the average full expenses of producing it.

It is clear that changes in the average full expenses of producing a commodity are the resultant of changes in the supply prices of the factors of production and changes in the quantities of the factors employed per unit of product. If, therefore, a correction is applied for changes in the prices of the factors of production, the remaining variations in normal price indicate changes in the quantity of resources consumed per unit of product, the several factors being assigned constant weights proportionate to their prices in the base year. In the studies which follow the year 1910 has been chosen as base for British industries and 1913 for American industries, because these were years of moderate prosperity and near the end of the period under investigation.[1] My index numbers therefore reflect changes in the real cost of production from the point of view of people accustomed to pre-War conditions. In theory two measures of the trend of real cost should be computed, the two base years being chosen so that the divergence between the two measures is a maximum. The actual change in real cost (in terms of resources) must necessarily lie between the limits set by these two measures. Experiment with the data used in Parts II–VI shows that the course of real costs in the industries investigated is much the

---

[1] The index numbers for British industries had already been calculated to the base 1910 when I discovered that 1913 would be a better base for my American studies, since much material had already been worked to this base. The effect of the change of base from 1910 to 1913 is negligible.

same whichever year is chosen as base. *Ex post facto* it appears that index numbers constructed with the year 1910 or 1913 as base may be used as index numbers of real cost without serious error. Index numbers have therefore been compiled for each industry studied, which reflect, as truly as the data will allow, the course of selling prices *as it would have been* if the prices of the factors of production had been the same throughout the period as in the base year (1910). It is contended that the trend of these corrected prices is a measure of changes in the normal real cost of production in terms of resources. Index numbers of the physical volume of production and, in certain cases, of the average output per firm, etc., complete the statistical material available. The existence of correlation, slight though it be, between the course of real costs and the trend of output, or of output per firm, suggests a causal relationship, but the coincidence may be purely accidental. Until we can enumerate the economies to which the changes in real cost are attributed and eliminate other probable causes, it is unsafe to draw such conclusions. Each case must be discussed on its merits. The measurement of the changes in real costs and their correlation with changes in size is but the starting point for discussion by those who have a detailed knowledge of the industry concerned. But it is a beginning.

The statistical problem thus resolves itself into the construction of index numbers which will show the ratio between the selling prices of a given product over a period of years, their correction for changes in the money cost per efficiency unit of the factors engaged in its production, and the correlation of the index of changes in real cost thus obtained with changes in the physical volume of production in the industry and in the several firms.

II

The method of deriving index numbers of real cost from selling price data is more easily explained by the use of symbols[1]:

Let p = the price of the product;

x = the output of the product;

$y_1, y_2, y_3, \ldots$ = the amounts of the various factors 1, 2, 3, $\ldots$ employed in the production of x units of product;

$\pi_1, \pi_2, \pi_3, \ldots$ = the supply prices of factors 1, 2, 3, $\ldots$;

$A_1, A_2, A_3, \ldots$ = the prices of the factors 1, 2, 3, $\ldots$ (i.e. values of π) in the base year.

Then on the Marshallian theory we have in equilibrium:

$$px = \pi_1 y_1 + \pi_2 y_2 + \pi_3 y_3 + \ldots = \Sigma \pi y.$$

Let e' = the elasticity of return to resources engaged in the production of the product.[2]

Then

$$e' = \frac{\delta x}{x} \div \left\{ \frac{\dfrac{\Sigma Ay}{x} - \dfrac{\Sigma A (y + \delta y)}{x + \delta x}}{\Sigma Ay / x} \right\}$$

$$= - \underset{\delta x \to 0}{\mathrm{Lt}} \; \frac{\Sigma Ay}{x^2} \div D_x . \frac{\Sigma Ay}{x}.$$

But if e = the elasticity of supply of x, we have

$$e = p/x \div D_x . p = - \frac{\Sigma \pi y}{x^2} \div D_x . \frac{\Sigma \pi y}{x}.$$

When the supply prices of the factors of production remain constant: $\pi = A$.

Therefore   Elasticity of Return = Elasticity of Supply.

In problems of maximum welfare it is the rate at which aggregate real costs increase with output, the marginal real cost of production, which is significant.[3]

---

[1] I have followed Dr Bowley's notation as closely as convenient. Cf. his book, *Mathematical Groundwork of Economics*, chap. iii, especially sections 5 and 6.

[2] The elasticity of return is measured by the rate of increase in the normal physical volume of production divided by the rate of fall of the normal real costs of production.

[3] *Vide* Professor Edgeworth's *Collected Papers*, pp. 71–4.

Let $\epsilon' = \dfrac{\text{the relative increase of output}}{\text{the relative increase in aggregate real costs}}$.

Then $$\epsilon' = \operatorname*{Lt}_{\delta x \to 0} \frac{\Sigma Ay}{x} \div D_x . \Sigma Ay.$$

Also $$1 = \frac{1}{e'} + \frac{1}{\epsilon'}.$$

Thus we have increasing, constant or diminishing return according as

$$e' \gtreqqless 0 \quad \text{or} \quad \epsilon' \gtreqqless 1.$$

Fortunately it can be shown that conflicting results are not given by the two definitions except near points of inflexion on the integral real costs curve.

Let p_a = the average real cost of production of a unit of the product, i.e. the cost in terms of resources; the unit of resources being computed by weighting the various factors according to their prices at a chosen time (the base year).

Thus $\Sigma Ay = \Sigma y$ units of resources.

Let p = the money cost of production = the normal selling price of x in same year.

Then $p_a x = A_1 y_1 + A_2 y_2 + A_3 y_3 + \dots = \Sigma Ay,$

and $px = \pi_1 y_1 + \pi_2 y_2 + \pi_3 y_3 + \dots = \Sigma \pi y.$

In general π is a function of x and is therefore variable. The most economical distribution of resources, and that assumed to be adopted, will equate the money values of the marginal net products of £1 spent upon each factor of production.[1]

---

[1] *Vide* Bowley, *Mathematical Groundwork of Economics*, p. 29.

The industry is here taken as a unit, land and business ability are assumed to be subject to the same process of substitution as labour and capital. This implies a determinate supply price for land and business ability, which may appear to involve circular reasoning—the return to land and to the entrepreneur being sometimes conceived as a surplus. If there were only one opportunity for the land and business ability concerned there would be truth in this objection. But in fact, from the long period point of view, there are numerous uses competing for a limited supply of land and of business ability. Each plot of land, each entrepreneur might be engaged in a number of employments. Consequently there is a supply price, per efficiency unit of each factor, which is necessary to secure its use in a particular employment.

There may be several ways of combining the factors of production which

In equilibrium therefore

$$\frac{1}{\pi_1}.F_{y_1} = \frac{1}{\pi_2}.F_{y_2} = \frac{1}{\pi_3}.F_{y_3} = \dots ,$$

where the F_y's = the partial differentials of $F(x)$ with respect to the y. In general F_y is a function of x.

If as a result either of a change in the scale of production, i.e. of x modifying the ratio $F_{y_1} : F_{y_2} : F_{y_3}$, or of a change in the relative prices of the factors, this equation of the marginal net products of money spent upon the different factors is disturbed, reorganisation will be necessary and in the new equilibrium different proportions of the factors will be employed. There will thus be a change in the internal constitution of the unit of resources.

Consider two proportionate combinations of the factors given by y and y'.

Let $\qquad p_a x = A_1 y_1 + A_2 y_2 + A_3 y_3 + \dots = \Sigma Ay,$

and $\qquad p_a' x = A_1 y_1' + A_2 y_2' + A_3 y_3' + \dots = \Sigma Ay'.$

The combination $y_1 + y_2 + y_3 +$ etc. is more or less "efficient" from the point of view of the present enquiry than the combination $y_1' + y_2' + y_3' +$ etc., according as $p_a \lessgtr p_a'$,

i.e. as $\qquad\qquad\qquad \Sigma \dfrac{Ay}{x} \lessgtr \Sigma \dfrac{Ay'}{x}.$

satisfy the condition that marginal net products are proportionate to supply prices. Such different combinations may exist side by side in equilibrium provided that the rate of return to each factor is the same, per efficiency unit, in each case. The coexistence of large and small firms in the same line of business is often to be regarded in this light; the entrepreneurs associated with the larger firms may be of higher quality than those responsible for the small and their efficiency earnings be in reality equal in spite of wide differences in their individual incomes. But the age of the ventures in question and their relative good fortune also modify actual efficiency earnings; the analysis of the text only applies to *normal* costs and selling prices. (Cf. Appendix III.) Taking the industry as a whole, there can only be one combination of resources at a given time but there may be better ways of organising the industry for the same output. For equilibrium to occur under these circumstances the producers must be prevented from establishing the better systems by ignorance, lack of foresight, or failure to obtain collective action. If one producer discovers business methods which, while not dependent for their success upon his peculiar genius, are more efficient than those prevailing, the other producers will be compelled to effect equal improvements though they need not necessarily follow the same methods.

A part of the tendency to increasing or diminishing returns indicated by my index numbers of real costs may therefore be attributed to changes in the proportions of the factors employed. In so far as these changes are due to relative changes in the price of the factors *not* caused by the increased output, they are external to the industry and are not properly to be included in an estimate of the elasticity of return.

We are now in a position to make the transition from selling price to real cost of production:

$$px = \pi_1 y_1 + \pi_2 y_2 + \pi_3 y_3 + \ldots = \Sigma \pi y$$
$$= A_1 y_1 + A_2 y_2 + A_3 y_3 + \ldots = \Sigma A y.$$

Clearly the real cost of production p_a may be derived from the money cost of production p by deducting from p the sum of a series of terms such as $\dfrac{(\pi - A) y}{x}$. We then have

$$p - \Sigma \frac{(\pi - A) y}{x} = \frac{\pi_1 y_1}{x} - \frac{(\pi_1 - A_1) y_1}{x} + \frac{\pi_2 y_2}{x} - \frac{(\pi_2 - A_2) y_2}{x}$$
$$+ \frac{\pi_3 y_3}{x} - \frac{(\pi_3 - A_3) y_3}{x}$$
$$= \Sigma \frac{A y}{x}$$
$$= p_a.$$

Notice that the y's must be the same throughout this calculation in order to preserve the identity, i.e. they must represent the amounts of the factors actually used in the production of x in the year to which the price p refers.

Let $y_{a_1}, y_{a_2}, y_{a_3}, \ldots =$ the amounts of the factors used in the production of x_a units in the base year.

In the British industries studied this is all the information available for weighting, so that my actual calculation of index numbers of real cost from selling price in any year is given by

$$p - \Sigma \frac{(\pi - A) y_a}{x_a} = p_a',$$

the index number of real cost, instead of

$$p - \Sigma \frac{(\pi - A) y}{x} = p_a,$$

the real cost as defined above.

The assumption that the amount of each factor employed per unit of product remains constant throughout the period studied, introduces an error in the index numbers of real cost which varies directly as:

(*a*) the differences between the actual prices of the factors and their prices in the base year;

(*b*) the changes in the amounts of the factors employed per unit of product as compared with the base year, i.e.

$$p_a' - p_a = \Sigma \, (\pi - A) \, (y/x - y_a/x_a).$$

The quantity of a given factor employed in an industry per unit of product may change because there is a change in the quantity of resources required to produce a given output, or because the proportion of the resources used which consist of the particular factor changes. The second variation may be due to a change in the relative prices of the factors or to technical progress.

If minute classification of the factors of production into approximately homogeneous categories were attempted these changes in the constitution of the unit of resources would be a source of serious error in the weighting of the corrections for price changes. In the present enquiry, however, the factors of production are divided into three groups, namely:

Labour: which does not include salaried staff in most cases.

Raw materials: covering the principal items.

Other Expenses: including standing charges, profit, earnings of management and all items not covered by labour and materials.

With this broad classification the error involved in constant weighting is not so serious: the difficulties now arise in the construction of index numbers to measure changes in the supply prices of these heterogeneous factors, a problem which is not unfamiliar to the modern statistician. It so happens that one can generalise concerning the direction of the error in the index numbers of real cost due to the constant weighting of the corrections for changes in the prices of these three factors of production. Technological improvement tends continuously to reduce the amount of labour and raw materials of given quality employed in production per unit of output. The progressive subdivision of labour increases the cost of management per unit of product, while the adoption of more roundabout processes of production necessitates an increase in the quantity of capital employed relative to labour. There is evidence in the industries studied that the more continuous use of equipment (e.g. the extension of the building season and the speeding up of blast furnaces and looms), combined with general economies of organisation, have offset the multiplication of uses for capital so that the quantity of the factor engaged per unit of product has probably not increased appreciably and may have diminished. The base year being near the end of the period, one may conclude that the corrections to the trend of selling prices for changes in the supply prices of the factors of production will generally be underweighted; i.e. $y/x > y_a/x_a$. The corrections will, therefore, be too small, the error in the index numbers of real costs being of the same sign as, but increasing faster than, the deviations of prices of the factors from those of the base year; i.e. error $> k\,(\pi - A)$, where k is constant.

From another point of view one may say that constant weighting of the corrections, the base year being at the end of the period, eliminates changes in the supply prices of the factors so far as they affect the resources employed in the base year, but economies effected during the period are valued at the prices prevailing in the years to which the index numbers refer.

This method of eliminating a large part of the effects of price changes is extremely simple in use. Index numbers of the selling price of the product are calculated to the base 100 in the year chosen (1910). The percentages of receipts normally expended upon each group of factors about 1910 at the prices prevailing in the base year are then calculated. This gives the values of

$$\frac{A_1 y_{a_1}}{x_a},\ \frac{A_2 y_{a_2}}{x_a},\ \frac{A_3 y_{a_3}}{x_a},$$

required. Index numbers of the supply prices of the several factors are then constructed to the *corresponding bases*, namely:

$$\frac{A_1 y_{a_1}}{x_a},\ \frac{A_2 y_{a_2}}{x_a},\ \frac{A_3 y_{a_3}}{x_a}.$$

These numbers give directly the values of

$$\frac{\pi_1 y_{a_1}}{x_a}, \frac{\pi_2 y_{a_2}}{x_a}, \frac{\pi_3 y_{a_3}}{x_a}, \dots$$

for any year. Hence the deviations of the index numbers of prices of the several factors from their base year values are equal to the quantities

$$(\pi_1 - A_1)\, y_{a_1}/x_a,\; (\pi_2 - A_2)\, y_{a_2}/x_a,\; (\pi_3 - A_3)\, y_{a_3}/x_a,$$

which are the required corrections.

The correction is thus effected in a single operation: the algebraic sum of the deviations of the index numbers of supply prices of the factors in a given year from the base numbers is deducted from the index numbers of selling price of the product in that year, and the real cost index number is obtained.

The index number of real cost then exceeds the *defined value* by the sum of the products of changes in the supply prices of the factors from the base year, and the changes in the amounts of the factors employed per unit of product. In other words, economies and diseconomies are entered in the index number of real cost at the values corresponding to the prices in the year to which the index number refers.

In the British industries studied the method of constant weighting of corrections was applied in every case except the joinery trade; moreover, real costs in these industries were so stable that the error involved probably did not amount to more than 2 % even in the index numbers over fifty years distant from the base year (i.e. *circa* 1845–50). When dealing with American industries one finds the frequent censuses of production supply material for a redetermination of weights every few years; moreover, the rapid development of these industries makes constant weighting very inaccurate. The case of varying weights, made to vary smoothly by interpolation between the successive censuses, is readily assimilated to the above discussion; for the real cost index numbers calculated with varying weights for the factors approximate closely to the defined value of "real cost". The error takes the form:

$$\Sigma\,(\pi - A)\,(y/x - y'/x)$$

with varying weights, whereas it is

$$\Sigma \, (\pi - A) \, (y/x - y_a/x_a)$$

with constant weights, where

$y'/x' =$ the weights assigned by interpolation,

$y_a/x_a =$ the weights according to the base year observations, i.e. those used in constant weighting of corrections,

$y/x =$ the amounts of the factors actually consumed per unit of product in the year to which the index number in question refers, i.e. the correct weight.

The use of varying weights makes the process of derivation of the index numbers of real cost from those of selling price rather more complicated, although the principle is the same as with constant weights. It is simplest to regard the selling price index numbers as average annual prices of a unit of a constant composite commodity which was worth 100 units of money in the base year; I shall refer to them simply as the prices of the product. The census returns give the proportion of the receipts of the industry going to pay for labour and for materials. Hence it is easy to calculate the expense per unit of product on account of labour and of raw materials in the census years and, with the aid of appropriate index numbers of efficiency, wages and prices of materials, to deduce the equivalents of these items of expense at the prices prevailing in the base year. By interpolation between the census years approximate values may now be obtained for the average cost of labour and of materials per unit of product in each year *at the prices prevailing in the base year*, i.e. annual index numbers showing changes in the physical quantity of labour and of raw materials required to produce a unit of the product may be computed, upon the assumption that the changes take place smoothly and continuously in the intercensal periods. By a reverse use of the index numbers of efficiency, wages and cost of materials, the amounts actually spent upon labour and upon materials per unit of product in the successive years can now be estimated; while the margin by which the price of the product exceeds the cost of labour and materials is available for other expenses: the equivalent of this margin at the prices prevailing in the base year may be computed with the aid of an appropriate index number of general prices.[1] In this way estimates can be made of the outlays per unit of product for labour $(\pi_1 y_1'/x')$, materials $(\pi_2 y_2'/x')$, and other expenses $(\pi_3 y_3'/x')$, in a given year, and the equivalents of these outlays at the prices prevailing in the base year computed (i.e. $A_1 y_1'/x'$; $A_2 y_2'/x'$; $A_3 y_3'/x'$). The algebraic sum of the differences between the outlays required at current prices and at the prices prevailing in the base year is then deducted from the selling price index number to obtain the index number of real cost (i.e. the required correction is

$$minus\ \{(\pi_1 - A_1)\, y_1'/x' + (\pi_2 - A_2)\, y_2'/x' + (\pi_3 - A_3)\, y_3'/x'\}).$$

For convenience of exposition I have distinguished sharply between those cases in which constant weights are given to the corrections for changes in the supply prices of the factors and those in which varying weights are used. In practice the two methods are combined opportunistically, the choice between constant and varying weights for a particular factor being decided (*a*) by the magnitude of the changes occurring during the period in the quantity of the factor employed per unit of product, (*b*) by the character of the data available for weighting. For example, variable weights were given to labour in British joinery while raw cotton received a constant weight in Massachusetts cotton manufacture. The general rule for finding the net error in the index numbers of real cost due to improper weighting of the corrections for price changes is simple: the corrections are too small by an amount equal to the algebraic

[1] When using the method of constant weighting in the British studies it would have been more accurate to determine the margin available for other expenses in this way, since wage rates and prices of materials generally move in sympathy with general prices. The constant weighting of all three factors (labour, materials, and other expenses) leaves a margin, equivalent to the net economies effected between the year to which the index number refers and the base year, entirely uncorrected for price changes; while the method employed in my American studies corrects this margin for the major price changes. Experiment shows that the trends of index numbers of real cost in the British industries would not be appreciably different if recalculated by this residual method; but some of the annual index numbers of corrected selling prices would be modified considerably by recalculation. As the trends alone are used in the present enquiry, I have not thought it worth while to refigure the British index numbers.

sum of the products of the price changes (as compared with the base year) and the differences between the weights given to the several factors and the amounts actually employed per unit of product. Detailed examination of the statistics used in Parts II–VI shows that this error in the index numbers of real cost probably does not exceed 2 % in any of the industries investigated.

Throughout this section I have used the term index number of real cost to describe the equivalent of the average annual selling price of the product in terms of the factor-prices prevailing in the base year. But average annual selling prices are not normal prices, and corrected average annual selling prices therefore fail to measure real costs. Cyclical fluctuations and random variations have to be eliminated from these corrected selling price index numbers before they can be used to measure changes in real cost. The known methods of determining statistically the secular trend of a time series are all unsatisfactory. For my purpose the centred-moving average is the best-known device. I have used a ten-year interval for the British industries (the number being placed opposite the sixth year) and an interval of seven years in the American studies. The fact that the cycles vary in amplitude and frequency calls for a moving average based upon a long period; while the fact that the trend of real costs is usually non-linear calls for an average with a short interval to lessen upward or downward distortion.[1] In some cases marked cyclical fluctuations remain in the moving averages (*vide* the charts of real cost of cotton manufacture in England and of iron smelting in America). Since output and prices move in sympathy in most industries, moving averages with equal intervals may be used to correlate the trend of output with the trend of corrected selling prices without serious error; and it is this correlation which is useful in estimating the elasticity of return.

---

[1] Upon the use of the moving average as a measure of secular trend *vide* F. C. Mills, *Statistical Methods*, pp. 260–70.

III

The sources, manipulation and significance of the data used in this enquiry are discussed in detail under the several industries (Parts II–VI); but there are certain general observations to be made at this point about the construction of the constituent price series, their manipulation to obtain the real cost series and the significance of the result.

The selling price index numbers are based upon quotations made for standard products in the official records of the principal (organised) markets of the several industries. There was a change in the standard grades of grey cotton cloth quoted in the Manchester market about 1900, and an uncertain transition has therefore to be made from the old to the new series. Owing to incomplete records there is also a splice (about 1890) in the American pig iron selling price index. Fortunately these interruptions are not serious, and the selling price index numbers for each industry may be assumed to measure changes in the price of a composite commodity of constant quality without appreciable error. Consequently the index of real cost derived therefrom registers directly changes in the efficiency of production of this composite commodity or, more accurately, changes in the efficiency of those processes of production which are performed in the industry under investigation. Is it legitimate to conclude that the index measures changes in the efficiency of the entire industry? In general, the answer is in the affirmative. It is true that there are constant changes in the quality and relative importance of the different items in the product of an industry and that these changes, though small, are often cumulative; but industrial development usually effects similar economies in the production of all the varieties of the product, if the industry is a natural unit, so that approximately proportionate changes take place in the real cost of each variety. There is no evidence, for example, of appreciable relative movement of the real costs of spinning 32's and 36's yarn between 1850 and 1910. In an industry such as the Lancashire cotton trade, which is subdivided into numerous branches covering a wide variety of products, improvements in the technique of certain divisions may effect permanent changes in the relative costs of the different products; but even these developments are likely to be copied and adapted to serve the allied branches of the industry, e.g. the automatic loom has gradually been perfected until it is used in America to weave all but the finest cotton piece goods. When studying the gradual development of an established industry in periods free from revolutionary changes in technique, it is reasonable to assume that changes in the real cost of producing the standard products of the industry provide a measure of changes in the efficiency of the industry as a whole which is adequate for the purposes of the present enquiry. It is necessary, however, to weight the corrections made to the selling price index for changes in the supply prices of the factors according to the quantities of the several factors employed in the production of the composite upon which the index is based. If census data showing the relative expenditure upon the different factors in the entire industry are used to weight these corrections, it is necessary first to demonstrate that the particular composite and the product of the entire industry are similar in respect of the relative quantities of the different factors employed in their production. This is likely to be the case when the composite is a representative sample of all the products of the industry, as in the Lancashire cotton study, unless considerable changes occur in the relative importance of the different branches of the industry; but it is dangerous to use data relating to the entire industry to correct a selling price index based upon a single commodity, e.g. Cleveland pig iron.

The construction of price index numbers for the three factors of production, labour, materials and other expenses, raises similar difficulties. These indexes are used to calculate the equivalents at base year prices of a given set of expenses. The ideal index number for this purpose would be the weighted arithmetic average of a number of series of price relatives (a series for each variety or quality of the factor employed in the industry at any time during the period)—weights being re-apportioned each year according to the amounts spent in the industry upon the several varieties of the factor in that year. This is, of course, an impossible ideal, if only for the reason that some varieties of the factors used in 1850 were unknown in 1910, and *vice versa*. The only resource is to group the numerous varieties of the factor into categories such that there is very little relative movement of the prices of items in the same category, while each category contains at least one standard variety of the factor for which continuous price records are available. The index for the factor is then based upon a sample containing items representative of each category, constant or varying weights being assigned according to the relative price movements of the several categories and the material available for weighting. In most cases the relative efficiencies (and therefore the relative prices) of the different varieties of raw materials used in an industry are determined by some physical characteristic such as the length of the staple in cotton manufacture and the percentage iron content of ores used in the blast furnaces, so that there is very little relative movement of the prices of the various qualities of material. Revolutionary discoveries such as the Bessemer process may change the relative efficiencies of different kinds of material, but these are the creators of new industries rather than incidents in the development of old.[1]

The case of labour is more serious. The substitution of unskilled for skilled labour has been an important feature of the industrial progress of the last fifty years; while the state regulation of working conditions (especially for women and children) has also progressed rapidly during this period. Both these developments tend to shift the relative wage rates of different grades of labour. Where possible series of relative wage rates have been constructed for every important occupation in the industry in question, and the index numbers of price per efficiency unit of labour derived from these series by weighting according to the numbers employed in the various occupations. The *Aldrich Report* provides material for reweighting each year the various occupational series in Massachusetts cotton manufacture from 1845–90; but in most cases constant weights only

---

[1] The value of Bessemer Lake Superior ore was still rising relative to that of Non-Bessemer in the early 'eighties; but the ratio of the price of Standard Bessemer ore to the price of Standard Non-Bessemer ore was precisely the same in 1910 as in 1888.

are available. In yet other industries, e.g. American pig iron and British cotton manufacture, the only index numbers available are weighted averages of actual wage rates; even these series approximate closely to the required index numbers because the range of the wage rates paid in the industry is not large, while only small changes occur in the relative numbers employed in the different occupations.

Changes in quality also make the choice of the constituent series of relative wages difficult. The index numbers of supply price of labour should measure changes in the wages received for an effort of given intensity and quality. Such efficiency wages are difficult to estimate: hourly wages make no allowance for changes in the intensity of work, while the same piece rates may yield a man a great or a very small income according to the state of the firm's plant and managerial staff. In general, time wages, properly interpreted, seem to provide the more reliable basis for indexes of efficiency wages, but in the building industry, where quotations exist for the labour cost of jobs in which the method of procedure has remained substantially unchanged for many years, a better index can be based upon "piece-rates". There is a tendency to attribute a large part of the increased earnings of workers, in the Lancashire cotton trade for example, to greater *personal* application. It would seem, however, that much of the improvement listed under this head is properly to be regarded as technical rather than personal progress. The speeding-up of the mules and looms may cause a worker—without greater effort on his part—to do twice as much piecing in the hour, while the assignment of two or three looms to a single weaver in the stead of the traditional one or two is made possible by mechanical improvements, and may involve little or no greater effort on the part of the weaver. The successful substitution of comparatively unskilled for skilled labour is also to be regarded as a technical economy. Only those changes in wages that are due to greater, more intense, personal effort are to be attributed to increased "efficiency" of the worker in the present use of the term. During the period under review hourly wages in the British building, pig iron and cotton trades seem to have moved roughly parallel to efficiency earnings. Some increase in efficiency probably took place in the cotton industry when hours were reduced to 56½ per week in 1847, while in the building trade efficiency wages have been rising more rapidly than weekly wage rates since 1890. The successive reduction of hours of work in American cotton factories appears to have had little effect upon *weekly* output until hours were reduced from 56 to 54 per week in 1912. From 1845–1912 I have, therefore, used weekly wage rates as the basis for my index numbers of efficiency wages. The index of changes in the supply price of the United States blast furnace labour is based upon puddlers' piece rates from 1880–90 and upon average hourly earnings from 1890.

The title "other expenses" covers a miscellaneous group of charges individually too small to demand separate treatment, but accounting in the aggregate for 10 to 20 % of the total costs of production in the base year. Rent, rates, insurance, salaries and profits, including interest charges, are the chief items. Again, it is changes in the supply price of a unit of effort expressed in these various services which should be reflected in the index numbers used to correct the selling price index for the price changes of the group of factors. In the absence of fuller information, I have assumed that the *real* price per efficiency unit of these factors remained constant; up to the War, at least, there is no evidence of appreciable change in the supply price (in terms of goods) of managing ability, the rate of interest fluctuated but little during the latter half of the nineteenth century, rents and rates rose somewhat, while insurance probably cheapened. It remains to correct for fluctuations in the supply price of this miscellaneous group, the real price being assumed constant. For this purpose an index of retail prices is desirable, since rates and salaries are more sensitive to the cost of living than to changes in the price of imported timber. Unfortunately no satisfactory index of the cost of living in England existed prior to 1914. For the pre-War period, therefore, a very rough correction has been made for changes in the general value of money, using the ten years' moving average of Sauerbeck's index number in preference to the annual numbers because rents, rates and salaries generally respond very slowly to such changes. In continuing the index numbers through the War period the annual average of the Ministry of Labour's Cost of Living Index has been used, and the gap between 1910 (the last Sauerbeck ten years' average employed) and 1914 bridged by interpolation. In the studies of American industries I have used Mr Carl Snyder's index of the general price level, because it includes wages (salaries), rents and other items of the type which constitute the margin of "other expenses". Unfortunately Mr Snyder's index does not begin until 1875; the index of general prices used for the period 1845–75 is based upon the *Aldrich Report* upon Wholesale Prices, Wages and Transportation.

§ 3. INTERPRETATION

I

The concluding sections of Parts II–VI are devoted to analysis of the statistical results industry by industry, while in Part VII I have gathered together those results which are of general importance and attempted to indicate their bearing upon economic problems. It will be convenient, however, at this point to describe in general terms the nature of the information made available by these statistical enquiries and the kind of interpretation of which it is capable. In the course of my investigations index numbers have been computed, for each industry studied, which reflect:

1. Changes in the supply prices of the factors of production.
   (*a*) Labour, i.e. efficiency wages.
   (*b*) Materials (sometimes subdivided, e.g. coke and iron ore).
   (*c*) Other expenses (i.e. a general price index).
2. Changes in the price of the product.
   (*a*) Uncorrected.
   Annual average, i.e. "Selling Price".
   Trend by moving average, i.e. "Money Costs".

(*b*) Corrected for changes in the supply prices of labour, materials and other expenses.
Annual average, i.e. "Real Price".
Trend by moving average, i.e. "Real Cost".

3. Changes in the physical volume of production.
Annual average.
Trend by moving average.

In addition, where material is available, we have index numbers showing:

4. Changes in the outlay made upon the several factors per unit of product.

(*a*) At current prices, i.e. expense upon account of labour, materials, and other items.

(*b*) At base year prices, i.e. a measure of changes in the physical quantities of the several factors consumed in the production of a constant composite commodity.

5. Changes in the average size of establishments and firms indicated by output, number of workers employed, or units of machinery (e.g. cotton spindles) engaged.

For convenience of reference the continuous data have been systematically tabulated and placed together in the Statistical Appendices. The appendices are arranged as follows:

I. The London Building Industry 1845–1913.
II. The Lancashire Cotton Industry 1845–1913.
III. The Cleveland Pig Iron Industry 1883–1925.
IV. The Massachusetts Cotton Industry 1845–1920.
V. The American Pig Iron Industry 1883–1925.

Each section contains ratio charts showing curves of real cost and of expansion of the industry, obtained by plotting the corresponding index numbers upon a semi-logarithmic scale. The special student will find other interesting material together with a detailed description of my sources and statistical methods in Parts II–VI, but the general reader may omit these dreary parts entirely and confine his attention to the Introduction (Part I), the Conclusion (Part VII), and the Statistical Appendices.

The defects of the data and errors arising in the process of manipulation are discussed in detail in Parts II–VI. It is there shown that the trend of the index numbers of selling price of the product corrected for changes in the supply prices of labour, materials and other expenses probably measures changes in the real cost of production (as defined above) in the several industries within 5 %, even in the periods remote from the base year. It can be stated with confidence that the index numbers exaggerate the decline of real costs during the period 1850–1910 in both the American and the British industries, because the bulk of the economies effected during the period took the form of labour saving. Since wages rose relative to the prices of the other factors of production almost continuously during this period, these economies are valued at a higher figure, the base year being at the end of the period, than they would have been had an earlier year been chosen as base.

II

Though computed for the purpose of measuring elasticities of return these time-series are useful in other problems. The annual index numbers revealing the fluctuations of "real prices" about the trend of "real costs" throw a good deal of light upon the phases of the trade cycle. There is often a discernible tendency for real prices to reach maxima before and minima after selling prices, while output shows the contrary tendency: the relative movements of these three series are in accord with current theories of the trade cycle. Unfortunately one cannot conclude from the concomitant variations of selling prices and real prices that real costs do or do not vary during the trade cycle, because there is no means of distinguishing between variations in real prices due to changes in the quantity of resources consumed per unit of product and fluctuations in gross profit: one cannot ascertain from the available data whether a rise (or fall) of real price represents a rise (or fall) of real cost or an increase (or decrease) in the quasi-rent earned byrsupplementary costs. It is interesting to note that a compa ison of the annual index numbers for Massachusetts cotton manufacture with the statements of financial and trade journals shows that the real price of the product is a better index of the prosperity of the industry than the selling price. A conclusion which may be extended to other industries.

III

The United States Bureau of Labour Statistics has recently begun a series of investigations into changes in the productivity of labour in various industries.[1] It is proposed to publish from time to time figures showing the physical output of product per man per unit of time (hour, week or year, according to convenience) in the principal American industries. The avowed purpose of these investigations is to record changes in the average "efficiency" of the labour employed in American industries, but the figures are frequently cited as a measure of the productivity of labour and even of the efficiency of the industries. The index numbers of real cost and of labour cost at the base wage rates provide a useful check upon these records of output per man. The case of the United States blast furnaces is a good illustration of the points at issue. The table on p. 49 brings into direct comparison the three series:

(*a*) Output per man per year, i.e. the weight of pig iron produced in the United States during the census year divided by the average number of wage earners employed as recorded by the United States Census of Manufactures. These figures have been taken from the *Monthly Labour Review*, July 1922, p. 6, and expressed as a percentage of the output per man per year in 1909 instead of 1850 as in the *Labour Review*.

(*b*) Productivity of labour, i.e. the reciprocals of the labour

---

[1] *Vide Monthly Labour Review*, August 1922, p. 109.

cost at 1913 wage rates per unit product as given in Appendix v, Table II, column 6, expressed as a percentage of 1909.

(c) Productivity of resources, i.e. the reciprocals of the index numbers of real cost of pig iron given in Appendix v, Table III, column 6.

The efficiency of United States blast furnaces 1890–1914

Census	Output per man	Productivity of labour[1]	Productivity of resources
	(1)	(2)	(3)
1889	40	67	86
1899	51	70	89
1904	70	99	88
1909	100	100	100
1914	118	128	109

It is clear from a comparison of columns 1 and 2 with column 3 that much of the labour saving in American blast furnace practice has been offset by additional outlays upon other factors of production, namely, capital in various forms. The difference between columns 1 and 2 may be due in part to the fact that the census returns of average number of wage earners employed are unreliable, especially in the early years; but the principal difference between the two series is that column 2 is constructed to show changes in output per efficiency unit of labour, the different kinds and qualities of labour being weighted according to their relative prices in the base year (1913), whereas column 1 makes no distinction between the good and the bad workers, the skilled and the unskilled. In this particular industry much common labour was displaced by machinery during the first

---

[1] Commenting upon the relation between coefficients of production $(a/p, b/p, ...)$ and the marginal productivities of the factors $(\delta a/\delta p, \delta b/\delta p, ...)$ M. Zotoff states (*Economic Journ.* 1923, p. 116) that the coefficients of production are *equal* to the marginal productivities of the corresponding factors, i.e. $a/p = \delta a/\delta p; b/p = \delta b/\delta p; ...$, but offers no proof. The identity is clearly untrue but it may be shown, if the production function is homogeneous, that

$$1 = a/p \cdot \delta p/\delta a + b/p \cdot \delta p/\delta b + ...$$

Therefore $\quad\quad a/p \propto \delta a/\delta p; b/p \propto \delta b/\delta p ....$

Hence my index numbers of productivity of labour (which measure changes in the labour coefficient of production) also measure changes in the marginal *private* net product of labour in the industry.

decade of the present century, so that the labour force contained
a larger proportion of skilled and semi-skilled workers in 1910
than in 1890. The output per worker rose 18 % between 1909
and 1914, whereas the productivity of labour increased 28 %.
This difference is largely explained by the reduction of average
hours worked per week from (about) 80 in 1909 to 74 in
1914.[1]

It appears that changes in the effectiveness of labour are
measured more accurately by the reciprocals of the index numbers of labour costs at base wage rates per unit product than by
figures showing output per man-hour irrespective of changes in
the composition of the labour force or the length of the working
day. Moreover, the reciprocals of the index numbers of real
cost measure changes in the efficiency of an industry better
than any device which neglects the fact that the machines which
make economies in labour costs possible are themselves
costly.

The time-series of selling prices, corrected and uncorrected,
supply prices of factors and outlay upon the several factors at
current and at base year prices provide material for a thorough
investigation of the process of diffusion of the benefits of industrial progress among the producers and consumers of the
products of particular industries. To yield fruit, however, such
a study would require to cover groups of industries competing
directly for the same resources and to take account of external
influences.

IV

Index numbers showing the movements of real cost in the export
industries of countries which trade *inter se* may be used to verify
the theory of international trade. My own studies do not cover
a sufficient number of industries or countries to be of value for
this purpose, but will serve to show the possibilities of the
method. My index numbers show that there was little, if any,
net change in the efficiency of the British cotton and pig iron

---

[1] *Vide* recent *Bulletins* of United States Bureau of Labour Statistics upon
Wages and Hours of Labour in the Iron and Steel Industry.

manufacturing industries during the period 1885–1910: whereas the real cost of manufacturing cotton in America in 1885 was 120 % of the cost in 1910; the corresponding figure for pig iron was 140 %. *Ceteris paribus*, we may conclude that America had a greater absolute advantage over England in the manufacture of both iron and cotton textiles in 1910 than in 1885, and a greater comparative advantage in the manufacture of pig iron.

It is generally admitted that the real rate of interchange turned against Great Britain at the end of the nineteenth century. Whether measured by the *gross* or the *net* barter terms of trade England had to offer an increasing volume of exports in exchange for a given volume of imports during the first decade of the twentieth century.[1] Moreover, it is commonly held that this tendency will again assert itself when the repercussions from the War of 1914–18 have died down. Optimists are prone to argue that this movement of the real rate of interchange was not significant, because British export industries were yielding, upon the whole, an increasing return to human effort. Unfortunately there is very little evidence to support this statement. Exports of iron and cotton manufactures bulk large in Great Britain's foreign trade. According to the index numbers presented in the Statistical Appendices, the real cost of smelting iron ore in England was declining very slightly, if at all, during the first decade of the present century, while the real cost of manufacturing cotton began to increase about 1900 and continued to rise until the outbreak of war in 1914. It is possible, but unlikely, that sharply increasing returns in the finishing processes of cotton and iron manufacture (which are neglected in the index numbers) or in other export industries may have been sufficient to offset the adverse movement of the rate of interchange. It is well known that the real cost of raising coal (Britain's third export in order of value and an important factor in her other export industries) from British mines has been increasing since the early 'nineties; it would require very large economies in other export industries to counterbalance this tendency. One cannot avoid the conclusion that the British people were paying

---

[1] Taussig, *International Trade*, p. 253.

an increasing *real* price for their imports during the first decade of the twentieth century.

V

It must be obvious from the two preceding sections that a valuable index of the industrial progress of a nation, or of any group of industries, might be constructed if index numbers of real cost, similar to those tabulated in the Appendices, were available for the principal industries of a country. In applying the method to the extractive industries one would have to ignore the national loss arising from the exhaustion of mines and quarries, measuring simply changes in the average real cost of extracting the mineral; the technical obstacles to such a measurement might conceivably be surmounted, for there are excellent records in many countries of the rentals and royalties paid for particular farms, mines and quarries. Manufacturing and distributing industries having no standard products present a more serious difficulty. It is almost impossible, for example, to construct a significant index of changes in the selling price of automobiles or of houses, because the variety and quality of these products change so rapidly.[1] In general, the selling price index numbers have to be based upon intermediate products such as grey cotton cloth, pig iron, steel ingots, common brickwork and doors, soda and permanganate, flour, coal, etc., which are exchanged wholesale at rates proportionate to the prices prevailing for standard grades. The method of investigation developed above cannot be applied to the advanced stages of manufacture nor to the distributing industries, because the progressive differentiation and the ever-changing quality of the product defy the technique of index numbers. Any measure of economic progress based upon enquiries similar to those attempted in

---

[1] Professor Irving Fisher tells me that he has overcome the difficulty in the case of automobiles by the device of chain index numbers. Records are available of the prices charged in adjacent years by the leading American manufacturers for their successive annual models, hence:

$$\frac{\text{Price of automobiles in 1927}}{\text{Price of automobiles in 1925}} = \frac{\text{Price of 1926 model in 1927}}{\text{Price of 1926 model in 1926}}$$
$$\times \frac{\text{Price of 1925 model in 1926}}{\text{Price of 1925 model in 1925}}$$

Parts II–VI, therefore, fails to record changes in the efficiency of the later processes of production.

When combining index numbers of real cost for several industries care is necessary to avoid duplication. In general, economies in the construction of machines for use in home industries are recorded in the industries using the machines and must not be counted a second time; while improvements in transportation and in the general financial and commercial organisation of the country (as by the development of insurance and banking facilities) are registered in the decline of real costs in manufacturing industries, since the index numbers are based upon market prices. In short, a thorough investigation (defective data aside) of a country's principal manufacturing and extractive industries by the method outlined above would give a valuable indication of the industrial progress of the nation, but would not take account of economies in the processes of finishing and distributing the consumer's goods.

VI

The manipulation of the time-series tabulated in the Appendices to obtain relationships of the type discussed in Parts II–VI is interesting, but it is not the main purpose of this essay. My primary object is the discovery of certain causal relations between these historical sequences; in particular that relation between the decline of the real cost per unit and the increase in the output of the product which is designated increasing return. No great discoveries occurred to revolutionise the five industries investigated in the present enquiry.[1] At the beginning of the period they were conducted in essentially the same way as at the end (1913); but division of labour has been pushed further and numerous technical improvements made in all five industries. Many of the inventions which have contributed to the decline of real costs in these industries would probably have

---

[1] Namely: The London Building Industry 1845–1913. The Lancashire Cotton Industry 1845–1913. Cotton Manufacture in Massachusetts 1845–1920. Pig Iron Manufacture on the North-East Coast of England 1883–1925. Pig Iron Manufacture in the United States 1883–1925.

been made if there had been no increase in the normal output of the industries. The elasticity of return should really measure the ratio between the rate of expansion of the industry and the increase in the rate of fall of real cost per unit of the product above that historical decline of real costs which occurs independently of the expansion. Both the elasticity of return and the independent decline of real costs are functions not only of the nature of the particular industry but also of the character of the environment: the inventiveness and vigour of the people within the industry and in neighbouring industries. Comparison of the elasticities of return in different industries will not yield useful results unless this environmental factor may be assumed constant without serious error.

The independent decline of real costs in the five industries studied was almost certainly continuously positive during the period under review (1850–1910); so that estimates based upon the ratio between the actual rate of fall of real costs and the expansion of the industry must necessarily give low values for the elasticity of return, thus exaggerating the tendency to increasing return. Moreover all arbitrary decisions upon questions of technique have been such as to exaggerate the tendency to increasing return. The values for the elasticity of return in certain industries presented in the table on p. 55 must therefore be regarded as minima.

These results are discussed in greater detail in the final sections of Parts II–VI and in Part VII, but certain features may be noted here. First, values have *not* been computed for the elasticity of return in periods of secular depression, but only at times of normal growth as indicated by the smooth upward trend of output and smooth (downward) trend of real cost. This is necessary to avoid the complicating influence of economic lag.[1] The low index numbers of real cost of American pig iron for 1890 to 1900, for example, are largely explained by the fact that many producers, caught in the depression of the early 'nineties, were compelled to take heavy losses and all earned abnormally low profits. One cannot assume that the index

[1] For business men anticipate depression and boom normal to the trade cycle but are surprised by periods of secular (i.e. continued) depression.

TABLE

Date	Rate of fall of real costs (% per annum)	Rate of expansion of industry (% per annum)	Elasticity of return, i.e. Rate of expansion of industry ÷ Rate of fall of real costs
The London Building Industry			
1850–60	$\frac{1}{2}$	2	4
1890–5	1	3	3
The Lancashire Cotton Industry			
1850–60	(1)	(5)	5
1870–80	$\frac{1}{2}$	$2\frac{1}{2}$	5
1890–1900	$\frac{1}{2}$	1	2
The Cleveland Pig Iron Industry			
1902–10	1	1	1
The Massachusetts Cotton Industry			
1850–4	$\frac{4}{5}$	4	5
1869–74	$4\frac{1}{3}$	8	2
1876–80	1	2	2
1880–5	2	4	2
1889–94	$1\frac{1}{2}$	$3\frac{1}{2}$	$2\frac{1}{3}$
The Pig Iron Industry of the United States			
1885–90	5	$8\frac{1}{2}$	$1\frac{7}{10}$
1907–12	$3\frac{1}{2}$	$3\frac{1}{2}$	1

N.B. The brackets indicate that the moving averages were smoothed by hand.

numbers of real cost measure changes in the quantity of resources employed per unit of product unless the industry is expanding continuously. It is also necessary that the trend of real costs and of output be smooth and fairly constant for several years on either side of the point at which the elasticity of return is measured: for the benefit of improvements, whether they be internal or external economies, will remain with the established producers until the competition of new investments compels them to transfer the benefit to the consumers in the form of lower selling prices. These quasi-rents are part of the returns necessary to maintain the investment of capital and business ability in the industry, but they create a gap between the introduction of economies and the consequent fall in the index numbers of real cost.[1]

Second, the apparent decrease in the elasticity of return in these industries during the latter half of the nineteenth century may represent a growing tendency to increasing return, but is more probably to be explained by the relative growth of independent economies (so-called external influences) with the decline in the rate of expansion of the industries.

Finally, it will be observed that I have made no attempt to divide the advantages of production on a large scale into external and internal economies. Though it is true that "the economic use of specialised skill and machinery requires that they should be fully occupied", it does not require that they be under the same management; while that subdivision of labour (including the work of management), which is the dominant feature of the tendency to increasing return, may be achieved by the progressive specialisation of firms upon narrower ranges of production or by the multiplication of departments within the financial unit.[2] In point of fact there is evidence, in these industries, that the size of both the manufacturing and the commercial unit has increased *pari passu* with the size of the industries, but the fact is irrelevant to our immediate purpose. So long as the returns to the several factors of production including management are determined by the competitive process (i.e. the principle of substitution) all the economies effected

[1] The general manager of a large firm which has been manufacturing cotton textile machinery in Massachusetts since 1838 claims that the manufacturers of improved textile machinery have always charged prices which absorbed nearly all the benefit of the improvements. Upon reflection it is clear that it will often be to the advantage of the manufacturer of a new machine to charge the highest price he can get for his output when he is producing to capacity. For this, among other reasons, many years may elapse between the invention and general adoption of an improvement.

[2] The choice between trustification and proliferation as a process of industrial growth is determined by the commercial and legal habits of the community in which the industry is located rather than the relative (social) efficiency of the two types of organisation. Whichever line of development is followed the fundamental relation between the trend of prices and costs which I have assumed may be expected to hold unless a trust establishes a monopoly of natural resources for which no satisfactory substitute is available; for the principle of substitution may work through the competition of different industries as readily as through the rivalry of similar enterprises.

will be registered in the index of real cost. Some business geniuses may require a very large enterprise to keep them fully employed upon the highest work of which they are capable, while others may exercise their skill to best advantage in the manipulation of a comparatively small concern. It is an accident if the expansion of an industry is *always* accompanied by an increase in the optimum size of the business unit. All that the development of the economic organism necessarily involves is an increasing subdivision of functions between its separate parts on the one hand and on the other hand a more intimate connection between them.

This conception of increasing return as a process of industrial growth varying in importance with the technological character of the industry is supported by the statistical results of the present enquiry. The values obtained for the elasticity of return in the period 1890–1910 suggest (*a*) that the strengths of the tendencies to increasing return in the manufacture of iron and cotton and the construction of buildings are in the ratio 3 : 2 : 1 respectively, which is precisely what one would expect *a priori* from the character of these industries; and (*b*) that the elasticities of return were about equal in the corresponding English and American industries in spite of the fact that the manufacturing and financial units were much larger in American iron and cotton manufacture than in the corresponding English industries.

Note. An attempt has been made to continue the index numbers through the War and up to the present time but no reliance is placed upon them after 1913. The calculations are correct but it is doubtful if the results have any meaning owing to the abnormal conditions of trade since 1914.

PART II

THE LONDON BUILDING INDUSTRY
1845–1913

§ 1. INTRODUCTION

EIGHTY YEARS of progress in the housebuilding and allied trades have seen little change. Ferro-concrete has largely replaced the massive carpentry which characterised large buildings in the middle of the nineteenth century. To some extent this new process has also displaced the bricklayer and stonemason, but as yet it is used mainly in floors and ceilings or in the manufacture of artificial stone which requires fixing by a competent mason. Specialities such as patent tiles and flooring often replace the plain work of the local artisans in modern buildings. These developments have been accompanied by great changes in architectural technique while the fittings of houses, hospitals, etc., now demand almost as much attention as the main construction. Such changes have profoundly modified the demand for labour in the trade, specially trained workmen displacing the old-fashioned journeyman while even among the labourers a high degree of specialisation is discernible in London and other cities. Mr N. B. Dearle discusses the significance of these developments from the labour point of view in his book on *Unemployment in the London Building Trades* (chap. iv). They need only be mentioned in the present connection.

The modern architect has thus a wide and more varied choice of materials for the creation of beautiful and useful structures than his predecessors of the 'fifties and 'sixties. The new processes made their first appearance for the most part in the 'seventies, 'eighties and 'nineties, but it was not until the present century that they won favour with builders generally, while it required the stimulus of war to weaken the public's prejudices against them. In tracing changes in the efficiency with which plain brickwork, joinery, slating, tiling, plastering, painting and plumbing were executed from 1845–1913, we are approximating to a measure of the progress made by the building industry during that period. In addition to economies in the execution of the architect's instructions, which are included in this measure, considerable improvements have been made in design. Doors, windows, floors and walls are now combined with greater skill than aforetime, so that more satisfaction is obtained from the same material. This group of architectural improvements does not enter into my index of real costs, nor is any allowance made for the wide choice of colours in decorating, of varieties of bricks or tiles, etc. The index numbers reflect only changes in the cost of constructing a building in which the architect's specifications as to brickwork, masonry, joinery, etc., are given.

In the wage census of 1906 the "building trades" were taken to include the construction of houses, factories, hospitals, and such public works as involve a large proportion of brick, stone, and woodwork. The construction of harbours, docks, roads and sewers was excluded, as also the work of the sewager. Unique as it is, this definition describes as well as may be the group of trades I have in mind when talking of the building industry. The workers covered by the definition numbered approximately one million in 1906, and rather less than half that number at the beginning of our period. The boundaries of the industry are necessarily ill-defined, for it ranges from the speculative house builder and small builder engaged largely upon jobbing repairs to the London master builder who contracts for public works, etc., subletting parts of his contracts to specialised firms. In London the house builders and the master builders are sharply divided, having separate associations and not often encroaching upon one another's territory; the recent incursions of munici-palities into the market have led indeed to large firms under-taking the mass production of houses, but this is an abnormal development. In the provinces, on the other hand, there are but few firms which do not build houses as well as contracting for large work.

The search for unity in such diversity seems futile. There is no standard product, house or factory, upon which to base selling price index numbers, nor any convenient record of the values of the principal types of building. The key to the problem lies in the fact that the work of the carpenter and joiner, bricklayer and mason, plumber, plasterer and painter enters largely into the construction of both the hospital and cottage, and into the repair of the railway station and country mansion. Fortunately the relative importance of the various trades in the industry did not change very much in spite of the growth of ferro-concrete. While the mason gradually gave way to the bricklayer and the concretor, decorating, repair, and alteration probably gained upon new construction; by 1907 they accounted for half the receipts of the industry (census of production). These are but small changes to occupy a half century and they have been ignored.

The index numbers of selling price or money cost of building have been computed by combining prices quoted for a unit of brickwork, joinery, plumbing, etc., of standard type and uniform quality, weighting each according to the relative expenditure upon the several trades in years adjacent to the base year (1910). Separate series of index numbers of selling price have been constructed for the several trades and corresponding "real cost" indexes derived therefrom by correcting for changes in the supply prices of labour and materials. By combining these in fixed proportions index numbers of selling prices of building (a) uncorrected, (b) corrected, for labour and materials are obtained. A final correction to the margin absorbed by "other expenses" for changes in the value of money gives an index of the "real cost" of constructing an imaginary building into which the various trades enter in fixed proportions corresponding to their relative importance in the industry (including alteration and repair) in the years first preceding the War. Changes in the real cost of producing this composite product of uniform quality will be a guide to the course of real costs of production in the building industry as a whole. The statistical work which follows has been based upon figures relating largely to the London building trades but, as this market dominates the building industry of England and Wales, the general trend of costs will be much the same in the provinces.

The prices used in these calculations have all been extracted from Laxton's *Builder's Price Book* which is recognised by the trade. All agree that, though Laxton's prices may be wrong, his error is constant. The publishers claim that their quotations are "fair" for first-class work in the London district and provide the acknowledged standard to which in any disputed cases in the various Law Courts reference is made. It has seemed best to use Laxton's prices for labour and materials in correcting the index numbers, since they are appropriate to the quoted prices. The items used have been chosen in consultation with experts as representing the several trades, and remaining uniform in quality throughout the period 1845–1922. At the latter date (1922) the *Annual* was drastically revised and some of the vital quotations omitted, other quantities being substituted, so that I have been unable to bring the index numbers up to date for the industry as a whole. However the growing importance of ferro-concrete, which has been entirely omitted from my calculations, requires that a new "imaginary building" be constructed to serve as standard for the post-War period.

In determining the relative expenditure, and thence the appropriate weights, upon the different items within each trade and upon the several trades, also in analysing costs for each quotation, I have had the advice of a professional builder's estimator of thirty years' experience and the criticism of the heads of leading firms in London and Manchester. These firms have supplied me with confidential information upon which my ratios are based.

The base year chosen is 1910. In that year all my selling price index numbers equal 100; while the index numbers of wages, cost of raw materials, and the value of money in that year equal the percentage of total costs going to labour, materials, and miscellaneous charges in the base year. It seemed best to lump together all miscellaneous charges rather than attempt to correct separately for such items as rates, salaries and interest charges. The material for separate correction is not available, save on the item interest charges, which is so small a proportion of the whole that the correction is negligible. It is generally reckoned that capital can normally be turned over three times a year, which gives us at 10 % a figure of 3½ % of turnover for interest charges. In the case of a London firm with a turnover of £300,000 in 1910 the capital value of the works was reckoned at £70,000, while interest charges on circulating capital borrowed from the bank amounted to £450 for the year. If we reckon gross interest on fixed capital at 10 % per annum, we get an interest charge of £7000 and £450 = 2½ % on turnover. The firm had also a moderate amount of private circulating capital and was doing a brisk trade at the time. A provincial company with a paid up capital of £8600 had an average turnover during the years 1915–24 of £45,400 per annum and an overdraft at the bank of approximately £1000. If this were all the capital employed the rates of turnover in this case would be nearly five times per annum. Again there was but little private circulating capital employed, but trade was good. The tradition in the building trade that capital is generally turned over three times in a normal year seems to be supported by these figures.

The reduction of wage index numbers and prices of raw materials to bases corresponding to the percentage of total costs that they represent brings into the limelight the effect of, say, a rise of wages upon the cost of building. For a rise of one whole number in the index of efficiency, wages will correspond approximately to a rise of one integer in the index numbers of money cost of building. In short, the absolute changes in the indexes of efficiency wages and cost of raw materials are approximately equal to the percentage change in the cost of building caused thereby. The relation is a rough one for years distant from the base because the weight appropriate to each factor may have changed while the index numbers of cost of building will deviate considerably in remote years from the 100 of 1910.

There follows a summary of the material used in the construction of the several trade index numbers and their combination into indexes for the industry. An estimate is made on pp. 78–81 of the magnitude of the errors involved in the calculations. A brief discussion of the significance of the curve of real cost of building closes this section of the essay. A more detailed analysis of the arrangement will be found in the table of contents.

Note. The columns quoted in brackets in the following sections refer to the columns in Appendix I, Table A.

§2. BRICKWORK (INCLUDING EXCAVATOR AND CONCRETOR)

I. The selling price index (col. 1) for this trade has been constructed from Laxton's quotations thus:

(*a*) Price per rod reduced of brickwork of stock bricks (known in the North of England as "common bricks" being also slightly larger) laid in mortar of stone lime and Thames sand (3 and 1) up to 40 ft. high, principally 9 and 14 in. work.

I am told that a very large proportion of all brickwork is covered directly by this quotation while architects reduce all brickwork to its equivalent in stock bricks.

(*b*) The price of concrete work was derived from quotations

(1) Concrete of Portland Cement and Thames ballast in ratio 1 : 7 in foundations, per cu. yd.

(2) Concrete of Portland Cement and Thames ballast in ratio 1 : 4 in floors per ft. super

by simple addition, since it is estimated that before the War about five times as much was spent on concrete for foundations as for floors. This happens to be the approximate ratio of the above prices.

In the absence of quotations the prices for 1845–75 have been assumed to move parallel to the price of Portland cement.

These prices have been reduced to pence and divided by 48·5 and 18·3 making the 1910 numbers 80 and 20 respectively which is the estimated pre-War ratio of expenditure on brickwork and concrete at 1910 prices. Addition then gives index numbers of selling price of "brickwork" (including excavation and concrete) expressed as percentages of price in 1910.

II. The index of cost of materials in the trade has been constructed by combining Laxton's prices for:

(*a*) Stock bricks, prime cost per thousand (col. 19).

(*b*) Chalk lime, per cubic yard (col. 20),

(*c*) Thames sand, per cubic yard (col. 21),

(*d*) Portland cement, per bushel (col. 22),

weighting then according to the amounts required in I, thus:

Concrete, 1 cu. yd. (1 : 7) { 3 bushels cement / 1 cu. yd. sand (ballast) }

Brickwork, 1 rod reduced { 3 cu. yds. sand / 1 cu. yd. lime / 5·5 thousand bricks (allowing for fact that price of bricks is prime) }

Combined in expenditure ratio 1 : 4 as in I above, dividing concrete material weights by 18·3 and brickwork by 48·5. Finally reduce index to base of 1910 = 50, which is the percentage of expenditure in the trade going to raw materials in 1910.

I thus calculate that to derive an index of cost of brickwork materials, I require to reduce all prices to pence and multiply:

$$\left.\begin{array}{l} (a) \times \cdot 0887 \\ (b) \times \cdot 015 \\ (c) \times \cdot 089 \\ (d) \times \cdot 126 \end{array}\right\} \text{ and add. For 1910 I get } \left\{\begin{array}{l} 36\cdot2 \\ 2\cdot3 \\ 8\cdot3 \\ \underline{3\cdot2} \end{array}\right.$$

Total   50·0

III. The measure of efficiency wages for this trade has been derived from Laxton's quotations for labour only per rod reduced of stock—brickwork (col. 28). This policy is justified because the method of bricklaying has remained practically the same throughout the period and the wages of concretors (where specialised to the work) move parallel to those of bricklayers.

IV. Figures 50 and 35 for the percentages of expenditure in this trade going to pay for materials and labour respectively in 1910 are derived as follows:

(a) An analysis of three large and representative contracts executed by a London firm in or about 1910, namely:

		Total contract
(1) New construction	... ...	£60,000
(2) Alterations and additions	... ...	44,000 } approx.
(3) Alterations and additions	... ...	2,500

gives a ratio of:

Materials   ...   56 % } For brickwork (including
Labour   ...   44 % } excavator and concretor).

(b) An analysis of the expenditure of a representative Manchester firm with an average pre-War turnover of £100,000 per annum shows an average ratio of:

Materials   ...   58 % } For brickwork (including
Labour   ...   42 % } excavator and concretor)

for the period 1906–13 inclusive.

(c) An experienced estimator in the eastern counties suggested, quite independently, that:

Materials	...	60 %	Would represent the trade
Labour	...	40 %	in pre-War days.

(d) Laxton, in 1916, gives:

Materials	...	66 %	For bricklayers' work
Labour	...	34 %	only.

(e) Laxton reckons 15 % for establishment charges, profit, etc., and this is confirmed by the above authorities.

After allowing for the fact that London wages are higher than in the provinces, that excavator and concretor are grouped together with bricklayer, and that Laxton's estimate was made in 1916 when prices of materials were rising faster than wages, I arrive at the following estimate for 1910:

Materials	...	...	50 %
Labour	...	...	35 %
Profit, etc.	...	...	15 %

It is interesting to note that a calculation based on memoranda given by Laxton (1910–25) as to the derivation of his quotations we get, at 1910 prices, for:

(a) Brickwork, labour equals 27 % of costs.
(b) Concretor,   ,,   16 %   ,,
(c) Excavator,   ,,   100 %   ,,

Combining these in ratio 4 : 1 : 1, which is in close accord with fact, we get labour = 37 % of costs, which agrees closely with the estimate given above.

§3. CARPENTRY & JOINERY

I. The selling price index (col. 2) has been constructed from the quotations given by Laxton for:

(a) Rough boarding, 1 in. thick, per square.

(b) Floors, 1 in. best yellow deal, wrought and laid folding, per square.

(c) Doors, 4-panel deal, square framed, moulded both sides, 2 in. thick, per ft. super.

(*d*) Windows, deal sashes and frames with weights, single hung, brass cased axle pulleys, etc., 2 in. sashes per ft. super.

(*e*) Windows, deal casement sashes and frames, 2 in. sashes, per ft. super.

It is estimated that expenditure upon carpentry (*a*) was about one quarter of the expenditure on joinery (*b*)–(*e*) in 1910, taking the trade as a whole; while expenditure upon floors, doors, sash windows and casement windows was in the ratio 4 : 5 : 1 : 1. Index numbers to the base 1910 = 100 in accordance with these ratios are computed by reducing to pence and dividing:

$$\left.\begin{array}{l} (a) \div 11\cdot3 \\ (b) \div 9\cdot9 \\ (c) \div 1\cdot91 \\ (d) \div 2\cdot63 \\ (e) \div 2\cdot89 \end{array}\right\} \text{ and adding.}$$

II. The price for Petrograd standard of deals in the London docks (col. 26) gives the measure of cost of materials in carpentry and joinery.

I am assured that no appreciable error is involved in the neglect of hard woodwork since it constitutes a very small proportion of the trade. Further changes in efficiency of that section of the industry dealing in hard wood must be closely related to changes in the soft wood trade.

III. (*a*) The index of efficiency wages of carpenters and joiners is derived by adding Laxton's quotations for labour only per foot super in ceiling floors (joists only) and lean-to roofs (col. 32).

These prices are chosen because continuous records are available and the method of doing the work has remained practically unchanged.

(*b*) Owing to the introduction of machinery to the joiners' shop during the 'seventies the physical amount of labour required to do a given piece of work has changed considerably during the period 1845–1922. Fortunately it is possible to allow for this, since Laxton gives quotations for labour only to each of the items used in constructing the selling price index for carpentry and joinery. Combining these labour items in the proportions employed in calculating that index, index numbers of the labour cost of the same job in successive years to the base 1910 = 40 are obtained (col. 3). These index numbers are corrected for changes in efficiency wages by the index calculated above to give figures showing the labour cost of the same job in successive years at 1910 wage rates, i.e. an index of the physical volume of labour required to do a given job in successive years. The differences between these two sets of index numbers measure the deviations of labour costs from the base year number 40 due to changes in wages, i.e. the required correction to the selling price index on account of labour.

IV. The evidence for the figures 40 and 40 as percentages of total expenditure on carpentry and joinery in 1910, going to pay for labour and materials is essentially the same as in the case of brickwork (ref. pp. 64-5).

(a) The London analysis gives a ratio:

Materials	...	...	50 %
Labour	...	...	50 %

(b) The Manchester analysis gives a ratio:

Materials	...	...	70 %
Labour	...	...	30 %

but the figures probably refer very largely to carpentry, in which the cost of materials accounts for a considerably higher proportion than in joinery. Further, wages are 5 % to 10 % lower in the Manchester area than in London.

(c) The expert estimator gives:

(1) Carpentry:	Materials	...	...	75 %
	Labour	...	...	25 %
(2) Joinery:	Materials	...	...	40 %
	Labour	...	...	60 %

Combining these in the ratio 1 : 4 we get:

Materials	...	...	47 %
Labour	...	...	53 %

(d) Laxton in 1916 estimates:

(1) Carpentry:	Materials	...	...	74 %
	Labour	...	...	26 %
(2) Joinery:	Materials	...	...	42 %
	Labour	...	...	58 %

Combining these in the ratio 1 : 4 we get:

Materials	... ...	48·4 %
Labour	... ...	51·6 %

(*e*) Laxton reckons 20 % for profit, establishment charges, etc., in carpentry and joinery, which is confirmed by other authorities.

I therefore estimate the distribution of costs in carpentry and joinery in 1910 to be approximately:

Materials	... ...	40 %
Labour	... ...	40 %
Profit, etc.	... ...	20 %

N.B. Laxton quotes two series of prices from 1870 to 1892 for joinery, the one for work done with and the other without the assistance of machinery in the shop. Thereafter he quotes only prices involving the use of such machinery as is in use in first-class joiners' shops. It has been assumed that the introduction of machinery took place uniformly over this period, and the prices used for labour and for the finished product have been derived by interpolation.

§4. MASONRY

I. The selling price index (col. 4) is derived from Laxton's quotation for Portland stone in block, plain face work, including hoisting and setting, per cubic foot by reducing to pence and multiplying by 1·59, which brings the index number for 1910 = 100.

II. The mason's materials cost is obtained from Laxton's prices per cubic foot of Portland stone in block at Nine Elms Station (col. 25).

III. Laxton's labour cost per foot super of mason's ordinary moulded work (i.e. greater than 2 in. diameter) (col. 31) gives a measure of the efficiency wages of masons.

This index is open to considerable criticism, since very little working of stone has been done in London for many years, the custom of ordering stone ready worked from the quarries where labour is cheaper having developed largely in the last decade of the nineteenth century and the first of the present. Consequently the quotations for moulded work seem to have been revised, but infrequently. The index is still probably better than hourly wages for my purpose, because the falling demand for mason's work during the last forty or fifty years has had the effect of weeding out the less efficient so that efficiency wages have risen slowly compared with time wages. The absence of stone building work during the War prevented the rise even of prices charged at quarries for labour, the stonemason who works largely on piece-rates being badly hit in spite of the rise of his hourly rates of pay parallel to the bricklayer. The stability of the mason's efficiency wage index from 1912–19 is thus confirmed.

IV. The evidence for estimated percentages of costs going to labour and to material in the trade in 1910 is much the same as for brickwork, etc.

(a) The London analysis does *not* allow of the separation of mason's work from that of the slater, it gives for the two:

Materials	... ...	54 %
Labour	... ...	46 %

(b) The Manchester analysis provides no evidence on this point.

(c) The estimator gives the ratio:

Materials	... ...	40 %
Labour	... ...	60 %

(d) Laxton in 1916 gives:

Materials	... ...	38 %
Labour	... ...	62 %

(e) 15 % is recognised by all as the correct allowance for establishment charges and profit, pre-War.

I therefore estimate the distribution of costs in masonry in 1910 to be approximately:

Materials	... ...	35 %
Labour	... ...	50 %
Profit, etc.	... ...	15 %

N.B. It will be clearly seen that the index numbers used in this trade cannot pretend to the accuracy of those for brickwork and carpentry, etc. Mason's work only accounts for 7 % of the industry, however, so that only a small fraction of the error is carried forward to the final index. Further the figures used throughout are strictly comparable so that the index numbers probably reflect *changes* fairly accurately.

§ 5. ROOFING (Tiling & Slating)

I. The roofing selling price index has been built up from Laxton's quotations:

(*a*) Price per square of best Bangor slating, countesses, copper nails.

(*b*) Price per square of plain tiling with wrought nails, showing 4 in. on the face.

Expenditure upon slating and tiling is estimated to be in the ratio 4 : 1 at 1910 prices. Reducing to pence and dividing

$$(b) \div 25 \cdot 2 + (a) \div 5 \cdot 7,$$

gives the required index numbers to the base 1910 = 100 (col. 5).

II. The raw materials' costs for this trade are based entirely upon Laxton's prices and memoranda.

(*a*) Prices of countess slates, per dozen (col. 24).

(*b*) Prices of plain tiles, per thousand (col. 23).

It requires 155 countess slates to cover one square with $2\frac{1}{2}$ in. overlap, while 600 plain tiles laid 4 in. to the face will cover the same area.

After making a small allowance for the greater waste of slates, we derive the raw materials index numbers by reducing to pence, dividing (*b*) by 8·8, multiplying (*a*) by 1·09, and adding. The base 1910 = 65 represents the estimated percentage of expenditure going to pay for raw materials in 1910.

III. The method of tiling and slating having remained very largely the same, the efficiency wage index has been obtained by adding Laxton's prices for Bangor slating and plain tiling, labour only (col. 29).

IV. The distribution of costs in this trade is based upon two estimates only, no information being available from the London or Manchester analyses ((*a*) and (*b*) in previous trades).

(*c*) The expert estimator gives the ratio:

Materials	... ...	75 %
Labour	... ...	25 %

(*d*) Laxton, in 1916, gives the ratio:

Materials	... ...	80 %
Labour	... ...	20 %

(*e*) Laxton agrees with other authorities in allowing 15 % for profits, etc.

I therefore suggest as the approximate distribution of costs in the trade at 1910 prices:

Materials	... ...	65 %
Labour	... ...	20 %
Profits, etc.	... ...	15 %

§ 6. PLUMBING

I. The selling price index is derived from Laxton's price per cwt. for milled lead cut to dimensions and laid in flats (col. 9) by reducing to pence and dividing by 3·12 to make the 1910 index number = 100.

II. The raw materials' costs are derived from the prime cost of milled lead in sheets (col. 27).

III. Laxton does not begin to quote a price (col. 33) for plumbing labour until 1898, but we have Dr Bowley's authority (*J.S.S.* 1901, p. 103 n.) for believing the movements of carpenters' and joiners' wages to reflect closely the movements throughout the industry. In the absence of better figures I have used the index of carpenters' and joiners' efficiency wages as an efficiency wage index for plumbers.

IV. The evidence for the percentages of costs attributed to the various factors is much the same as for brickwork.

(*a*) London analysis shows the ratio:

Materials	... ...	60 %
Labour	... ...	40 %

(*b*) The Manchester analysis gives:

Materials	...	...	79 %
Labour	...	...	21 %

(*c*) The estimator gives, for the trade as a whole:

Materials	...	...	70 %
Labour	...	...	30 %

(*d*) Laxton, in 1916:

Materials	...	...	73 %
Labour	...	...	27 %

(*e*) 15 % is the agreed allowance for establishment charges, etc.

I therefore estimate that the following proportions may be taken as representative of the trade in 1910:

Materials	...	...	60 %
Labour	...	...	25 %
Profit, etc.	...	...	15 %

§7. PAINTING

I. The decorating trade is represented by this selling price index (col. 6) which is derived from Laxton's prices per yard super of painting plain new work in common colours, three coats, the knotting and priming being counted as one coat by reducing to pence and multiplying by 8·33.

II. The prime cost of lead (col. 27) is the basis of the index numbers of cost of painters' materials since lead enters very largely into the manufacture of paints.

III. As for plumbers, the efficiency wage index is derived from that of carpenters and joiners.

IV. The evidence as to the distribution of costs in this trade is unsatisfactory.

(*a*) The London analysis only gives figures for painter and glazier combined:

Materials	...	...	57 %
Labour	...	...	43 %

(b) The Manchester analysis gives the ratio for painter:

Materials	...	...	30 %
Labour	...	...	70 %

(c) The estimator's figures are:

Materials	...	...	40 %
Labour	...	...	60 %

(d) Laxton, in 1916, gives the same ratio:

Materials	...	...	40 %
Labour	...	...	60 %

(e) Laxton allows 15 % for establishment charges, profit, etc., in this trade.

The distribution of costs in the trade at 1910 prices is approximately:

Materials	...	...	30 %
Labour	...	...	55 %
Profit, etc.	...	...	15 %

This estimate allows a rather low proportion for materials, following the Manchester analysis closely, because the selling price index has been based on work in which the value of materials used is small, and further the Manchester firms' figures are based on a wide variety of work actually done by the firm since 1910. In any case the error, if it be in allowing too small a proportion for raw materials, would accentuate the marked rise of the corrected selling price index of painting, reducing the strength of the tendency to increasing return indicated by the final index numbers.

N.B. This trade alone in the industry shows an upward trend of real costs of production from 1845-1910. Taken at their face value the figures indicate a 35 % fall in efficiency during this period. Any likely error in weighting of the correction would accentuate this apparent fall of efficiency. The use of the prime cost of lead as a guide to changes in the cost of paints, etc., possibly accounts for part of the apparent rise of real costs; the margin charged for the manufacture of paints from the raw material may have increased: the rise of wages would lead one to expect as much, on the other hand technical progress has been considerable in the chemical and allied industries. I do not think that appreciable allowance is necessary under this head. The time explanation of the rise is, I think, twofold. The index numbers refer to the amount charged for painting new work in common colours. In 1850 there was little variety in house decoration, the painter was invited to contract for " doing a place through " in solid fashion calculated to last rather than to please the artistic senses. Such work was done very largely by unskilled or semi-skilled labour, while the master painter and decorator could carry on a brisk trade with but a small stock of colours, etc. Now all is changed—we have our houses re-decorated frequently and are exacting as to colour and finish, unskilled workers are no longer satisfactory and the journeyman painter has but recently been recognised by the trade and granted the same wages as the bricklayer and plumber. On the other hand, I think there is little doubt that the rapid growth in demand for decorating has opened the door to inferior talent among both masters and men, and that the economies reaped from the specialisation of firms upon particular branches of the trade have not sufficed to offset this slackening of effort.

It appears, therefore, that a part of the rise of corrected selling price index numbers in this trade is apparent rather than real, being offset by the wider range of qualities obtainable and the greater satisfaction derived from a more varied scheme of decoration. Nevertheless there has probably been a consider-able fall in the efficiency of master and man in the trade.

§8. PLASTERING

I. Three items enter into the composition of the selling price index (col. 7) for this trade, all from Laxton.

(a) Price for rendering one coat rough on brick, per yard super.

(b) Lathing and plastering one coat, set with fine stuff, per yard super (lath and a half to partitions).

(c) Portland cement plastering (3 : 1) plain face on brick, floated, per yard super.

The third item is intended to cover outdoor work. It is estimated that the ratio of expenditure upon these three items, at 1910 prices, is 3 : 2 : 1. Hence the index numbers are calculated by reducing the prices to pence and multiplying (*a*) by 6·25, multiplying (*b*) by 1·66, dividing (*c*) by 1·77, and adding. The base number is 1910 = 100.

II. In constructing the raw materials' index (col. 8) I find that "plaster" in the technical sense is very little used so that the index numbers are based upon the prime cost of (*a*) sand (col. 21), (*b*) lime (col. 20), (*c*) laths, i.e. deal (col. 26), and (*d*) cement (col. 22). Hair, etc., accounts for less than 1 % and has been neglected. The appropriate weights have been calculated from J. T. Rea's *How to Estimate* (1913) used in conjunction with Laxton. I have weighted sand, lime, cement, and laths in the ratio 20 yd.³ : 10 yd.³ : 10 bushels : ¼ Petrograd standard.

III. The efficiency wage index for plasterers is derived from Laxton's labour price per yard super for rendering one coat rough on brick (col. 30).

IV. The evidence for distribution of costs in plastering is slight, the Manchester and London figures giving no guidance on the point.

(*d*) The estimator gives the ratio:

Materials	...	...	40 %
Labour	...	...	60 %

(*e*) Laxton, in 1916, gives the ratio:

Materials	...	...	46 %
Labour	...	...	54 %

(*f*) Laxton allows 15 % to cover profit, etc.

The percentages allotted to the different items in cost in the base year 1910 are:

Materials	...	...	35 %
Labour	...	...	50 %
Profit, etc.	...	...	15 %

§9. THE BUILDING INDUSTRY—COSTS

I. *The relative importance of the several trades in the building industry.*

(*a*) An analysis of three contracts executed by a London firm in or about 1910 (see above) gives the following ratios for the seven trades under consideration.

A	B	C, D
	Carpenter and	Mason and
Brickwork	joiner	slater
35 %	24 %	23 %*
E	F	G
Plumber	Painter	Plasterer
5 %	6 %	7 %

* Abnormal amount of stonework in contracts.

(*b*) An analysis of the trading accounts of the Manchester firm shows the following apportionment of expenditure.

A	B	C*	D†	E	F	G
45 %	36 %	3 %	2 %	8 %	2 %	4 %

* Mason.   † Slater.

After consulting several builders, etc., I have decided to apportion the expenditure in my imaginary building as follows:

A	B	C	D	E	F	G
40 %	30 %	7 %	2 %	8 %	7 %	6 %

The divergencies from the two analyses ((*a*) and (*b*)) are largely explained by the facts (*a*) that there is a larger proportion of stonework in the London district than in Manchester, hence the 7 % for masonry; (*b*) that the decorating trade which is important specially in London engages many specialised firms, and therefore comes out low in the analysis of particular builder's costs.

II. *Derivation of the index numbers for the whole industry from the trade indexes.*

The index numbers for the industry as a whole (Appendix I B, p. 268) have been constructed by multiplying the corresponding trade index numbers by the weights decided upon above (I), adding and dividing by a hundred. This gives us:

(a) The index of selling price of building ... ...   Column B 1
(b) The index of selling price of building corrected for changes in the cost of labour and materials ...   ,,   B 2
(c) The index of cost of materials in the building industry   ,,   B 5
(d) The index of efficiency wages in the London building industry ... ...   ,,   B 6

Dr Bowley's index of average summer weekly wages in the London building trades (B 7) has been reduced to the base 1910 = 38·8 for comparison with the efficiency wage index. Although Dr Bowley's index numbers cease at 1900 it is possible to bring them to the base 1910 = 38·8 because wages remained stable from 1900–10.

A final index of selling price of building corrected for changes in the cost of labour, materials, and in the value of money (B 3) has been obtained by adding to or subtracting from the corrected index (B 2) the deviations of the index numbers of the trend in general prices (B 4) from the base number 16·5, which is the percentage of costs taking the industry as a whole devoted to establishment charges, profits, etc., to which no correction has so far been made.

N.B. The index B 4 of the trend of general prices is derived (a) from the ten years' moving average of Sauerbeck's index number of general prices, e.g. the index number for 1850

$$= \frac{\text{Av. Sauerbeck } 1845\text{–}54}{4\cdot8} = \frac{85}{4\cdot8} = 17\cdot7.$$

The index numbers for 1845–1910 inclusive have been derived in this way. The base year 1910

$$= \frac{\text{Av. Sauerbeck } 1905\text{–}14}{4\cdot8} = \frac{79}{4\cdot8} = 16\cdot5.$$

(b) During the War the Ministry of Labour cost of living index numbers have been used. The averages of the monthly numbers for each year from 1915–25 are 126, 146, 176, 203, 215, 249, 226, 183, 174, 175 and 176 respectively.

The Sauerbeck index number for July 1914 (when the cost of living index number was 100) was 82·4. The cost of living index numbers have therefore been multiplied by $\frac{82.4}{100}$ to reduce them to the Sauerbeck base. The figures for 1911–14 inclusive have been obtained by interpolation. Thus in continuation of the Sauerbeck moving average from 1910 to 1925 we get 79, (81), (83), (84), (86), 104, 120, 145, 167, 177, 205, 186, 151, 143, 145, 145. Dividing these numbers by 4·8 to reduce to the base 1910 = 16·5 gives the index numbers for the years 1910–25 used in correcting for changes in the value of money, etc.

Several considerations have decided me to use the cost of living index numbers for the War period.

(a) The Sauerbeck index, based on average import values, became very unreliable as the War proceeded owing to changes in the quality of our imports.

(b) The items of costs under the heading Profit, etc., include rent, rates and salaries, items which tend to move in sympathy with the cost of living index rather than the Sauerbeck.

(c) The rapid changes in the value of money which characterised the War and post-War period were met by frequent changes in wages, salaries and prices. To correct for these changes the sensitive cost of living index number is preferable to the comparatively inert Sauerbeck index.

III. *The accuracy of the index numbers of costs for the building industry.*

It will be convenient first to discuss errors due to the inadequacy of the data, and then to consider the difficulty of interpreting the index numbers of real cost of building.

Statistical errors.

(a) *Prices.* The accuracy of the indexes of prices of the product, of raw materials and of labour depends upon the consistency of Laxton's quotations. There seems little doubt that the prices in this annual are compiled by men in close touch with market conditions, and that great care is exercised to secure comparable quotations as regards quality, etc. The figures probably do not represent actual contracts, but are reliable as a measure of changes in market prices. The value of Sauerbeck's index number of general prices is too well known to call for comment. It is the best measure of changes in the value of money available for the period. I have already indicated my reasons for preferring the ten years' moving average to the annual index numbers in applying a correction to the item "other expenses". They are twofold: first, it is improbable that the value of money to the entrepreneur actually fluctuated in the violent manner indicated by Sauerbeck's annual numbers; second, salaries, rents, rates and interest charges, which comprise the bulk of this group of costs, are slow to adapt themselves to such changes. Their course will, therefore, be better represented by the moving average than by the annual index numbers. In any case the item is quite small, the maximum correction under this head between 1845 and 1913 is 5 points in the index numbers of selling price. An error of 1 % in the measure of the value of money would thus involve an error of less than ·05 % in the measure of costs of building.

An allowance of 1 % would probably be more than adequate to cover the maximum deviation in the index of real cost attributable to errors in the constituent prices.

(b) *Weighting*. Given the prices of the product and of the factors, the index numbers of real cost deduced may err because inappropriate weights are assigned in correcting the selling prices for changes in the supply prices of the factors of production. This may happen in two ways:

(i) The distribution of costs in the base year may be inaccurate.

Corrections were applied to the several trade index numbers for changes in the cost of labour and of materials before combining them into index numbers for the industry. The distribution of costs in the construction of an imaginary building may be computed from these trade analyses. We get:

Materials	...	...	...	44·7 %
Labour	...	...	...	38·8 %
Other expenses	...	...	16·5 %

Fortunately there is other evidence in support of these proportions:

(1) An analysis of the balance sheets of a representative firm for the years 1915–24 shows an average expenditure of 49 % of

turnover upon wages and salaries, including the salaries of the staff and directors which are grouped with "other expenses" in my analysis. The difference of 10 % is close to the usual cost of "salaries of staff and directors".

(2) The net output of all firms covered by the *Building and Contracting Report of the Census of Production* (1907), after allowing for duplication, was approximately forty-three million pounds and the total cost of materials thirty-eight and a half million pounds. The census returns thus indicate a proportion of 47½ % for cost of raw materials in the building and contracting trades. This compares favourably with the figure of 44·7 % for building alone.

(3) The analysis of a number of contracts executed by a London firm between 1909 and 1911 gives an overall ratio of 53·7 : 46·3 for materials : labour. This agrees closely with my ratio of 53·5 : 46·5 at 1910 prices.

5 % seems to be a generous allowance for error in apportioning costs in the base year. This would probably not cause a variation of more than ½ % in the corrected index numbers, when allowance is made for the sympathetic movement of prices (ref. (ii) below).

(ii) The use of constant weights in correcting for changes in the supply prices of the factors involves inaccuracy in the index numbers of real cost.

This is probably the source of greatest error. It has already been fully discussed in general terms in the introduction, and was there shown to be equal to "the algebraic sum of the products of the errors in weighting and the deviations of the prices of the factors from those of the base year". Taking the maximum value of these deviations (pre-War) we find that an error of 1 % in the weight given to each factor would raise or lower the index numbers of real cost by less than

·1 in the case of materials;

·2 in the case of labour;

·05 in the case of other expenses (corrected for changes in the value of money).

Supposing these errors to be superimposed, a maximum variation of ·35 would occur in the index of real costs on account of an error of 1 % in the weighting of each of the three factors of production. In other words, a change between 1845 and 1913 of 1 % in the amount of labour or material or managing ability consumed in the production of an imaginary building would cause, on the average, a variation of not more than ·1 % in the index of real cost of building. In Part I, Section 2, II, I endeavoured to show that constant weighting left the "economies" made during the period uncorrected for these changes in prices. Between 1845 and 1910 the index numbers of real cost of building fell from about 120 to 100, so that net economies amounted to 20 %. Thus, the net error upon this count in the final index number of real cost in the building industry was probably not greater than 2 % at any time between 1845 and 1910.

Collecting together these three types of error I conclude that 3 %–4 % will cover any inaccuracy in the measure of changes in the real cost of building the imaginary structure from 1845 up to the outbreak of the War. The error is greater in the early years, falling gradually to about 1 % in the early part of the present century.

N.B. It has been assumed that constant weights were used in each of the seven trades. In point of fact the data in the carpentry and joinery allowed me to estimate the physical volume of labour required for the same job in successive years, and the weight attributed to this factor was modified accordingly. As this trade accounts for a very large proportion of the economies realised during the period the allowance made above for statistical error is too generous.

IV. *Interpretation of the corrected selling price index.*

Assuming that we can now measure changes in the real cost of producing an imaginary building from 1845–1910 within 3 % or 4 %, we have to ask the further question how far this cost curve represents changes in the efficiency of the building industry as a whole.

(a) *The composite product*. First the weights given to the various trades have been based upon the relative expenditure upon brickwork, joinery, masonry, slating and tiling, plumbing, decorating and plastering in years round about 1910. Clearly there may have been considerable changes of fashion between 1845 and 1910, in which case the imaginary building appropriate to the latter date will not represent the industry at the former. This difficulty would remain were all relevant information as to the relative importance of the several trades available, for one could not attach any simple meaning to index numbers which reflected changes in the real cost of producing a variable product. Fortunately there is evidence that no great changes did take place in the relative demands for the different trades prior to the outbreak of war.

(1) *The census returns for the decades* 1841–1921. In spite of changes in the method of enumerating and grouping census returns, fairly comparable figures can, I think, be obtained for the numbers employed in the principal sections of the building industry—accuracy is not required. The table in Appendix 1 c summarises the results of the censuses of 1841 to 1921.

It appears from these figures that the number of masons employed in the industry reached a maximum in the 'seventies, and declined thereafter both absolutely and relatively save for a slight recovery in actual numbers during the abnormal prosperity of the late 'nineties. The output of stonework did not fall off so markedly as the number of masons, for the efficiency of the trade increased nearly 20 % during this period, largely on account of the labour-saving devices introduced, e.g. mechanical stone-cutting, hauling, etc. The gap left by the mason has necessarily been largely filled by the bricklayer, although ferro-concrete has recently replaced both to some extent. I am told that there are signs of a revival in masonry.

The numbers employed in the trades grouped together—plumbing, painting, plastering, etc.—have increased rapidly and continuously ever since 1840; they are now more important than ever, relative to the other trades. The explanation is found in the multiplication and elaboration of house fittings, etc., and the growth of a taste for frequent and varied decorations. Output has probably changed with the numbers employed in these trades, for plumbing was about as efficient in 1910 as 1845, plastering nearly 20 % more efficient, painting 20 % less, according to the index numbers. Slaters and tilers increased until the beginning of the present century, according to the census returns. Care is, however, necessary in interpreting this result, for in many districts bricklayers and plasterers now perform the work previously reserved for the specialised roofing artisan. It seems probable that were allowance made for this fact and for a 10 % fall in the real costs of roofing, the trade would be found to have increased *pari passu* with the expansion of the industry.

Following the general introduction of machinery to the joiners' shop in the 'seventies the proportion of carpenters and joiners to other workers engaged in the industry declined. The demand of the government during the War for huts, shell boxes, etc., stimulated the trade so that the proportion of carpenters and joiners in the industry rose by 5 %–10 % between 1911 and 1921. The fall in numbers of carpenters and joiners employed from approximately 35 % of the total in 1870 to 25 % in 1910 was largely offset by a fall of 20 % in the physical volume of labour required to perform a given job of work in this trade, so that no great change occurred in the output of the trade relative to the size of the industry.

So far the evidence seems to point to a considerable decline in stonework and a considerable increase in the decorating trades, but otherwise the relative outputs of the various trades were much the same throughout the period 1840–1910.

(2) *The wage census of 1906 and returns of wages 1836–86.* The report upon the wage census of 1906, in so far as it affects the building trade (Cmd. 5086/1910, pp. ix–xxvii), is based upon returns covering only 12 % of the people employed in the industry. Since, however, firms doing all types of building in all parts of the country are included, the information concerning the relative numbers employed in the different trades may be taken to represent the industry in the United Kingdom.

The relevant information contained in the report may be summarised briefly:

It is estimated that there were about a million males engaged in the industry in 1906, of whom a large proportion were skilled workmen who had served an apprenticeship varying from three to seven years.

The detailed analysis of the returns is set out in the following table:

Percentage distribution of men among the different occupations in the building industry of the United Kingdom 1906

Foremen	4 %			
		Bricklayers	8·7 % = 15·8 %	of skilled men
		Masons	6·7 % = 12·2 %	,,
		Carpenters and joiners	17·2 % = 31·3 %	,,
Skilled men	55 %	Slaters	1·4 % = 2·5 %	,,
		Plumbers	4·5 % = 8·2 %	,,
		Plasterers	3·0 % = 5·5 %	,,
		Painters and decorators	13·5 % = 24·5 %	,,
Other skilled and semi-skilled men	3·5 %			
		Bricklayers' labourers	10·6 %	
		Masons' labourers	4·3 %	
		Plasterers' labourers	2·1 %	
Labourers	30·8 %	Plumbers' mates Painters' labourers }	2·3 %	
		Excavators	3·9 %	
		General labourers	7·6 %	
Other men	6·7 %			
Total men	100 %			

N.B. These proportions cover only "men" who numbered 86 % of the total returns. The remaining 14 % were either:

(a) Improvers or apprentices of all ages.

(b) Lads and boys under twenty years of age.

This table may be compared with the following table which was reproduced in the Returns Relating to Wages 1836–86.

Proportion of craftsmen per 100 hands employed in building trades in different districts in 1877

Miscellaneous Stat. 1879. pp. 409–13.

Occupation	Estimated average of districts recorded
Foremen	4
Bricklayers	14
Masons	8
Joiners } House carpenters }	24
Plasterers	6
Slaters	2
Painters	4
Plumbers	2
Glaziers	2
Smiths } Gasfitters } Bellhangers }	4
Paperhangers	1
Labourers generally	25
Scaffolders and hoisters	4

Each section includes lads and boys as well as journeymen and labourers.

From these two tables we obtain the following comparable figures:

Percentage of total men engaged in building in the United Kingdom

Date	Foreman	Brick-layer and labourer	Mason and labourer	Carpenter and joiner	Painter, plasterer, glazier, etc.	Slater and tiler	Others
1877	4	18	8	24	15	2	29
1906	4	19·3	11·0	17·2	25·4	1·4	21·7

This table confirms the conclusions drawn from the census returns in striking fashion. Between 1877 and 1906 the output of the plumbing and decorating trade increased considerably relative to the others; while the numbers employed in carpentry and joinery fell from 24 % to a little over 17 %, a fall which was offset by the economy of 20 % effected in labour costs. The slight rise in percentage of workers who were masons is contrary to the indication of the census returns for England and Wales, but the explanation lies in the abnormally high proportion of stonework done in Scotland. The wage census found that the ratio of masons : bricklayers was, for *skilled* men:

9 : 1 for Scotland.
5 : 6 for Northern England.
4 : 1 for the rest of England, Wales, and Ireland.

It seems clear, however, that the census returns indicate a too rapid reduction in the number of masons even for England and Wales: they are complicated by the diverse classification of monumental masons and others in the successive censuses. Still the direction of the indication is almost certainly correct, stonework did not keep pace with brickwork in England between 1880 and 1910.

Finally I return to the earlier conclusion that the composite building which adequately represents the condition of the British building trades in 1910 is not greatly out of touch with the industry during the latter half of the nineteenth century. Changes in the real cost of constructing such a building may, therefore, be used as a guide to changes in the efficiency of the industry without serious error.

(*b*) *Quasi-rent*. Fluctuations in the margin between the prime costs of production and the selling price of the product which are generally associated with the trade cycle have been eliminated as far as possible by taking a ten years' moving average of the annual index numbers as a measure of the trend of costs in the industry. It is these averages which are to be regarded as index numbers of normal costs at the date corresponding as near as possible to their middle year: thus the average of the annual index numbers of selling prices from 1875–84 would be tabulated as ̇index number of normal prices in 1880, i.e. the trend of prices. Interesting conclusions as to industrial efficiency at different stages in the trade cycle might be drawn from a study of the annual numbers, but care is necessary in making allowance for fluctuating profits which are equivalent to uncorrected changes in the supply price of capital, managing ability, etc.

For the present we are concerned only with the trend of real costs.

(*c*) *Proportion of building work covered by composite product.*
The seven trades represented in the imaginary building selected

for study account for a large part of the total turnover of the industry. The three London contracts analysed attributed 75 % of the costs to these trades, but were rather abnormal contracts, including special work in alteration and repair. The Manchester firm's trading account associated 92 % of the turnover in 1910 with the seven trades selected. Up to the War, at least, it is apparent that the error involved in neglecting other trades (steel work, gas and electric fittings) is small.

I conclude finally that my index numbers of selling price of building corrected for changes in the cost of labour and materials, and for changes in the value of money, measure changes in the real cost of building construction in London from 1850-1910 to within 5 %. The error is probably much smaller, say 2 %-3 %.

§ 10. THE BUILDING INDUSTRY—SIZE

(a) *Absolute size.* The *Final Report of the Census of Production* taken in 1907 gives £81 to £82·5 million for the total annual output of the building and contracting trades after allowing for duplication in the returns (*loc. cit.* p. 763). Of this grand total, building, including repair work, covered £66·5 to £68 million, while building done on private account, etc., by firms not included in this figure raised it £79·5 million. The total output of the building industry of the United Kingdom in 1907 is therefore estimated to have been approximately £80 million, distributed between new construction and alteration or repairs in the ratio 3 : 2.

(b) *Changes in the size of the representative firm.* I have been unable to obtain any information as to the number of firms engaged in building even in London; nor have I any direct evidence concerning changes in the size of the business unit.

Mr E. J. Brown, Director of the London Master Builders' Association, has supplied me with the following record of their membership:

Date	No. of firms in membership
1872	278
1882	237
1892	272
1902	182
1912	137
1922	340
1926	348

He assures me that, with the one or two exceptions, all the large building firms in London were members of the association during this period; but unfortunately one can conclude very little from the figures, except that the number of important building concerns in London fell considerably in the decade 1890–1900. This seems to have been due largely to a growth of the representative firms, combination, etc., being stimulated by the severe depression of the 'eighties. The exceedingly high post-War figures are probably due largely to the mania for association which possesses business men to-day, rather than to changes in the number of firms operating in London, though this figure has also risen.

In Mr Brown's memory, extending over nearly fifty years, there have been practically no additions to the ranks of the very big builders, while the old-established large firms produce very little more than in the middle of last century. Progress has been seen in the number of small firms which have expanded and now do a moderately large business without stepping into the first rank. It appears impossible to obtain the information necessary to distinguish between internal and external economies in the building industry; there is little doubt, however, that the representative firm produces but little more at the present time than it did in the 'seventies.

§ 11. PROVISIONAL CONCLUSIONS CONCERNING THE BUILDING INDUSTRY

The series of index numbers which have been obtained in the manner described in the preceding sections have been collected together on a ratio chart (Diagram I) for convenience in correlation, i.e. they have been plotted on a semi-logarithmic scale which has the property that the gradient of the curves (with dates as abscissae) at any point varies as the *rate* of change of the ordinate. A comparison of the relative rates of change of two quantities, say the real cost and the volume of employment can easily be made by eye from these charts since the relation

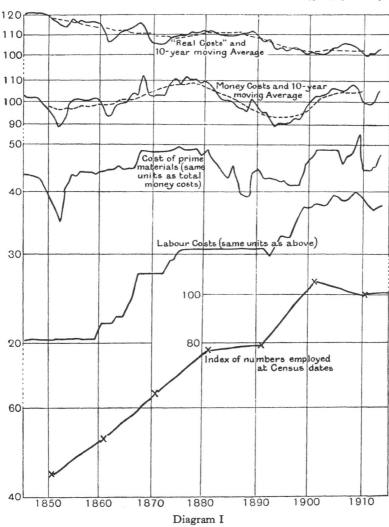

Diagram I

Costs of Labour and Materials, Total Money costs and Real Costs in the London Building Industry, 1845–1913. Numbers employed in the Building Trades at Census dates in England and Wales, 1851–1911.

is given directly by the ratio of the vertical distances traversed by the two curves between the same dates.

I. *Short period fluctuations.*

Having so painfully collected together the materials for judgment, it remains only to consider the significance of the curve of real costs of building construction and to relate it to changes in the scale of the industry. Here I must be content with provisional remarks of a very general character. It requires an intimate knowledge of the history of these trades and of the progress of industry generally to interpret the curves in detail. Time has not permitted me to undertake this investigation, but I hope to do so in the future. As far as short period problems are concerned it is noteworthy that real costs fluctuate less than money costs, while the prices of raw materials oscillate more violently than either. Efficiency wages were remarkably stable prior to 1913, rising almost continuously until 1909. Comparison with Dr Bowley's index numbers of weekly earnings in the London building trades shows that time and efficiency wages moved almost parallel until the 'nineties, when efficiency wages began to rise more rapidly than weekly earnings. In other words, the effort put in the full week's work began to decline. Between 1890 and 1910 efficiency wages rose from 30·7 to 38·8 while weekly earnings only rose from 34·9 to 38·8. It appears that the efficiency of the worker declined about 14 % during the twenty years.

The annual index numbers of real cost fall in depression and rise in periods of boom. A part of this variation is doubtless to be explained by fluctuations in gross profits or quasi-rents which are equivalent to changes in the supply price of capital, managing ability, etc., for which no correction has been made; but when allowance is made for this there seems still to remain slight periodic changes in the index numbers of real cost which must be attributed to varying efficiency. Laxton is published annually and the prices are calculated to be "just" and "equitable" in the period considered, so that one would not expect them to indicate those extreme variations in the margin of profit which occur at critical points in the trade cycle.

Broadly speaking, the course of the annual index numbers of prices and of output in the building industry suggest that the trade is subject to cyclical fluctuations having a period of about ten years, shortening to seven as the nineteenth century draws to a close. Output fluctuates in sympathy with selling price, while the efficiency of the industry appears to decline slightly in prosperity and to rise in periods of depression.

The index numbers for the period 1913-22 are subject to grave error and have not been entered into the chart. They are nevertheless suggestive. The fall of real costs between 1913 and 1918 may be explained to some extent.

(1) The value of money was falling rapidly.

(2) Large firms were fully employed upon public works, etc., under government contracts, their plant being in continuous use and their attention concentrated upon construction. Thus capital was turned over quickly and a low rate of profit upon turnover yielded a high dividend.

(3) Building materials were under government control (D.B.M.S.) and private contracts were limited after 1916 to less than £1000. Thus small builders, housebuilders, etc., were without work; little alteration or repair work was done and the small private builder was compelled to pay high wages and high prices for materials and to sell in a weak market. In fact speculative building was brought almost to a standstill.

The rapid rise of real costs in 1919, 1920, 1921, is largely explained by the high profits reaped from the abnormal conditions of demand and the limited supply of materials and labour. Some of the rise is, however, undoubtedly due to actual inefficiency; the truculence of labour and the slackness of master and man combining with the shortage of raw materials, etc., to render plant idle in spite of the brisk demand, while the habit of reckoning profit and establishment charges as a percentage of turnover undoubtedly leads to some unnecessary rise in selling price in times of high prices. Interesting evidence upon the subject of the inefficiency of labour as compared with pre-War has been supplied by a large London firm. They kindly analysed their bricklaying contracts in certain years between 1883 and 1926 with the following results.

Labour allowed per rod of brickwork by a London firm 1885–1926

Year	Hourly wages Brick-layer	Hourly wages Labourer	Labour cost per rod	Labour cost per hour	No. of hours' labour per rod	No. of bricks laid per hour
	s. d.	s. d.	£ s. d.	s. d.		
1885	8	6	3 15 0	1 0	75	
1890	8½	6½	4 0 0	1 1	74	
1895	9	6½	4 5 0	1 1½	75	
1900	9¼	7	4 5 0	1 2	73	60
1905	9½	7	4 5 0	1 2	73	
1910	10½	7	4 10 0	1 3	72	
1915	11½	8	5 10 0	1 5	78	
1920	2 4	2 1	18 0 0	3 9	96	44
1921	2 2	1 10	20 0 0	3 5	117	
1922	1 10	1 5	16 0 0	2 9	116	36
1923	1 7½	1 2	14 0 0	2 5	116	
1924	1 8½	1 3	14 0 0	2 6	112	
1925	1 9½	1 4½	12 0 0	2 0½	88	49
1926	1 9½	1 4½	12 0 0	2 8½	88	

N.B. The table has been compiled upon the assumption that three bricklayers have the assistance of two labourers plus a scaffolder, or three labourers, and that there are 4300 bricks to the rod.

The sixth column provides a sensitive index of changes in the hourly efficiency of bricklayers and their labourers, while in the last column the changes are thrown into bold relief in the popular form of "bricks laid per hour" by a bricklayer with the assistance of one labourer. The changes occurring between 1915 and 1926 call for no comment, but the extraordinary steadiness of the workers from 1885 to the outbreak of War is remarkable.

II. *The trend of building costs* 1850–1910.

Note. For the remainder of this section the terms "real costs" and "money costs" refer to normal costs, i.e. to the ten years' moving averages of the annual index numbers, unless otherwise indicated.

Perhaps the two most striking facts about the cost curves of the industry during this long period are: first, the wide divergence between the trend of money costs and of real costs, between apparent changes in the efficiency of the industry and changes which actually took place; and secondly, the stability of real costs, the smoothness of the curve. The latter is in itself a strong testimony to the success with which changes in selling prices not due to changes in the efficiency of the industry have been eliminated.

After falling slightly, money costs remained steady from 1851 to 1855 whence they rose almost continuously until 1873—a total rise of 10 %. From 1873 to 1878 they were again steady, but began to fall rapidly in that year. The fall continued until 1892 and amounted in the aggregate to 15 %. After five years' stability the cost of building (measured in money) began to rise, by 1905 it had risen 10 %. From 1905 to 1910 costs were almost uniform.

Real costs were falling when our period commenced (1850) and continued to fall until 1875, though the rate of fall began to decline midway between 1850 and 1875. In the decade 1850–60 the building industry was thus increasing in efficiency at the rate of $\frac{1}{2}$ % per annum (as measured by the gradient of the real costs curve upon the ratio chart), while in the decade 1865–75 the rate of improvement had fallen to $\frac{1}{3}$ % per annum. Between 1875 and 1878 real costs rose slightly (2 %) and were then stable until 1886 when they again began to fall, continuing downward until 1900. After rising 1 % between 1901 and 1902 the real cost of building remained constant during the first decade of the present century. In 1911 War conditions began to influence the trend of costs as measured by the ten years' moving average. Between 1890 and 1895 the building industry increased in efficiency at the rate of 1 % per annum. Taking the whole period the real cost of building fell from 120 in 1850 to a minimum of 102 about 1900, rising to 103 during the first decade of the present century. It is interesting to discover how the constituent trades contributed to this increase of 17 % or 18 % in the efficiency of the industry. Before reviewing the course of real costs in the several trades it will be well to restate the amounts spent upon the different trades in the composite product—they were:

Brickwork	Carpentry and joinery	Masonry	
40 %	30 %	7 %	
Slater and tiler	Plumber	Painter	Plasterer
2 %	8 %	7 %	6 %

In consequence a change of 1 in the brickwork index number will only effect a change of ·4 in the index number for the industry, and similarly the other trades influence the industrial figures only in proportion to the weights attached to them.

(1) *Brickwork* (including concretor and excavator). Increased 10 % in efficiency between 1850 and 1900, when the real cost of production reached a minimum (94 as compared with 104 in 1850). By 1910 real costs had risen to just over 100, leaving a net increase in efficiency of 4 %. The development of concreting technique was probably largely responsible for the improvement during the latter half of the nineteenth century, while the decline in the first decade of the present century may be attributed to the better conditions of work demanded by the now powerful unions and to the check to the expansion of the industry. Though some attempt has been made to improve the process of brick-laying, the method actually used has remained substantially the same for generations, the only scope for technical economy has been in the transport of materials, the skilful use of various cements in place of mortar, and the extension of the season.

(2) *Carpentry and Joinery*. This trade has shown a continuous improvement, efficiency increasing nearly 60 % between 1850 and 1910 (normal real costs falling from 162 in 1850 to 105 in 1910). Over four-fifths of this 60 % increase in efficiency is associated with the introduction of machinery into the joiners' shop in the 'seventies and 'eighties. This point is clearly brought out in the index numbers showing the physical volume of labour required to make a given piece of joinery. Beginning to fall in 1860, it drops slowly as the pioneers learn to use the new machinery; with the more general introduction of the machines in the 'seventies and 'eighties the fall in labour cost becomes rapid, only to slow down in the 'nineties and reach a minimum in 1908. Between 1860 and 1910 an economy of 30 % was effected in labour alone in the joiners' shop. A certain amount of woodwork is purchased by small builders ready joined, being manufactured in standard sizes by specialised firms, some working abroad where labour is cheap and importing doors, windows, etc., into this country ready for fixing; others im-

porting cheap wood and machining it in London. This ready-made joinery is not used in good work, the builder preferring to make to the architect's specification in his own shop. However, speculative house builders are using the ready-made article with greater freedom since the War. The competition, potential rather than active, of these specialised firms has doubtless contributed to the efficiency of the ordinary joiners' shop.

(3) *Masonry*. As in brickwork so in masonry efficiency reached a maximum about 1900. Real costs fell from 111 in 1850 to 91 in 1900, rising to 109 in 1910 (as measured by the average of the corrected selling price index numbers 1905-14). The annual index numbers show a rapid rise of both real and money costs between 1905 and 1913, the increase being most marked in 1912 and 1913. These sharp changes may have been due to the return of stonework to popular favour and the dearth of competent masons. The 20 % increase in efficiency which took place during the second half of the nineteenth century was made possible by the wide use of machinery for cutting or shaping stone and hauling it into position, and the custom of buying stone cut to order and shaped at the quarry which has grown up largely as a result of the use of machinery which can be more fully employed at the quarry, though the lower wages paid in the provinces (where the quarries are situated) have also encouraged this habit.

Care should be exercised in using the index numbers for mason's work. The trade is a small one and has a somewhat lethargic market. I am suspicious that Laxton's prices for stonework have not been revised with the same frequency or care as the other trades. However, the direction of the changes is doubtless in accord with the facts.

(4) *Roofing*. Efficiency in this trade seems to have reached a maximum about 1890, when real costs stood at 88 as compared with 110 in 1850 and 105 in 1910. There has been a further improvement in this trade which is not shown by the index—the wide variety of tiles now available constitutes in itself an addition to welfare. The 20 % increase in efficiency during the period 1850–90 is probably to be attributed to the speciali-

sation of men and firms upon roofing. In certain districts the bricklayers and plasterers have secured the tiling by custom, but it is generally done by skilled workers who do nothing else; while it is not uncommon for important roofing to be sublet by the contractor to special firms.

(5) *Plumbing*. Apart from cyclical fluctuations there was practically no change in the real cost of plumbing throughout the period 1850–1910. This is as one would expect, for improvements in the quality and variety of fittings which are installed by the plumber are not included in the measure of real costs. Apart from such changes the trade has remained much the same as in the middle of the last century.

(6) *Painting*. The index numbers of real cost of painting (ten years' average of the annual numbers) rose continuously from 76 in 1850 to 112 in 1910. In a note added to my remarks upon the derivation of the trade index numbers I explained that the great variety of decorations available and the superior skill of the workman must be offset against this apparent fall of over 30 % in the efficiency of the trade. When full allowance has been made for this fact, it still seems probable that the decorating trade is not as efficient as it was in the middle nineteenth century. Masters have enjoyed an urgent demand for their wares while the good "brush" has been sure of a market for his labour; so great has been the expansion of the trade to meet the growing demand for frequent and varied decorations that enterprise has not kept pace with it, and the inefficient master or man has found a comfortable niche. The shorter working day alone means a great increase in costs, for the painter is often held up by the weather and to be economical must work long hours when he may. This is but one way in which the organisation of the painters to secure better conditions of work, desirable as these may be, has raised the real cost of decorating.

(7) *Plastering*. In plastering, as in brickwork and masonry, efficiency seems to have reached a maximum about the turn of the century. Real costs stood at 116 in 1850, 97 in 1900 and 98 in 1910. The 20 % increase in efficiency between 1850 and 1900 seems to have been due in part to improvements in the

range of cements and plasters available for different kinds of work, in part to improved technique of master and man. Latterly mechanical mixing devices have been used upon some large work, but this is not general. The plasterers themselves have a reputation for truculence in the trade, their unions seem to have been very aggressive, and the rise in real cost during the early part of this century may be attributed to labour troubles.

When the results are collected together and weighted it appears that the efficiency of British building construction rose between 17 % and 18 % during the sixty years 1850–1910. The wood-working trades (carpentry and joinery) contributed 17·1 % to this reduction of real costs, brickwork (including concretor) 1·6 %, plastering 1·1 %, masonry ·1 %, roofing ·1 %, plumbing ·0 %, and painting 2·5 %. Thus the industry may be regarded as suffering no net change in efficiency, save for an increase of 17 % almost entirely due to the introduction of machinery to the joiners' shop. This conclusion does not imply that other developments such as the use of electric derricks and cranes to haul materials into position, or of motor transport on the road, have not effected considerable economies *per se*. The evidence is simply that economies arising from the progress of industrial technique and from inventions have been neutralised by dis-economies associated perhaps with growing discontent among the workmen leading to increased cost of supervision, to a shorter working day even in fine weather, and to the direction of the masters' energies to meet trade union requirements. It may be argued that these are desirable changes, though they involve some check to industrial efficiency. If so, then it is clear that, apart from such developments as the mechanising of wood-working which cannot be expected to recur at frequent intervals, industrial progress has only just sufficed to support the burden of these amenities.

Finally we come to the relation between changes in efficiency and the expansion of the industry. It seems impossible to dis-tinguish in practice between inventions which are, and those which are not, the result of growth in the scale of production.

One would expect to find technical progress more rapid in an alive and inventive generation shaken from its sloth by a war or a revolution in some basic industry such as transport. So the fact that an industry is subject to rapidly falling real costs of production does not in itself constitute a claim for special encouragement by bounty or other device, for the economies being effected may be in no way dependent upon the scale of production. Indeed after the stable period of the 'eighties the real cost of building began to fall in 1887, five years before the receipts of London surveyors showed a recovery. Even allowing for a delay of a year or two in these receipts, it appears that industrial progress anticipated the expansion of the industry by two or three years. In these circumstances it is clear that the lumping together of all inventions and economies, internal or external, dependent or independent of industrial expansion, will give a value for the "elasticity of return" which is probably considerably greater than the true value, for it is very unlikely that diseconomies, which are not properly associated with the change in the scale of production, have outweighed the positive economies reaped from inventions in no way dependent upon the size of the industry. The data now available will, therefore, give a lower limit to the elasticity of return in the building industry at intervals during the period 1850–1910.

Apart from a slight check about 1870 the building industry was expanding continuously from 1860 to 1875, and the real cost of production was falling. The rate of expansion slowed down in the late 'seventies and the industry ceased to expand about 1880, declining steadily until 1890, whence it recovered and expanded rapidly until the turn of the century. It then became stable, except for a slight expansion in 1907–8. During the hard times of the late 'seventies and 'eighties, no increase in efficiency took place, real costs rising a little between 1875 and 1880 to remain constant until 1887 when they began to fall. From 1890–1900 real costs fell rapidly only to rise slightly and remain steady to the end of the period.

At the risk of straining the evidence I have made a calculation of the relation between the rate of fall of real costs and the rate of expansion of the industry in certain periods:

Date	Rate of fall of real costs of building (% per annum)	Rate of expansion of the building industry (% per annum)	Elasticity of return, i.e. Rate of expansion ÷ Rate of fall of real cost
1850–60	$\frac{1}{2}$	2 (census returns)	4
1865–75	$\frac{1}{3}$	$2\frac{2}{3}$	8
1890–5	1	3	3

Thus, *if we include the invention and use of machinery* among the economies of large-scale production, the British building industry was working under slightly increasing return during the sixty years preceding the War. The elasticity of return was positive and the strength of the tendency to increasing return (which varies as the reciprocal of the elasticity of return) was greatest in the period 1890–5. Even allowing this upper limit for the elasticity of return to stand as fact, there is no evidence of a sufficient increase in efficiency consequent upon expansion of the building industry to justify state interference. The net economies of large scale production are very small; apart from the use of machinery in joinery the industry provides an excellent example of constant returns.

PART III

THE LANCASHIRE COTTON INDUSTRY
1845–1913

§ 1. INTRODUCTION

DELIMITATION of industries involves the erection of barriers which do not naturally exist. The placing of the boundaries appropriate to the present purpose round the cotton industry is even more difficult than the definition of the building trade. Before the introduction of the roller mill, warps for strong cloths were spun from wool or flax, but by 1845 the water frame had replaced these coarse woollen or linen yarns by cotton twist, and during the latter part of the nineteenth century the great bulk of cloth manufactured in Lancashire was from cotton yarns alone. The recent development of artificial silk manufacture in Lancashire has stimulated the mixing of cotton and silk in light fabrics, but cotton goods are still the standard textile product of the district. For a long time considerable quantities of yarn have been used in the hosiery and lace trades or exported as such, so that more cotton is spun in this county than is consumed by the weavers. Moreover spinning and weaving are normally conducted by separate firms; but the paucity of data and other considerations have determined me to lump together the two processes in a single industry. I, therefore, define the "Cotton Industry" for my present purpose, as the process of transformation of "raw cotton", as sold in the Liverpool market, into "grey cloth", as sold on the Manchester exchange. Thus the spinning and weaving of cotton together with such preparatory processes as are generally performed in this country are covered by the "industry". Cotton is "ginned" before it is shipped, while bleaching, dyeing and finishing are excluded for statistical convenience.

The method of procedure in compiling the various index numbers for the cotton industry is similar to the derivation of the corresponding indexes for building, and the general assumptions are the same in principle. A less detailed description of the calculations will, therefore, suffice to make clear the meaning of the cost curves and their relation to changes in the scale of production. Reference may be made to Parts I and II of this essay if further explanation is required.

There follows a summary of the statistical work, arranged as in Part II, and then a brief discussion of the significance of the changes in efficiency indicated by the trend of real costs of production. A detailed analysis of the arrangement will be found in the table of contents.

Note. The references in the following sections are to Tables which will be found in Appendix II.

§ 2. INDEX NUMBERS OF PRICES

[Ref. Table I, Col. (1)]

I. *Selling price of grey cloth.*

The index of selling price of grey cloth has been based upon the weekly returns from the Manchester market as published in the *Economist*. These returns are, I understand, supplied by experts on the spot and are compiled so as to give comparable prices. Unfortunately the series is not continuous.

(*a*) From 1845–1902 prices are quoted for:

26 in. 66 reed printer 29 yd. (4 lb. 2 oz.)
27 in. 72 reed printer 29 yd. (5 lb. 2 oz.)
39 in. 60 reed cold end shirting 37½ yd. (8 lb. 4 oz.)
40 in. 66 reed cold end shirting 37½ yd. (8 lb. 12 oz.)
40 in. 72 reed cold end shirting 37½ yd. (9 lb. 4 oz.)
39 in. 44 reed red end long cloth 36 yd. (9 lb.)

(*b*) From 1899 onwards prices are quoted for:

32 in. printers 116 yd. 16 × 16, 32's and 50's (15 lb. 5 oz.)
32 in. shirtings 75 yd. 19 × 19, 32's and 40's (12 lb. 15 oz.)
38 in. shirtings 38 yd. 18 × 16 (10 lb.)
39 in. shirtings 37½ yd. 16 × 15 (8¼ lb.)

The change-over in February 1903 to the new series was due apparently to the fact that the old series had ceased to represent the market. Further, the prices for the new series were given retrospectively. It has been thought best therefore to make the change in 1899 according to the ratio of the two series in that year. This also gives the smoothest transition.

These price quotations were accordingly extracted from the *Economist* for the first weeks in February, June and October of each year from 1845–1925. The three weeks chosen are free from holiday and other anomalies. The prices in shillings for each year were summed and reduced to the base 1910 = 100 by multiplying by 1·414 in the case of the first series (1845–99) and by 1·549 in the case of the second series (1899–1925).

The index numbers thus reflect the changes in price of a composite bundle of grey cloth. The bundle is different in the two series, but in both may be taken to represent the course of the market for grey cloth, i.e. we have the required index of changes in the selling price of grey cloth generally.

II. *Cost of materials.*

[Ref. Table I, Col. (3)]

The index numbers of cost of materials were obtained simply by expressing the yearly average price of mid-American raw cotton in the Liverpool market as a percentage of the average price in 1910. Tattersall's *Cotton Trade Review* gives the required average for 1845 to 1908 inclusive, but all calculated averages subsequent to that date seem to have been made up for the seasonal year. I have therefore calculated the averages for 1909–25 from the weekly returns of the Liverpool Cotton Association.

III. *Efficiency wages.*

[Ref. Table I, Col. (4)]

G. H. Wood's index numbers of average weekly wages in cotton factories (*J.S.S.* 1910, pp. 598–9) have been used as a measure of changes in the cost of labour so far as they go (1906). The index has been continued from the Bolton and Oldham spinning list prices and the uniform cotton weaving price list (i.e. piece rates of wages) weighting in the ratio spinning (2) and weaving (3). These were the weights used by the Ministry of Labour in their pre-War textile wage index numbers. No allowance has been made for the change of hours (55½–48) per week in 1919, since there is no evidence of appreciable change in the intensity of work. Indeed short time has been so common that shorter hours would in any case have been worked. Mr Vernon (*Fatigue and Industrial Efficiency*) agrees that the evidence is conflicting and that it can only be asserted that hours in excess of sixty per week do not necessarily yield a greater output than sixty hours. He is of the opinion that some increase in the average efficiency of the workers has taken place.

It seems to me that there has been little change either in personal application or in technical equipment, therefore changes in piece rates may fairly be used to continue Mr G. H. Wood's index numbers of time rates.

Apart from this recent change, hours of work in the industry were reduced from sixty-nine to sixty in 1847, from sixty to fifty-six and a half in 1875, and from fifty-six and a half to fifty-five in 1901.

I have assumed that these reductions had no appreciable effect upon *weekly* output. It is probable that improvements in time keeping and personal application sufficed to make good the loss of hours in 1847 and 1875, while the slight reduction in 1901 was neutralised by changes in the regulations concerning "clearing time, etc."

Mr G. H. Wood (*J.S.S.* 1902, p. 284 *et seq.*) finds that though there was a slight reduction in earnings due to reduced hours in 1847, yet by 1849 (after allowing for a reduction of 10 % in piece rates) wages were about the same, i.e.

Reduction of hours	... ...	16 %
Rise in hourly earnings due to increased application	... ...	16·6 %

The case is not so clear in 1875. Mr Wood (*J.S.S.* 1910, pp. 604–6) is of the opinion that, though wages "would have been higher" if hours had not been reduced, "the operatives have soon earned as much in the short week as in the previous long one because they have drawn on their reserves of personal efficiency". This seems to me optimistic. Time rates remained the same for the fifty-six and a half as for the previous sixty hours, and piece rates were not altered till 1877–8. On the other hand the earnings of piece workers fell immediately by amounts varying from 1·5 %–5·9 %, while in one large mill they fell 7 %. Hours were reduced 5·83 %. As the workers would make great efforts to maintain their standard of living immediately after the fall of hours (i.e. before a rise of piece rates made it easy) I am of the opinion that intensity of work did not increase nearly in proportion to the fall of hours. The rise of weekly earnings taking place at the time was only checked for about a year, so that it is difficult to say whether the continued rise was due to increased personal efficiency or to improvements in machinery, etc.

Fortunately there is a tendency which offsets the error introduced by ignoring the reduction of hours in 1875. Adults steadily displaced children, while men often superseded women in the industry during the latter half of the nineteenth century. Mr Wood (*J.S.S.* 1910, p. 607) shows that owing to this cause alone we have an increment of 5 %–8 % in earnings from 1862 to 1907. This is of the same order as the concealed rise in efficiency wages due to reduced hours in 1875 and compensates the error, so that changes in weekly earnings provide a close measure of the course of efficiency wages.

IV. *Weighting.*

The costs of spinning in the cotton industry vary so widely with the counts spun, and the expenses of manufacture of cloth differ so markedly with the quality of the piece goods produced, that nothing short of a complete census of the industry can give an accurate analysis of the distribution of cost through the industry as a whole. One experienced manufacturer told me that he knew of two mills having about equal weekly wages bills and running 90,000 spindles each, yet the one produced 160,000 lb. of coarse yarn (16*s*.–24*s*.) per week and the other only 40,000 lb. of fine yarn (60*s*.–100*s*.); while he himself manufactured piece goods selling at 6*d*. per yard and others, of finer quality but the same weight per yard, at 13*d*. to 14*d*. per yard. The difference is due to the extra labour and other expenses involved in the spinning and weaving of the finer qualities of cloth.

Information is further limited by the division of labour between spinning and manufacturing firms. One is thus reduced to a "reasoned guess" at the distribution of costs appropriate to the composite commodity whose price changes are reflected in the index numbers.

The information upon which my analysis is based is summarised below:

1. An analysis of the trading accounts of an Oldham spinning and manufacturing firm, producing and using medium coarse yarns, gives (average for the period 1907–13):

Cotton	...	...	...	69 %
Wages	...	...	...	18 %
Other expenses		...	...	13 %

2. An estimate based on the *Board of Trade Report on Wages and the Cost of Production in* 1889 (C. 6535, 1891) when brought to 1910 price levels gives:

Cotton	...	...	...	53 %
Wages	...	...	...	25 %
Other expenses		...	...	22 %

3. The mean of these two estimates is:

Cotton	...	...	...	61 %
Wages	...	...	...	22 %
Other expenses		...	...	17 %

This analysis is confirmed in a rather striking manner:

(*a*) By a calculation from weight of cloth in the composite commodity whose price changes are reflected in the index numbers of selling price. Assuming that wastes in spinning and weaving (16 %) are equal to the weight added to cotton in sizing, etc., we find that cost of cotton valued at the average price of mid-American for the season 1909–10 accounted for 61 % of the total costs of production of the piece goods in 1910.

(*b*) In the *Census of Production* 1907 (*Final Report*) the cotton trade is largely treated as a whole, i.e. preparing, spinning, weaving, dyeing, bleaching, finishing, belt making, etc., so that it is difficult to extract information relating to spinning and weaving alone.

(i) On p. 286 it is estimated that the value of the total production in the trade during 1907, free from duplication, was between £131,000,000 and £133,000,000 while the net output of the trade was £45,007,000 (p. 285) without duplication, i.e. in 1907 wages, profits, establishment charges, etc., only accounted for about 34 % of the proceeds of the industry. At 1910 prices the proportion would be considerably smaller. It is clear, however, that this is too low an estimate for the net output of that part of the industry (spinning and weaving of staple cotton goods) with which we are concerned. Further it excludes all materials, whereas my analysis places all materials except raw cotton in with "other expenses".

(ii) It is argued on p. 289 of the *Final Report* that there is practically no duplication in the returns for piece goods. Allowing waste in manufacture as an offset to yarn sold at home to hosiery and lace makers, etc., we get approximately: 1,560,000 lb. of cotton costing £40,000,000 (at mid-American prices) used in the production of £82,000,000 of grey piece goods, i.e. cost of raw cotton = 49 % of the total costs of production in 1907.

Correcting to 1910 prices by average price mid-American 1909-10, we get £51,000,000 of raw cotton used in producing £84,000,000 piece goods, i.e. in 1910 cost of raw cotton = 61 % of total costs.

It appears therefore that the evidence is strong for the estimate of 61 %—cost of raw cotton in 1910.

Evidence as to the appropriate division of the remaining 39 % between labour and other expenses is scanty; but, allowing for the fact that Mr G. H. Wood's wages index rose from 88·66 in 1889 to 107·3 in 1910, while Sauerbeck's index of general prices rose only from 72 to 80, my estimate of wages 22 %, other expenses 17 %, is in accord with the opinion of the Board of Trade in 1889 (C. 6535—1891, p. 27): "In the process of conversion of raw cotton—into manufactured goods—a sum approaching if not exceeding a moiety of the increased value is directly devoted to the payment of wages".

V. *Calculation of the corrected index numbers of selling price.*

[Ref. Table I (*passim*)]

The index numbers of cost of raw cotton, of wages, and of general prices (ten years' moving average of Sauerbeck up to 1914 and Ministry of Labour cost of living from 1914 as in

building and pig iron industries) have accordingly been calculated to the bases 1910 = 61, 22 and 17 respectively, and the
corrections made to the selling price index numbers for changes
in the supply prices of the factors of production with the constant
weights corresponding to those expenditures in 1910.

In this way series of index numbers are obtained showing
changes in the selling price of grey cotton cloth, and the same
corrected for changes in labour costs, cost of raw cotton, and in
the value of money.

As for the building and pig iron industries the trade cycle has
been eliminated by calculating ten years' moving averages of
each of these series. The ten years' moving average of the latter
reflects the trend of real costs of production in the industry,
i.e. it is an index of changes in the efficiency of manufacture of
grey cloth from raw cotton.

VI. *Errors involved in the derivation of the index of real costs.*

Sources of error may be divided into two groups:

(*a*) Errors in the series of index numbers themselves.

(*b*) Errors in the weighting of the corrections for changing
supply prices of the factors.

(*a*) *Prices.* The accuracy of the index numbers of selling
price, cost of cotton and efficiency wages has been discussed a
little under the previous sub-headings.

(i) With regard to the selling price index there is little doubt
that the two series of price quotations given in the *Economist*
are strictly comparable within themselves, but the transition in
1899 from the old to the new series is less reliable. The *Economist*
published both series for 1902, 1901, 1900 and 1899, the ratio
of the prices in the first to those in the second series being:

$$1902 \quad \frac{\text{1st series}}{\text{2nd series}} = 1\cdot67.$$

$$1901 \quad \frac{\text{1st series}}{\text{2nd series}} = 1\cdot62.$$

$$1900 \quad \frac{\text{1st series}}{\text{2nd series}} = 1\cdot56.$$

$$1899 \quad \frac{\text{1st series}}{\text{2nd series}} = 1\cdot414.$$

There is evidence that the ratio in 1899 was better representative of the normal relation between the prices of the piece goods contained in the two series, for the business done in the constituents of the first series was already falling off in 1899, and their prices consequently failed to respond to the rapid rise in value of raw cotton in the first few years of this century. The transition has therefore been based upon the 1899 ratio; the resulting index numbers move in close parallelism with the price of cotton, thus justifying the choice of transition ratio.

I am of the opinion that the selling price index numbers are throughout in close touch with the prices of grey cloth in general in the Manchester market. Some small error may have been introduced by the assumption that the average of the prices in the first weeks in February, June and October is the average price for the year, but one would not expect error from this source to amount to more than, say, ·5 %, because the averages for corresponding weeks of successive years are comparable.

It would appear that the index numbers of selling price record changes in the prices of grey cloths within 1 % and that they are probably correct to ·5 %.

(ii) The index numbers of prices of raw cotton are accurate records of the changes in price of middling American cotton as the grade has throughout the period been standardised on the Liverpool exchange. The use of these index numbers as a measure of the changes in cost of raw cotton generally is justified because the great bulk of cotton used in Great Britain is American, and the yarns required to produce the piece goods entering into the selling price index would very probably be spun from American cotton.

(iii) The accuracy of Mr G. H. Wood's index numbers of weekly wages in cotton factories is beyond question. The errors involved in their use as an index of changes in efficiency wages have been discussed above (III, pp. 102–4). Men of long experience in the industry assure me that very little change has taken place in the amount of effort put into an hour's work. The error involved in the use of the index numbers of weekly wages as a measure of changes in efficiency wage rates is probably not greater than 1 % or at most 2 %, involving a variation of not more than 3 % or at most ·5 % in the index numbers of real costs.

(iv) The significance of the index numbers of general prices has already been discussed in Parts I and II. Though no separate correction has been attempted it is interesting to observe that about 7 % of the 17 % of turnover allowed for "other expenses" is normally absorbed by gross interest upon capital engaged in the industry, leaving 10 % to meet rates, salaries and incidental charges. The figure of 7 % is suggested by analysis of the accounts of an Oldham spinning and manufacturing firm, which turned over its capital between once and twice a year during the six years preceding the War. The Board of Trade enquiry into wages and the cost of production 1889 suggests that about half the item "expenses" is to be regarded as "profits", but they appear to include rather more earnings of management, in the category of profits, than is the custom in modern companies.

(b) *Weighting*. The great diversity of the industry lays the analysis of costs open to considerable error. The weighting of the corrections for changes in the supply prices of the factors is, therefore, less accurate in the cotton than the building industries.

An error of 1 % in the weights given to cotton, labour and other expenses would, by itself, cause a maximum variation of ·36, ·12 and ·03 respectively in the real costs index numbers. (The cotton famine of the 'sixties caused prices to rise very high for a few years, 1862–6; these abnormal years have been neglected in the determination of the extreme deviation of the prices of the factors from the base prices and the margin of error allowed is consequently insufficient to cover the cotton famine.)

If superimposed, errors of 1 % in the weights given to each of the factors would involve a maximum error of ·5 in the index numbers of real costs. In practice the extreme deviations of prices of the different factors from their base year numbers occur in the same sense for all factors; errors involved in underweighting one and overweighting the other factors will, therefore, offset one another. The probable error in the index of real costs due to an error of 1 % in the weighting of corrections will be of the order of ·1 %.

Errors in weighting may arise in two ways: (i) Inaccurate analysis of costs in the base year 1910. An allowance of 5 %, involving an error of ·5 % in real costs, seems adequate to meet this difficulty. (ii) The use of constant weights when the physical quantities of the factors concerned in the production of a unit of the product are changing. Since changes in the efficiency of the industry are indicated by the gradient of the curve of real costs, it follows that the weights appropriate to the several factors must also have changed during the period studied. Between 1850 and 1910 normal real costs of production in the cotton trade fell nearly 20 % so that an error of 2 % may occur in the measure of efficiency in the cotton trade on this account alone. In the latter years the allowance necessary under this head will be much smaller finally falling to zero as the base year 1910 is approached.

The statistical errors to which the index of real costs is liable may now be summarised:

		%
(a) Prices:		
Selling price index		1·0
Wages index		·5
Cotton		—
(b) Weighting:		
Inaccuracy in base year		·5
Constant weighting		2·0
Total error to which real costs index is liable		4·0

This is a generous allowance: it is probable that a ten years' moving average of the index numbers reflects changes in the real cost of producing grey cloth to within 1 % or 2 % except in the very early years. The annual numbers are subject of course to short period fluctuations which may easily amount to 10 % without any change in efficiency.

Note on the interpretation of the curve of real costs.

Though my index numbers measure changes in the cost of producing a bundle of grey cloth with but a small error, it does not follow that they represent the trend of costs for the industry as a whole. Bleaching, dyeing and finishing have by definition been excluded; for the rest I am assured that the piece goods which are quoted in the *Economist* are widely representative of the trade, so that no great error is involved in assuming that the curve of real costs provides a rough measure of changes in the efficiency of the industry.

The same precautions are necessary in the use of the annual index numbers as were emphasised in the discussion of short period problems in the building industry. The trend of real costs alone is discussed in the present part of the essay.

§ 3. THE SIZE OF THE INDUSTRY

I. *Yarn produced and consumed.*

[Ref. Table II]

The separation of spinning and weaving into two "industries" makes the choice of the appropriate index of size for the cotton industry as a whole difficult. Obviously economies associated with large-scale production may result from an increase in exports of yarn without any change in the scale of the weaving operations conducted in this country. Mr J. W. F. Rowe in his index of the *Physical Volume of Production* (London and Cambridge Service Special Memoirs 8, p. 22), lacking information as to the average value added to the cotton in each stage of production, simply adds together weight of yarn produced and consumed and takes the sum as a measure of the output of the cotton industry. I have simply extended his index number to cover the period 1845–1913.

The figures have been obtained as follows:

(*a*) *Yarn produced in Great Britain*

[Ref. Table II, Col. (3)]

(1) 1845–84. Mr T. E. Ellison, in the appendix to his *Cotton Trade of Great Britain*, gives the weight in millions of pounds of cotton consumed in Great Britain year by year from 1811–84. From these 6 % has been deducted for waste in spinning.

(2) 1884–1911. Mr T. E. Ellison has kindly supplied me with estimates of yarn produced in Great Britain year by year from

1884–1911, which are apparently arrived at by deducting 6 % from the estimated consumption of cotton by the mills. They are thus strictly comparable with the figures for 1845–84. The estimates were originally published in Ellison's *Annual Review* of the trade but ceased in 1911.

(3) 1913–20. In the absence of any estimates of cotton consumed during this period by the calendar year I have summed the weekly returns of the Liverpool Association of cotton forwarded to the trade and deducted 6 % for waste in spinning. The result gives figures for yarn produced, subject to changes in mill stocks.

(4) 1920–23 and 1912–13. Mr J. W. F. Rowe's figures have been used.

(b) *Net exports of yarn.*

[Ref. Table II, Col. (2)]

(1) Exports of yarn are given in millions of pounds in the statistical abstracts for the United Kingdom.

(2) Imports of yarn are also given in the statistical abstracts from 1890. The earlier figures have been taken from the *Annual Reports* of the Board of Trade. I was unable to find any record of the imports of yarn in 1845 and 1846, and so allowed 500,000 lb., an estimate based on the figures of 529,000 lb. and 413,000 lb. of yarn imported in 1847 and 1848 respectively. In 1882 and 1883 yarn imported was not distinguished from piece goods in the Board of Trade *Reports*. I therefore resorted to estimate by interpolation.

The assumption that net exports of yarn from the United Kingdom = net exports of yarn from Great Britain, involves very little error because the amount of spinning done in Ireland even in the earlier years was small. There is now, I am told, no spinning in Ireland. The *Tenth Abstract of Labour Statistics* (1910) gives the number of spindles in the British Isles, by countries, in certain years. From these returns I calculate that as early as 1870 Ireland possessed only ·334 % of the spindles in the United Kingdom and ·775 % of the looms. By 1903 the proportions had fallen to ·075 % and ·124 % respectively.

Thus no appreciable error is involved in treating the cotton industry of Great Britain as identical with the cotton industry of the United Kingdom.

(c) The yarn consumed in Great Britain.

[Ref. Table II, Col. (4)]

This has been calculated by deducting net exports of yarn from yarn produced. Mr Ellison made allowances for changes in stocks of cotton both at the mill and warehouse. The figures based on cotton forwarded to the trade ignore changes in mill stocks, i.e. 1912–20 inclusive, but allow for changes in ware-house stocks, while the recent figures based on the *International Cotton Bulletin* figures for mill consumption make due allowance for all changes in stocks of raw cotton. Changes in stocks of yarn have been ignored, but the error involved is very small. More serious is the neglect to correct for yarn consumed by the hosiery and lace trades, etc. The quantities consumed by this group are appreciable but changes in these quantities will be of "the second order of smalls". Changes in yarn consumed will thus be due almost entirely to varying activity of the weaving sheds.

II. Changes in the size of the representative firm.

[Ref. Table III]

There is very little information available as to the number of mills spinning, sheds weaving, or concerns operating, year by year. Tattersall's trade circulars give the number of spinning companies making stocktaking reports from 1884 onwards, but unfortunately these only include spinning firms and not all even of that group of concerns. The *Cotton Spinners and Manufacturers Directory for Lancashire* (includes Cheshire) publishes returns of firms operating in the district, and of the spindles and looms owned by them. In the absence of figures for yarn produced and consumed in Lancashire, as distinct from Great Britain, index numbers proportionate to the average size of firms operating in Lancashire have been compiled by adding together spindles and looms, counting one loom equivalent to sixty spindles. These numbers have been expressed as percentages of 1910 and entered in column 5 of Table III.

From these index numbers it appears that cotton concerns in Lancashire started to grow in 1890 after remaining steady for some years. They continued to expand, save for a check in 1900–5, until the outbreak of war in 1914. However, the expansion seems to have checked rather than accelerated the fall of real costs. There is no indication that the benefit of internal economies, if reaped, was handed on to the consumer in the form of reduced prices.

Note. The ratio 1 : 60 for weights appropriate to spindles and looms was derived from the Ministry of Labour returns of spindles and looms engaged in spinning and weaving in Great Britain (*Thirteenth Abstract of Labour Statistics*) in certain years and the figures for yarn produced and yarn consumed:

Date	Yarn produced per spindle (lb.)	Yarn consumed per loom (lb.)
1870	29	1970
1874	32	2100
1878	28	1680
1885	32	1850
1890	38	2130
1903	33	1930
Average 1870–1903	32	1943

I.e. Taking the average of the years 1870, 1874, 1878, 1885, 1890 and 1903 the output of yarn per spindle engaged in spinning was to the consumption of yarn per loom as 1 : 61.

§4. PROVISIONAL CONCLUSIONS

The index numbers, derived in the manner described in the previous sections of this part, have been collected together upon a ratio chart, Diagram II, as in the case of building. Again the scale is such that a gradient of 1 in 1 represents an increase of $2\frac{1}{2}$% per annum.

On the whole the annual index numbers of real cost fluctuate with money costs and with the volume of production, but less violently. There are, however, notable exceptions to this rule, e.g. during the cotton famine in 1860–5. There seems to be a general tendency for real costs to reach maxima *before* and minima *after* money costs, while output reaches minima before

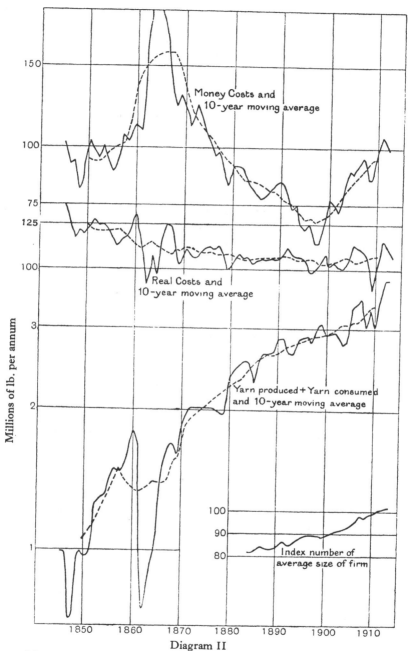

Diagram II

Money Costs and Real Costs in the Lancashire Cotton Industry, 1845–1913.
Amount of Output (yarn produced + yarn consumed) and average size of firms.

8-2

and maxima after money costs or selling prices. But production is closely and inversely correlated with the cost of raw cotton, i.e. output varies directly as the cotton crop. This complicates the relation, and when fluctuations in the margin between prime costs and selling prices are considered one wisely remembers that short-period problems are outside the scope of the present essay.

[For the remainder of this section the terms cost, money or real, may be taken to refer to normal costs, i.e. to the ten years' moving average of the annual index numbers, unless otherwise indicated.]

The money costs of manufacture of grey cloth show a very marked rise during the cotton famine of the 'sixties, whence they fall steadily to reach a minimum in the late 'nineties. They rose rapidly during the first decade of the present century, reaching a maximum in 1910. There is nothing remarkable in this history save the dependence of cloth prices upon the price of raw cotton. Though fluctuating less from year to year, cloth prices move in close sympathy with cotton prices over a number of years.

Again the most striking feature of the ratio chart is the stability of the curve of real costs.[1] The trend is not so smooth as in the case of building, but that is scarcely to be expected since technical development in the cotton trade takes place in spurts. The dismantling and refitting of mills and sheds with new machinery is an expensive item, and only takes place when improvements sufficient to justify it have accumulated. The shape of the curve of real costs is a strong testimony to the accuracy of the index numbers. Even during the abnormal price fluctuations of the 'sixties real costs remained steady.

After a stable period from 1850-5 the real cost of manufacture of grey cloth, including spinning, fell at the rate of approximately $1\frac{2}{3}$ % per annum for five years, and after a slight rise fell again at about the same speed from 1863-7. Rising to 111 in 1870,

---

[1] The ripples in the curve of real costs are undoubtedly due in part to the imperfections of the moving average as a measure of trend. Experiment with a seven years' moving average reveals essentially the same trend of real costs as the ten years' average, save that the rise of the curve between 1860 and 1863 shows five years later in the seven years' average. The ripples in the curve between 1860 and 1870 may therefore be attributed to changes in the amplitude and frequency of the fluctuations of the annual index numbers; for the purpose of the present study they may be smoothed by hand or eye.

real costs fell almost continuously from 1871 to 1882 at an average rate of $\frac{1}{2}$ % per annum. Thence there was a gradual rise to 108 in 1890 when efficiency began again to increase, reaching a maximum for the period in 1900. Between 1900 and 1910 real costs rose from 102 to 107, but there was a temporary improvement about 1905. Curiously this progressive fall in efficiency, at least so far as the consumer is concerned with the term, accompanied great expansion of plant and a rapid increase in the average size of firms operating.

During the early part of this sixty-year-period the Lancashire cotton industry was suffering the rapid introduction of machines similar in principle to the modern plant. The last quarter of the eighteenth and first half of the nineteenth century saw the gradual gathering together of spinners and weavers into factories. Mechanical power was early used to propel Arkwright's roller spinning mills but Hargreave's jenny was less cumbersome to handle while the skill of the spinner was all important, consequently small mills and hand jennies were the rule. In 1870 the mule, combining the advantages of the water frame and the jenny was first completed. By the turn of the century it was firmly established, though still in its infancy as a commercial proposition. Meantime the power loom had been invented in 1785 and was introduced commercially in the early nineteenth century. During the decade 1835–45 power looms increased rapidly.

At the commencement of our period (1845) factories had triumphed over the domestic system, the hand mule (which was driven *out* by mechanical power but had to be pushed back by hand) was the dominant spinning mechanism and the power loom was firmly established in the weaving trade. The fundamental features of the modern machinery were already known commercially—for the self-actor mule had been invented in 1825 and had by this time been adopted for coarse counts; while a patent had been taken out for ring spinning in the United States as early as 1828; by the 'fifties ring spinning for warp yarns was well established in the States. But it was a long time before these machines displaced the older types. Among medium and coarse counts the self-actor mule was completing its conquests between 1850–60 and may largely account for the fall of 10 % in the real cost of production of grey cloth which occurred between 1855–60. Then followed the cotton famine of 1862–4 when there was great inducement to adapt machinery to the spinning of East Indian and short-staple cotton, so that the self-actor mule was extended to the spinning of nearly all counts. This is probably associated with the fall of 3 % in the real cost of grey cloth between 1863 and 1867.

Throstle spinning was decaying between 1840 and 1875, but the adoption of the "ring" revived this process, for ring spinning steadily increased during the 'eighties and was rapidly adopted after 1890 for weft yarns. This development, however, has not had any marked effect upon the cost of production.

Improvements, such as increasing the number and speed of spindles in the mule, the invention of automatic devices enabling the weaver to mind ever more looms and the speeding-up of looms, have been taking place continually and have made possible the rapid rise of efficiency wages. Opening, cleaning and carding machinery has also developed greatly. But such improvements are perhaps to be expected with a growing industry and possibly to be listed as economies of large-scale production. Localisation, bringing with it considerable external economies, has also increased.

In spite of these developments, and a host of others, efficiency, as measured by real costs, only increased about 20 % in sixty years. In 1850 real costs stood at 124, in 1900 at 102, in 1910 at 107. In short, net changes in efficiency during this period seem to have been of the same order of magnitude in building as in spinning and weaving. The result is surprising. It would appear that economies resulting from the introduction of machinery into the joiners' shop have been as important as all the improvements in textile machinery since 1850. This, however, is an unwarranted conclusion; the lot of the cotton operative has improved in a thousand different ways since the middle of the last century, while the building trade workers have received little more than higher wages and shorter hours, which changes have been eliminated from the index numbers of real costs. The reasonable conclusion seems to be that a large proportion of the economies reaped from technical progress have been offset by the high cost of meeting the demands of the workers as regards hours and conditions of work. Changes in "efficiency wages" have been eliminated, but the cotton operative has benefited from the progress of the industry in other ways besides receiving higher pay for a given physical effort. Other diseconomies of organisation may also have accompanied the expansion of the industry, but an intimate knowledge of its history and present condition is necessary before they can be enumerated and assigned their true relative importance.

No significant correlation between efficiency and output is discernible. Prior to 1870 the effects of the cotton famine conceal normal changes in the scale of production. In the decade 1870–80 output increased at the rate of $2\frac{1}{2}$ % per annum, while real costs fell $\frac{1}{2}$ % per annum. If the changes proceeding be assumed to be due entirely to the expansion of the industry, the elasticity of return 1870–80 = 5.

Two decades later the industry was growing more slowly, output expanding only 1% per annum, while real costs were falling at about the same rate—$\frac{1}{2}$% per annum—giving an extreme value for the elasticity of return 1890–1900 = 2.

When a smooth curve is drawn through the seven and ten years' moving averages of the corrected selling price index numbers, it appears that real costs were falling, on the average, approximately 1 % per annum during the decade 1850–60, while output was increasing 5 % per annum. The ratio 5 is the same as the value computed for the elasticity of return during the decade 1870–80.

PART IV

THE CLEVELAND PIG IRON INDUSTRY
1883–1925

§ 1. INTRODUCTION

THE English economist naturally desires to obtain information concerning the industrial progress of the nation as a whole. Unfortunately the production of pig iron in Great Britain is divided between some half-dozen districts, which are separated from one another by industrial as well as geographical barriers. The coastal districts can export their iron and steel products cheaply, but the cost of transport prohibits the Midlands from exporting on a large scale. Again the nature of the local supplies of coal and ore and of the demand for iron and steel largely determines the character of the smelting industry in different districts. The hardness of Durham coke makes possible the large blast furnaces used on the north-east coast, while the poor coking qualities of Scotch coal, among other things, limits the size of the Clyde furnaces—coal is largely used in the raw state in this district and it soon sets hard if subjected to high pressure.

These considerations, together with the complications arising from the rapid changes in the relative importance of the different districts which have taken place during the last fifty years, have determined me to concentrate upon a single district. The Cleveland pig iron trade lends itself more easily to statistical treatment than other districts. Moreover, it has been expanding continuously, though rather slowly, during the whole period.

Rising rapidly in importance during the 'seventies the north-east coast produced nearly 3,000,000 out of the 8,500,000 tons of pig iron made in Great Britain in 1883. In 1913 almost 4,000,000 tons were produced in this district out of a total output of 10,000,000 for the United Kingdom. Writing in 1924 Mr M. S. Birkitt (*Ferrous Metals*, p. 23) says:

Among the pig iron producing districts of the country the pre-eminent place is held by the north-east coast. At present this area possesses in a higher degree than any other in the kingdom that combination of advantages which spells success in pig iron production, and as a result is responsible for approximately one third of the total production of the country. Cleveland ore and Durham coking coal laid the foundation of this prosperity, and the situation on the coast renders easy the importation of high grade Spanish ore for the production of haematite pig iron and the despatch of pig iron to overseas markets or on coasting vessels to other districts in the United Kingdom—e.g. Scotland's deficiency in pig iron is largely made good by coastwise shipping from Middlesborough. No district can attempt to rival the north-east coast in respect of output, which in 1920 amounted to 2,638,600 tons as compared with 1,009,200 tons produced on the west coast (Cumberland and North Lancashire) which ranks second among the pig iron producing areas.

Changes in the efficiency of the smelting industry on the north-east coast will, therefore, be a guide to the progress of the British pig iron trade as a whole. There is acute difficulty, however, in measuring such changes even for the Cleveland district, for there are many varieties of pig iron produced in the same area and the process of production of ordinary and basic pig iron differs very considerably from the making of haematite iron. However, all three types are produced side by side on the north-east coast, often at the same works, so that it is difficult to imagine appreciable changes of efficiency taking place in the production of one without effecting economies in the smelting of the other types (apart from certain fundamental inventions). In any case the only satisfactory price records refer to Cleveland No. 3 iron, and the index numbers of real cost have, therefore, been calculated to reflect changes in the efficiency of production of Cleveland pig iron, in the hope that conclusions of general application would result.

The distinction between the manufacture of pig iron and its conversion into steel was at one time sharply defined but it is rapidly disappearing, though still convenient for statistical work. In the following pages it is necessary to remember that the index numbers relate only to the processes occurring between the purchase of raw materials and the tapping of the blast furnace.

A very full statistical history of the pig iron trade of the

United Kingdom is contained in the *Statistical Report of the National Federation of British Iron and Steel Manufacturers* 1922; unfortunately the returns are not analysed by districts except for recent years. To obtain figures relating to the north-east coast alone (i.e. Durham, the North Riding of Yorkshire and, in the earlier years, Northumberland), it has been necessary to go to the *Annual Reports* of H.M. Chief Inspector of Mines (Statistical Appendix, Part III, Output: after 1920 the *Reports* are published together with the *Annual Reports* of the Secretary for Mines and the relevant figures continued in the Statistical Appendix of these two *Reports*). The information obtained from the Home Office records has been supplemented and, where possible, brought up to date by the kindness of the Secretary of the Cleveland Ironmasters' Association, while the Secretary of the Durham Coal Owners' Association supplied me with the ascertained prices of Durham coal 1914–25, required to bring the Labour Abstracts records up to date. I have indicated the authorities for my figures under each heading.

§ 2. INDEX NUMBERS, ETC.

[The references are to "Tables" and List in Appendix III]

I. *Selling Price.*

[Ref. Table I, Col. (1)]

The selling price index numbers have been derived from the ascertained prices of No. 3 Cleveland pig iron by taking the average of the quarterly ascertainments for each year, and expressing as a percentage of the price in 1910. It is generally agreed that these prices are typical of pig iron prices throughout the country, and it is certain that they are closely in touch with the movements of pig iron prices on the north-east coast. They relate to a definite quality of iron.

II. *Cost of materials.*

The index numbers of cost of materials to the ironmaster have been based upon: [Ref. Table II, Col. (6)]

(a) *Ore.* The average price of Cleveland ore raised from mines under the Coal Mines Act (i.e. deep mines as opposed to foot-rills). Only three-quarters of the ore used in the district was raised locally in 1883, while by 1910 the proportion had fallen to two-thirds. However the weights given to the different factors in applying corrections for changes in price have been calculated on the assumption that a 30 % ore alone is used; this is appropriate to the selling price index based on No. 3 Cleveland pig iron. The Home Office estimates that the average iron content of Cleveland ore was approximately 30 % from 1880–1920, 28 % in 1921, 29 % in 1922 and 28 % in 1923–4. Thus it may be assumed that the prices used relate to ore of constant quality.

[Ref. Table II, Col. (7)]

(b) *Fuel.* The ascertained pit-head prices of Durham coal as given in the *Tenth Abstract of Labour Statistics* 1883–93, the *Seventeenth Abstract of Labour Statistics* 1893–1913, and by the Secretary of the Durham Coal Owners' Association 1914–20.

From 1922 the figures used are "pit-head weights" supplied by the Secretary of the Durham Coal Owners' Association, determined presumably by dividing the ascertained proceeds of the industry by the amount of coal sold.

The use of this index to correct for changes in the cost of fuel is open to criticism, since the great bulk of fuel used is in the form of coke. The weight applied to the prices in correcting has been based upon the coal equivalent of coke used in smelting, but this is not the whole difficulty. It is by no means certain that the cost of coke to the ironmaster has moved parallel to the price of coal.

(1) Many ironmasters own their own coal mines so that only a part of the coal produced is thrown on the market, and ascertainments of coal prices based upon these limited sales may be widely out of touch with the cost of coal to ironmasters owning their own collieries. On the other hand, miners' wages have been based upon these ascertainments and, in view of the high proportion of the proceeds of the industry going to labour, it is improbable that any great error is involved in their use as index numbers of *changes* in the *cost of coal* to the ironmaster.

(2) Much more serious is the possibility of movements in the cost of coke to ironmasters relative to the cost of coal. In so far as such movements are due to changes in wage rates, they

will be eliminated by giving additional weight to the correction to changes in labour cost, thus covering labour at the coke ovens and at the furnaces. In so far as they are due to changes in the efficiency of coking or in the value of the by-products, the real cost of producing pig iron, as indicated by the final index numbers, will be modified, i.e. a part of the changes in efficiency indicated will be attributable to the coking process rather than the smelting. Since the majority of ironmasters run their own coke ovens in connection with the furnaces, little harm is done by treating the two processes as one industry in measuring changes in internal efficiency. Unfortunately it is not clear that my index numbers will serve as a measure of changes in the efficiency of the industry so defined. Coke and its by-products being jointly produced, changes in the demand for the one relative to the other should in theory cause corresponding changes in their relative prices. There is, however, reason to suppose that the ironmaster in calculating the cost of fuel with which to debit his furnaces has, at least in the past, taken little account of the market price of coke. He has probably made a rough calculation based upon the cost of coal and the labour of coking, regarding any income from by-products in the nature of a perquisite. Competition would gradually force him to take account of the increasing yield of coke from a given weight of coal and also of by-products valued at normal prices, but it seems highly improbable that his accounting would be adapted to short-period fluctuations in the market price of by-products. I am therefore of opinion that the use of the price of coal in correcting for changes in the cost of fuel to the ironmaster may mean the inclusion of certain changes in the efficiency of coking together with changes in the efficiency of smelting itself, but that no appreciable error due to fluctuations in the market price of by-products need be anticipated.

The above argument is general. It is considerably strengthened, when the Home Office Records tabulated below are studied.

Of the coking works making returns only 27·5 % worked up their by-products in 1906, 31·5 % in 1910, and 37·6 % in 1913. By 1924 the proportion had risen to 64·8 %. The yield by

Production of coke—Durham district. Home Office records

Date	Coal coked (thousand tons)	Coke produced (thousand tons)	Value of coke (£000)	Works recovering by-products, i.e. proportion of coking firms (not including gas works in United Kingdom)	Value of coke produced per ton of coal coked		Ascertained pit-head price of Durham coal per ton	
					s.	d.	s.	d.
1906*	9858	6291	4640	—	9	4	.6	11·51
1907	9451	5919	5120	—	10	10	8	8·54
1908	8497	5408	3641	69/251	8	7	8	8·28
1909	8846	5611	3710	71/248	8	3	7	6·44
1910	8748	5613	3987	77/244	9	1	7	11·62
1911	8280	5338	3556	81/224	8	7	7	6·53
1912	7785	5053	3892	89/234	10	0	8	5·28
1913	9153	5892	5581	88/234	12	2	10	1·56
1914	7608	4943	3790	103/211	10	0	9	6·46
1915	7193	4813	4852	166/211	13	6	11	0·51
1916	8178	5465	7705	115/200	18	8	15	1·82
1917	8448	5581	8487	123/200	20	1	16	4·16
1918	8126	5372	9837	116/201	24	2	19	4·69
1919	7507	4910	11076	117/196	29	6	26	6·50
1920	7584	5001	15952	125/193	42	0	34	7·45
1921	2792	1864						
1922								
1923	7376	5113†						
1924	6853	4778†						

* (a) The returns for 1906 were not statutory but are believed to be fairly complete.

(b) The difference between price of coal and value of coke yield is due partly to transport cost.

† Supplied by the Secretary of the Cleveland Ironmasters' Association.

Note. (1) The ratio weight of coal coked : coke produced for:

1906 = 100 : 63·9
1910 = 100 : 64·1
1924 = 100 : 69·8

Ignoring possible changes in quality of coal used or coke produced, this would seem to indicate that comparatively little change took place in the efficiency of pre-War coking. This is confirmed by the proportion of works in Great Britain recovering by-products, 27·5 % in 1906, 31·5 % in 1910, 37·6 % in 1913, and 64·8 % in 1924.

(2) Of the 5,613,574 tons of coke produced in Durham in 1910, only 273,887 tons were from gas works.

(3) The ratio price of coal : value of coke yield was:

1907 as 1 : 1·25
1910 ,, 1 : 1·15
1913 ,, 1 : 1·20
1919 ,, 1 : 1·11

weight of coke from coal coked in Durham district rose from 63·9 % in 1906 to 64·1 % in 1910 and 69·8 % in 1924. It appears that changes of efficiency at the coke ovens were small until the stimulus received during the War.

The ratio of pit-head price of Durham coal to the value of its coke yield per ton of coal coked (estimated at the coke yards according to the price of coke actually changing hands on the market) was:

1907 as 1 : 1·25
1910 ,, 1 : 1·15
1913 ,, 1 : 1·20
1919 ,, 1 : 1·11

N.B. A calculation from these ratios shows that the index numbers of real costs of pig iron will fall less than 1 % between 1907 and 1913 on account of changes in relative price of coal and coke. By 1919 the fall will be about 2 %.

This ratio showed that an increasing proportion of the cost of coking was borne by by-products, but that the development was not rapid until the War broke out.

I conclude that the changes in real costs of producing pig iron between 1883 and 1913 as indicated by my index numbers are affected very little by changes taking place in the coking industry.

Note. Mr M. S. Birkitt in his article on "The Iron and Steel Trades during the War" (*J.S.S.* 1920, p. 369) points out that the opportunity (i.e. arising from control) was taken to investigate the relation between the price of coke and its cost of production, and where substantial profits were found the subsidy was correspondingly reduced.

This, I take it, infers that the cost of metallurgical coke debited against the furnaces was out of touch with the actual cost of production in a considerable number of cases.

III. *Cost of labour.*

[Ref. Table II, Col. (8)]

The index numbers of cost of labour to the ironmaster have been based upon shift wages, all information with regard to wages being supplied by the Secretary of the Cleveland Ironmasters' Association.

Since the adoption of the first sliding scale in 1880 the wages of Cleveland blast furnacemen have been based upon the ascertained price of No. 3 Cleveland pig iron. Although there have been numerous changes in scales (the present being the ninth) they have operated continuously except for short periods in 1885-6, 1890, 1894-5 and 1897. During these periods, and at times of special stress, temporary agreements, fixing wage rates at a percentage above or below the scale rate, operated. Thus standard rates of wages have been in operation since 1880, calculated by adding a percentage to the basis shift rates (technically the "standard" rates of pay). Actual shift wage rates vary from firm to firm according to the local usage, but move parallel to the standard rates.

Basis shift rates remained constant from 1880-1919 as follows: keeper 6s., charger 4s. 6d., slagger 4s., mine-filler 3s. 8d., helper 3s. 6d., labourer 3s., but were raised at the end of 1919 to 9s. 3d., 7s. 5d., 6s. 10d., 6s. 8d. and 6s. respectively. In making allowance for this change of basis rates the wages of slaggers have been taken as representative, and this is supported by a calculation of the mean rate of pay in 1880 and 1883 (*Board of Trade Return, Wages* 1880-6, p. 155), viz.:

		1880		1883	
		s.	d.	s.	d.
8 keepers	at	6	8	6	9
4 keepers' helpers	,,	3	4	3	4
8 chargers	,,	5	0	5	2
1 charger's helper	,,	3	5	3	5
8 slaggers	,,	4	3	4	6
10 mire-fillers	,,	3	11	4	1
4 lime-fillers	,,	3	5	3	9
2 coke-fillers	,,	3	6	3	9
5 enginemen	,,	4	4	4	6
4 weighmen	,,	3	4	3	4

Average (weighted) shift wages: 1880 = 4s. 5d., 1883 = 4s. 7d.

Hours worked per shift were twelve from 1870-96, but in 1897 the eight-hour shift began in the Cleveland district and by the middle of 1897 had been adopted generally, three shifts per day being worked instead of one. There was no appreciable increase in output in the next few years, the hourly efficiency of the worker apparently remaining unchanged in spite of the promises of the Trade Unions.

My wage index numbers have therefore been derived by taking the basis shift rate = 100, adding the average percentage increment on base rates payable in each year (i.e. the mean of the quarterly percentage additions based on the ascertained price of No. 3 Cleveland pig iron in the previous quarter), as supplied by the Cleveland ironmasters, and reducing to the base 1910 = 15 (by dividing by 8·19). In the years preceding 1897 these figures have been reduced by one-third to allow for the reduction of hours, and raised 72 % after 1919 to correct for change in base rate. During the War period allowance has also been made for the various bonuses granted in addition to the standard rates as calculated from the price of pig iron. These were as follows:

Beginning:
    3rd Quarter 1915—First War bonus of 3d. to 7d. per shift worked according to base rate.
    2nd Quarter 1917—Further War bonus of 5d. to 9d. per shift worked according to base rate.
    1st Quarter 1918—Ministry of Munitions granted an increase of 12½ % which was merged in subsequent advances under the scale.
    4th Quarter 1918—Special War advance of 1s. 6d. net per shift.

Allowance has been made for these increments by percentage additions to base rates over and above the standard rates as follows:

		%
1915	... ...	4·6
1916	... ...	9·3
1917	... ...	19·0
1918	... ...	30·6
1919	... ...	55·5

When the present wages agreement was made in December 1919 all War bonuses being paid were wiped out. They then amounted to from 2s. 3d. to 2s. 10d. per shift according to base rate. My percentage additions for War bonuses are equivalent in 1919 to from 1s. 8d. to 3s. 4d. per shift according to base rate with an average of 2s. 6d.

My index numbers may thus be regarded as measuring changes in hourly wages from 1883–1925. Further it is probable that no great error is committed in using them as an index of efficiency wages, at least up to 1919. There seems to have been but little change in the effort put into an hour's work in spite of the adoption of the eight-hour shift.

Mr T. J. Atkinson (Secretary, Cleveland Ironmasters' Association) estimates that weekly wages for an average of seven and two-thirds shifts per week were:

	July 1914 £ s.	July 1915 £ s.	Increase on 1914 (%)
Keeper	3 10	5 0	43
Charger	2 12	4 10	73
Filler	2 3	3 19	83
Slagger	2 5	3 16	69
Helper	2 0	3 10	75
	Average increase (unweighted)		69

My index number, worked out for the second and third quarters of 1914 and 1925, would indicate:

			Index no.
Mid-1914	...	...	15·1
Mid-1925	...	...	23·3

indicating a rise of 55 % only.

The difference is probably explained by the increased use of bonuses on production after 1919. It is agreed that much better and steadier work has been forthcoming since the 1919 agreement, so that my index number is probably nearer to the ratio of efficiency wages in 1914 than in 1925.

In addition to the standard shift wage determined as described above, bonuses varying from firm to firm and worker to worker and based on production are customary, but I have been unable to make any allowance for changes in this item of labour cost. It is probable that the error involved is small, as the bonus is but a fraction of total pay and would in any case tend to move parallel to shift rates. Previous to the 1919 agreement, production bonuses were confined to keepers, fillers, slaggers, chargers and helpers, and were based upon the output of the furnaces. According to the new agreement, production bonuses are based upon output or input of the furnaces according to the worker and situation and are extended to all employees. All complaints of neglect or slackness in work have disappeared since this agreement came into force.

IV. *Changes in the value of money.*

[Ref. Table II, Col. (9)]

The index numbers of general prices used in correcting for changes in the value of money are derived from Sauerbeck's ten years' moving average of commodity prices and, for the period 1914–25, the Ministry of Labour cost of living index figure, as for the building industry.

V. *The weighting of corrections for the different factors.*

The distribution of costs of smelting iron ore so obviously depends upon the quantity of ore used and of pig iron produced that averages taken over the whole industry are meaningless. For the present purpose an estimate has been made of the cost of producing Cleveland pig iron from Cleveland ore and corresponding weights have been applied to the changes in price of the factors of production in order to obtain index numbers of real cost.

The analysis is as follows:

Distribution of cost of production of Cleveland No. 3 pig iron in 1910

	(%)
Cost of coal	36
Cost of ores	31
Labour	15
Miscellaneous charges	18
	100

The index numbers of prices of coal, ore and labour, and of the trend of general prices have accordingly been reduced to the bases 1910 = 36, 31, 15 and 18 respectively, and corrections applied to the selling price index with constant weights corresponding to these expenditures.

Note. (a) Coal and ore have been valued at the mine and transport charges included under the head of "miscellaneous expenses".

(b) Labour cost is estimated so as to include the wages of men employed at the coke ovens.

This analysis has been arrived at as follows:

The *Statistical Report of the Federation of Iron and Steel Manufacturers* gives the following table (p. 7, Table 12):

Materials consumed per ton of pig iron produced in the United Kingdom

1922

Materials consumed per ton of pig iron produced (all in cwts.)

Quality	Iron ore Home	Im- ported	Lime- stone	Other mate- rials*	Total charge	Coal	Coke	Total coal equi- valent
Haematite	9·31	23·98	8·56	3·64	45·49	1·04	21·87	35·70
Basic	37·23	6·99	5·20	9·67	59·09	0·15	27·09	42·55
Foundry and forge	43·10	6·06	9·59	3·80	62·55	11·26	20·56	42·50
Alloys	0·67	39·31	12·26	0·54	52·78	—	40·84	69·90
Total (all qualities)	28·07	13·67	8·16	5·35	55·25	3·87	23·74	40·94

* Cinder and scale, purple ore and scrap.

The table for 1922 has been used in preference to that given for 1920 because ordinary care was not taken in selecting materials, etc., in 1920.

Allowing for the fact that Cleveland is only a 30 % ore, and weighting so as to include all ores (including cinder, scale and scrap) required, it is estimated that 3½ tons of ore and the equivalent of 2¼ tons of coal would be consumed in the production of 1 ton of pig iron made from a 30 % ore.

The wages bill of blast furnacemen (including men employed at coke ovens at the furnaces) is stated in the same *Report* to have amounted to £3,338,266 for the United Kingdom in 1922, while the total production of pig iron was 4,902,300 tons. Thus the average labour cost per ton of pig iron produced in the United Kingdom in 1922 = £·68, but the average ascertained price of pig iron in 1922 = £4·35. Thus in 1922 approximately 15·5 % of the proceeds of the industry went to pay wages.

Reducing by means of my index numbers to 1910 prices, we get a figure of 12·0 % for average labour cost of smelting in the United Kingdom. After making allowance for the facts that (a) the weight of charge per ton of pig iron produced would be about 15 % above the average in the case of a 30 % ore, and (b) coke ovens are not all situated at the furnaces, we arrive at the figure of 15 % for labour cost in 1910.

The analysis may now be summarised:

Estimated analysis of costs of production of No. 3 Cleveland pig iron in 1910

	(%)
Ores (3½ tons at 4s. 5d. = 15s. 6d.)	36
Coal (2¼ tons at 8s. = 18s.)	31
Labour (including labour at coke ovens)	15
Miscellaneous charges (including transport, profit, etc.)	18
Total (mean ascertained price No. 3 = 50s. 6d.)	100

In support of this analysis I have:

(i) The general approval of Mr M. S. Birkitt as regards the items coal and ore (he is not in a position to divulge information as to labour cost but seems to consider that my estimate is high rather than low).

(ii) A letter from Sir Hugh Bell in which he says: "Speaking quite generally, I think the figures cited in your letter are approximately correct", and promises further criticism and evidence on the point later.

(iii) Mr T. J. Atkinson estimates that the average labour cost per ton of pig iron produced in the Cleveland district about 1883 was roughly 3s. 6d., the price of pig iron being about £2. This would indicate a wages bill of approximately 8·75 %. The wage index number stands at 9·1 in 1883 and the selling price index at 78·9, indicating a labour cost of 11·5 %.

The difference is probably largely accounted for by the facts: (a) that of the 8,000,000 tons of ore used in the district in 1883 nearly 1,000,000 was imported ore containing a high percentage of iron; (b) that the labour employed at coke ovens is included in my estimate but not in Mr Atkinson's.

Note

Further support for the above distribution of expenses comes from an unexpected quarter. The *Sixth Annual Report of the United States Commissioner of Labour*, Part I, is devoted to an analysis of cost of production in the iron and steel trades of the United States, Great Britain, and Europe. Eight or nine British iron smelting establishments made fairly complete returns for accounting periods in 1888 or 1889. Of these:

Establishments 36–9, producing Bessemer pig from haematite ores, average iron content *circa* 50 %, show approximately:

	% of current expenses
Labour cost of smelting	6–7
Ore, including cinder	58–62
Coke	23–27
Limestone, about	2
Taxes, supplies and repairs, etc.	3–6

Establishments 61–3, when making gray forge pig iron from mixed ores (haematite and ironstone):

	% of current expenses
Labour cost of smelting	8–9
Ore	44–48
Coke	30–38
Limestone	2–5
Other expenses	4–8

Establishment 116, making basic iron from poor ores:

	% of current expenses
Labour cost of smelting	7
Ore, including cinder	34
Coke	48½
Limestone	5
Other expenses	5½

On p. 242 an analysis of cost of coking in five establishments in Great Britain is given, viz.:

Average cost per ton of 2000 pounds

	($)
Coal	1·433
Labour (wages)	·339
Officials and clerks (salaries)	·010
Supplies and repairs	·123
Taxes	·010
Total cost, i.e. current expenses	1·915

Coal equivalent of 1 ton of coke = 1·65 ton.

This analysis gives a basis for computing the labour cost of coking, and thus bringing the returns into direct comparison with the analysis of the text.

Establishment 63 alone of the eight making returns appears to have been working under conditions comparable with those considered in the text, producing mainly gray forge pig iron of ordinary grade with incidental pockets of special grades from ironstone requiring 3·2 tons of ore to make a ton of iron. I have, therefore, reproduced the returns for this establishment in a convenient form, adding estimates of the items chargeable to coking. The returns are then brought into direct comparison with the analysis of the text.

Distribution of Expenses of Production of Pig Iron from Ironstone[1]

The returns refer to the production of 7980 tons of gray forge pig iron from a single furnace in Great Britain between November 1st, 1888, and October 31st, 1889.

Cost per Ton of Pig Iron Produced

3·200 tons of ironstone	3·427 (40 % of total costs)
·525 tons of limestone	·406
1·860 tons of coal (equivalent to 1·125 tons of coke plus ·013 tons of coal and valued at cost of coke minus labour of coking)	2·584 (30 % of total cost)
Labour:	
In smelting $ ·710 } wages ... ... In coking $ ·415 }	1·125 (13 % of total costs)
Officials and clerks:	
In smelting $ ·054 } salaries ... ... In coking $ ·012 }	·066
Supplies and repairs	·212
Taxes	·031
Total current expenses	7·851
10 % gross profit	·785
Total cost	8·636

The average ascertained price of Cleveland No. 3 for the last quarter of 1888 and first three quarters of 1889 was approximately 35s. 4d. as compared with 50s. 6d. for 1910.

This gives an index number 70 for price of pig iron during the period under review.

My index numbers for cost of materials and labour in 1888 and 1889 are: labour 7·9–8·3, ore 20·5–22·8, coal 20·1–23·3, whence we get the comparison:

Percentage distribution of full expenses of production of pig iron from ironstone, 1888–9

	A. Establishment 63 (%)	B. Analysis used in text (%)
Ore	40	32
Coal	30	32
Labour (including coking) ...	13	11½
Other expenses	17	24½

N.B. In A the ore and coal are valued at the furnace, while in B costs of transportation are included in the "other expenses", the ore and coal being valued at the mine.

[1] Based upon returns made by Establishment 63, *Sixth Annual Report of the United States Commissioner of Labour*, Part I, Table 1.

The agreement is really surprising when one allows for the fact that Establishment 63, although reporting ironstone as its chief ore, almost certainly used some admixture of better ores; for instance, in Establishment 116, the percentages going to ore and fuel are the reverse of those in Establishment 63. The comparison is of greatest value for the labour item; it will be noticed that the labour cost of coking is rather more than half that involved in smelting. Taking the returns given above for Establishments 36–9, 61–3 and 116, adding 50 % to the labour item to allow for the labour cost of coking, and expressing as a percentage of the full expenses of production, including 10 % gross profit upon turnover, we get:

	% of full expenses	
Establishments 36–9		
Labour cost of Bessemer pig iron, including coking	8–9	
Establishments 61–3		
Labour cost of gray forge pig iron	11–12	including coking
Establishment 116		
Labour cost of basic pig iron	9½	

Forge and foundry irons being very closely allied, the figure of 11½ % for the labour cost of Cleveland No. 3 is confirmed in striking fashion.

VI. *Statistical errors.*

Two series of index numbers have now been obtained:

(*a*) Index of the selling price of pig iron in the Cleveland district (Table I, Col. (1)).

(*b*) The same corrected for changes in the cost of labour and materials and the value of money (Table I, Col. (2)).

The errors to which these indexes are subject may be grouped under the two headings, prices and weighting.

(*a*) *Prices.* The ascertained price of No. 3 Cleveland iron may be taken as typical of ordinary iron sold upon the north-east coast without appreciable error. The index of efficiency wages is open to more serious error, for it is based upon the standard time rates of wages for the district. Bonuses upon output have varied from time to time and firm to firm, while there may have been changes in the amount of effort put into an hour's work by the blast furnacemen in this district. I understand that such changes in intensity of work have been negligible, while an allowance of 3 %–4 % for error due to changes in average bonus upon output would only involve an error of $\frac{1}{2}$ % in the cost of pig iron.

The use of the price of Cleveland ore and of Durham coal in correcting for changes in the cost of materials has already been discussed, and the error compensated as far as possible by suitable weighting.

An allowance of 1 % for the maximum error due to the price indexes seems reasonable.

(b) *Weighting*. An error of 1 % in the weight given to the corrections for changes in the prices of the factors would produce a maximum variation (pre-War) in the index numbers of real costs of:

·07 in the case of labour
·16　　,,　　,,　　coal
·12　　,,　　,,　　ore
·03　　,,　　,,　　miscellaneous charges.

In other words, an error of 1 % in the weight given to any one factor of production would on the average cause directly an error of ·1 % in the index of real cost of production of pig iron between 1883 and 1913.

The underweighting of one factor in the base year involves the overweighting of others, so that two errors will be superimposed. The prices of ore and coal moved in sympathy as did wages and general prices from 1883–1913, while after 1895 all four quantities moved in the same direction. When allowance is made for these facts it is clear that an error of 1 % in the weights given to each of the factors in the base year would probably not cause the real cost index numbers to vary more than ·1 % (pre-War).

Apart from inaccurate weighting in the base year, changes in the amounts of the several factors consumed in the production of a ton of pig iron will lead to errors in weighting (since the weights used are kept constant). Between 1883 and 1913 the normal real cost of smelting only varied about 5 % from the cost in 1910, so that the error due to constant weighting is probably not greater than ·5 %.

Allowing for 5 % error in the distribution of costs in the base year we get a figure of 1 % for the greatest error likely to occur as a result of inaccurate weighting.

It appears that the ten years' moving averages of the index numbers of selling price of Cleveland pig iron, corrected for changes in the cost of labour and materials and in the value of money, represent the course of real costs of production within 2 % and that the error is probably less.

It is difficult to attribute any significance to the annual index numbers in this industry. The group "miscellaneous charges" includes:

(1) Costs of transport, which probably absorb at least 5 % of the receipts of the industry.

(2) Rates and the cost of materials, such as limestone, which are not of sufficient importance to command separate correction.

(3) Earnings of management.

(4) Interest upon capital, etc.

The first two items are prime costs from the present viewpoint, while the fourth item and part at least of the third are properly regarded as quasi-rent, fluctuating violently from year to year. Beyond this variable margin, which the ironmaster expects to oscillate, further irregularity may occur in deep depression or in a period of boom. For it will often pay an ironmaster to produce at a loss rather than allow the works to come to a standstill, while the time taken to equip furnaces may enable producers who have furnaces in blast to benefit from an exceptional rise in demand.

In consequence the fortune of the ironmaster fluctuates violently. Moreover, there is no presumption that high prices mean high profits in this trade.

There is a tradition in this industry that capital can normally be turned over once a year, and this is confirmed by the enquiry of the Board of Trade into wages and the cost of production 1889 (C. 6535). An analysis of the accounts of four firms producing iron and steel separately are there reproduced. The two firms producing iron made a profit of 10·8 % on capital in 1889, those producing steel only 10·1 % on capital. This provides striking confirmation of the opinion of Sir Hugh Bell that, in the "iron and steel industry", capital is turned over once a year.

VII. *Interpretation of the index of real cost of pig iron.*

Statistical errors involved in the data and the calculations therefrom probably do not amount to more than 2 %. But a further difficulty arises in that these index numbers have been compiled for Cleveland No. 3 pig iron. What relation do the changes in real cost so indicated bear to changes in the efficiency of the industry on the north-east coast taken as a whole?

The Home Office records provide an analysis of the total production of the district into haematite, foundry, forge, basic and direct castings, etc., for the years 1920–5 and also show what proportion of this production was sent molten to the steel works. A similar analysis is available for the single year 1913 before the War, except that the iron sent molten is not analysed. I am assured, however, that almost the whole of the iron sent molten in 1913 was basic, so that comparable figures can be obtained. From 1886 to 1912 only:

> Haematite
> Foundry and forge and basic } Ore distinguished.
> Special qualities

The following table shows the percentages of the different kinds of pig iron produced in the district as indicated by these returns:

Production of pig iron in Cleveland district analysed by kinds

Date	Haematite	Foundry	Forge	Basic	Others	Sent molten to steel works
1925	—	—	—	—	—	—
1924	31·8	23·0	3·1	38·2	3·9	—
1923	34·6	21·4	4·2	34·4	5·4	38·8
1922	40·7	18·0	4·1	30·4	6·8	21·6
1921	37·8	20·9	5·6	31·8	3·9	27·9
1920	37·8	14·8	5·0	37·3	5·0	30·6

Returns not made during the War period

Date	Haematite	Foundry	Forge	Basic	Others	Sent molten to steel works
1913	34·2	28·8	6·5	27·0	3·5	26·0
1910	33·9		62·6		3·5	—
1905	35·2		61·8		3·0	—
1900	37·7		59·3		3·0	—
1895	37·9		60·0		2·1	—
1890	28·0		69·8		2·2	—
1886	20·2		77·5		2·3	—

Taking this table in conjunction with the table which analyses ore consumed in the district into Cleveland, foreign and home, as brought from other districts (Table III), we conclude that:

The production of ordinary iron (foundry and forge) has fallen off continuously relative to other sorts, the fall being very marked in the decades 1885–95 and 1914–24. Production of basic iron increased slowly 1900 to 1910, but was greatly stimulated by the War.

Of the ores used in the district in 1883 about 84 % by weight was raised locally, 12½ % imported and 3½ % brought from other home districts. In 1913 the proportions were 60 %, 33½ % and 6½ % respectively, while in 1923 only 44½ % of the ore used was raised locally.

Thus "Cleveland iron" has fallen steadily in importance among the production of the north-east coast. Fortunately the basic iron of the district may be classed together with the ordinary iron for our purpose, since it is produced from similar ores and employs the factors of production in about the same proportion (see Birkitt's table above). Grouping ordinary and basic iron together we find that the index numbers cover a large portion of north-east coast production directly (77·5 % in 1886, 62·3 % in 1913, 57·2 % in 1920 and 60 % in 1923), i.e. changes in the efficiency of production of about 60 % of the total output of the district are directly measured. Moreover, since the same iron-masters in many cases produce each of the three chief qualities (haematite, basic, and ordinary), it is inconceivable that changes in the efficiency of production of the one would vary without corresponding variations in the others.

We may therefore conclude that the index numbers of real costs will reflect changes in the general efficiency of the Cleveland smelting industry.

§3. THE SIZE OF THE INDUSTRY, MATERIALS USED, AND SIZE OF THE FIRMS ENGAGED THEREIN

[Ref. Table III]

(a) The table showing pig iron produced, ore used, coal used, Cleveland ore raised, etc., has been compiled from the Home Office records with the exception of the figures for Cleveland ore raised, which were supplied by Mr T. J. Atkinson. The imports of foreign ore into the district have been calculated by summing the imports into Middlesborough, Stockton-on-Tees, Sunderland, Hartlepool (including West Hartlepool), Newcastle-on-Tyne and Shields (South and North). I am assured that all ore imported via these ports would be used in the Cleveland district, and that no appreciable amount of foreign ore would be obtained by any other path. The figures for "Home ore brought from other districts" are simply the differences between the ore used in any given year and the Cleveland ore raised plus foreign ores imported. No allowance has been made for changes in stocks of ore.

The table brings out clearly the fall in the amount of Cleveland ore used, and the growing habit of bringing ores from the Lincolnshire and Northamptonshire mines.

[Ref. Table II]

(b) The information tabulated as to numbers of works and of owners operating has been collected from the detailed reports of H.M. Inspectors, except in the case of number of furnaces blowing; here we find the figures of the Ironmasters and H.M. Inspectors differ considerably. The difference between the returns of the Ironmasters' Association and the Home Office records is probably partly due to government information lagging behind the times. It must be noted that the phrase "number of owners" means the number of concerns having independent legal status.

I have compiled and tabulated from H.M. Inspector of Mines' reports a history of the ironworks of the district from

1885-1926, together with their changes of ownership in so far as revealed by changes of name of owning company. Effective combination *may* also have occurred by the interlocking of directorates, etc., but such developments are not recorded in the Home Office records, nor in my tables.

Table IV has been compiled to show the process of integration in the industry, and also the growth in output of each furnace. It may be possible incidentally to associate short-period changes in efficiency to some extent with variations in the output per furnace blowing.

§4. PROVISIONAL CONCLUSIONS

The ratio chart for this industry is somewhat overcrowded, but the advantages of having all relevant material conveniently to hand outweigh other considerations.

Upon this chart a gradient of 1 in 1 represents an increase of 5 % per annum—double the scale of the charts for the cotton and building trades.

Short-period problems are complicated in this industry by the high ratio of supplementary to prime costs. Being dependent largely upon foreign demand, output fluctuates considerably. The slump in production in 1892 was, however, due to the three months' strike of Durham miners. Costs, money and real, fluctuate much more violently than in the cotton or building industries. The depression in 1894 and 1895 was phenomenal, and led to a temporary rupture in the relations between masters and men; a new sliding scale was finally substituted for the old one.

It is interesting to notice that, contrary to the cotton and building industries, the prices of raw materials are quite as stable as those of the finished product. There is a general tendency for the output per furnace in blast to fall slightly in periods of prosperity (as measured by output) and to rise in depression. This supports the view that real costs of production fluctuate with the trade cycle. In depression only the larger and more efficient furnaces are kept blowing, while great care is

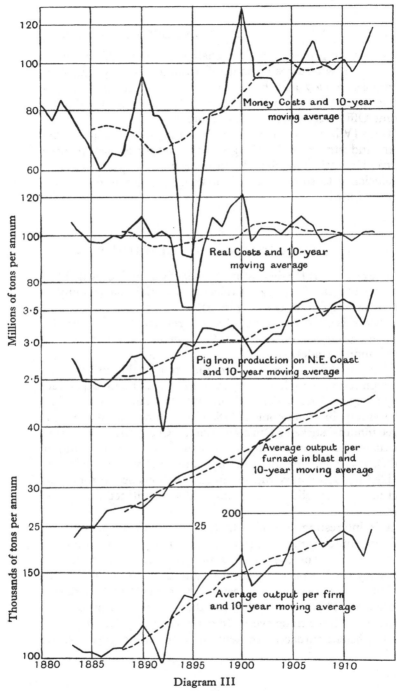

Diagram III

Money Costs and Real Costs in the Pig Iron Industry of the North-East
Coast, 1883–1913. Production, average output per furnace in blast and
average output per firm in same area.

exercised in the provision of a continuous charge of properly mixed ores, etc., for such furnaces as are in blast. These facts probably account for the fluctuation of output for furnaces in blast.

[For the remainder of this section the term "costs", money or real, refers to the normal cost of production, measured by the ten years' moving averages of the annual index numbers.]

Owing to the phenomenal depression of the early 'nineties, it is difficult to compute a satisfactory measure of the trend of real costs in this industry. If a ten years' moving average is used the index numbers from 1889 to 1901 are depressed by the abnormally low annual figures for 1894 and 1895; yet a five years' average does not eliminate cyclical fluctuations. Comparison of the five and the ten years' moving averages of the annual index numbers of corrected selling price shows that the real cost of smelting iron in the Cleveland district in 1888 was 102 % of the cost in 1910, and was declining very slowly (about $\frac{1}{3}$ % per annum) after falling during the early 'nineties to a record low level, real costs rose to 108 in 1900 and then declined gradually, approximately 1 % per annum, to 100 in 1910. The curve of real costs for the American pig iron industry follows a similar course.

In the conclusion to the American Study (Part VI), it is argued that the fluctuations of the index numbers of real cost of pig iron between 1890 and 1900 are due largely to variations in the returns (quasi-rent) earned by the capital "fixed" in the industry; but the argument does not provide a satisfactory explanation of the rise of real costs from 102 in 1888 to 108 in 1900 (or 106 in 1902, if the ten years' average is followed closely).

This rise followed the substitution of three shifts of eight hours per day for two shifts of twelve hours.

In a general survey any economic disadvantages of this change must be set against the social value of greater leisure. From the immediate point of view, however, it seems clear that the ironmasters, after a brief trial, found that output per man was not maintained and passed on the extra cost to the consumer. A correction has already been made for the concealed rise in efficiency wages; the rise of real costs must therefore be attributed to definite diseconomies of organisation following the reduction of hours, yet the ironmasters themselves assert that they have gained more from the more regular working of the furnaces than the additional cost of managing the larger body of workers.

Once recovered from the change in hours, technical economies began to assert themselves and real costs fell steadily until the end of the pre-War period. The substitution of by-product coking plant for the old beehive ovens had doubtless much to do with this increase in efficiency. The retort oven did not displace the beehive in the country as a whole until after the War, but in Durham it had already been widely introduced in 1913. Though yielding nearly 70 % coke from the best quality Durham coal, as compared with the 50 % yield of the beehive, the retort does not produce quite so good a coke from the iron-masters' point of view. It is difficult to point out the precise difference, but the fact remains that beehive coke resists the action of the ascending gases in the blast furnaces better than by-product coke.

Mechanical charging and other haulage devices made their appearance quite early in the period, but were not generally adopted. Even now there appears to be a doubt whether hand charging is not more economical—it depends upon the general organisation of the works, especially the use made of waste gases.[1]

---

[1] The most important technical developments in the Cleveland iron trade since 1880 have been:

(1) The substitution of firebrick stoves for the cast iron pipes previously used to preheat the gas, thus raising the temperature of the gas entering the furnace from 900° F. to 1400°–1500° F.

The adoption of firebrick stoves on the north-east coast began in the 'seventies and was almost complete by 1890.

(2) The increase in capacity of the furnaces. The tendency has been to enlarge the hearth (from 8 ft. in 1880 to 13 ft. in 1913), reduce the diameter and lower the height of the bosh. There has also been a steady increase in the pressure of the gases blown into the furnace.

(3) The employment of waste heat and gases, e.g. the firing of boilers, and in some cases internal combustion engines, with blast-furnace gas; and the employment of exhaust steam to blow the furnaces or, in low-pressure turbines, for the generation of electric power.

(4) The development of the Basic Bessemer process for making steel, demanding an iron differing somewhat from the ordinary Cleveland iron. Ironmasters who used to confine themselves to the production of foundry and forge iron now mix imported ores (Fe 50 %) with the local ores to make

There is no significant correlation between the expansion of the industry and the trend of real costs. When real costs were falling at the rate of 1 % per annum between 1902 and 1910, output was increasing at about the same rate, so that the extreme value of the elasticity of return would be unity (i.e. assuming that all the economies were due to the expansion of the industry).

Throughout the period the output per furnace in blast, and per firm operating, increased, though the rate of expansion of firms fell somewhat after the middle 'nineties. After the period of dismantling of old works which came to an end in 1892 the number of concerns operating remained almost constant (twenty-two in 1892 and nineteen in 1920) until the depression which followed the boom of 1920. In 1923 large amalgamations were effected, and there are now only ten concerns operating upon the north-east coast. The tabular history in Appendix III B shows clearly how the trade has remained in the hands of a few families who were already associated with it in 1883. The stability of British industry in the late nineteenth and early twentieth century is remarkable. The Cleveland pig iron trade seems to have yielded an almost constant return to human effort.

iron suitable for the basic steel process. The ironstone dug from the Cleveland mines is within measurable distance of exhaustion. In 1870 it averaged 32 % iron and 11 % silica but fell to 28 % iron during the 'eighties and by 1913 was as low as 26 % with silica contents as high as 17 %. The ironmasters are thus forced to go to the Lincolnshire and Northamptonshire iron fields for an economical home ore. They are naturally using a higher proportion of high grade Spanish ore for the manufacture of basic as well as haematite iron.

(5) The introduction of mechanical haulage, etc., etc., e.g. clay guns for stopping tapping holes; pig bed cranes and pig breakers equipped with electric magnets; mechanical charging. As a result of these developments the capacity of the furnace doubled in the thirty years preceding the War and has again doubled since 1913, e.g. the weekly output per furnace blowing at Clarence Iron and Steel Works rose from 440 tons in 1880 to 926 tons in 1913, an increase of more than 110 %; while the modern furnaces at this works have produced over 2000 tons of pig iron in a single week.

PART V

THE MASSACHUSETTS COTTON INDUSTRY 1845-1920

§ 1. INTRODUCTION

COTTON manufacture upon a commercial scale began in the United States during the last decade of the eighteenth century. After a slow start the industry developed rapidly in New England, supplies of cloth from Great Britain being curtailed during the Napoleonic wars and restrictions upon foreign trade providing a readier supply of capital. Assisted by the tariff, the young industry successfully encountered the severe competition of English manufacturers after the war; the best English machinery was introduced and adapted to local conditions. Moreover, the adoption of the power loom checked the growth of household weaving.

The census of 1840, though so crudely administered that the returns have been omitted from the tables in the Appendix, showed that there were over two and a quarter millions of cotton spindles in the mills of the Eastern States and that they consumed more than one hundred million pounds of cotton per annum. From 1845 to 1914 there was no fundamental change in the organisation or mechanical process of cotton manufacture in New England; its history is the story of continuous expansion under competitive conditions accompanied by such technical improvements and changes in the division of labour as one would expect *a priori*, and is likely, therefore, to throw light upon the relation between the size and efficiency of industries.

As in the studies of British industries, I have confined the statistical enquiry to a particular locality rather than attempt to compute from scanty information averages representative of the diverse conditions in the different states. Measured by all standards Massachusetts has been the leading state in the Union for cotton manufacture throughout the period; the general conditions of employment have changed little, except in respect of hours, for which allowance can be made, and the statistical records are more satisfactory than those of any other states. Moreover, in view of the concentration of the industry in the New England states, the mobility of labour and capital within this area, and the common market, it is inconceivable that the course of real costs in Massachusetts has differed appreciably from their trend in New England as a whole. The development of cotton manufacture in the Southern States would call for separate study were the statistics available, but as we are concerned with the normal growth rather than the laborious birth of industries, the New England study is more significant. The statistical investigation is therefore confined to Massachusetts, but the results are significant for New England, and with careful interpretation give a basis for broad conclusions concerning American cotton manufacture as a whole.

The following table shows the proportions of the industry concentrated in New England and Massachusetts as indicated by the federal census returns of spindles and looms in operation.

Percentage of the spindles and looms in the cotton mills of the United States which were situate in Massachusetts or New England at the federal censuses 1840–1920

	Massachusetts		New England	
	Spindles	Looms	Spindles	Looms
1840	29	—	70	—
1860	32	34	74	74
1870	37	35	77	73
1880	40	42	81	82
1890	41	41	76	77
1900	41	40	67	66
1914	34	34	54	57
1920	33	33	52	54

The percentages are given in round numbers, for neither the number of spindles nor the number of looms is an accurate measure of the resources employed. There is more labour employed per spindle, *ceteris paribus*, in mills spinning coarse yarns than is required in the fine counts because "mills spinning and weaving coarse goods require more machinery other than spindles, and consequently more hands than fine mills ". The amount of raw cotton consumed by spindles driven at a given speed varies inversely as the count of yarn spun, while the fabrics woven from the finer yarns cost more to weave and command higher prices than the coarser goods. These errors largely offset one another and the spindle is recognised as a good measure of capacity. [The loom varies considerably in width, but serves to confirm the indication of the number of spindles in a district which consumes its own yarns, so long as the general character of the fabrics woven does not change greatly. The bulk of the looms in all sections of the United States are plain looms of standard width.]

So much for machinery as a measure of the capacity of cotton textiles industries and the resources employed in different districts at a given stage of industrial development. In using the spindle or loom to make similar comparisons over long intervals of time or between industries at widely different stages of technical development, allowance must be made for changes in the speed at which the machinery is driven; the consumption of cotton provides a useful check in such cases upon the number of spindles producing yarn.

To return, after this somewhat lengthy digression, to the consideration of the table. The speed of the spindles operating in Massachusetts and New England has been somewhat above the average of the country, especially in the early years, the looms have also been wider, while the yarns spun and goods woven have been of rather finer grade. One can safely say that at least 30 % of the resources of the industry have been employed in Massachusetts since 1845, and that the New England states have together accounted for more than one-half. In 1909, for example, when New England was hampered by the scarcity of raw cotton suitable for medium or fine yarns, Massachusetts contributed 29·7 % of the value of cotton manufactures reported at the census and employed 28·7 % of the wage earners.

The separation of spinning and weaving which makes the statistical treatment of the Lancashire cotton industry so difficult, gives little trouble in New England. For the most part the cotton mills spin the yarn they require for weaving. The export trade in cotton yarns remains negligible, but sales of yarn for use in allied industries have recently assumed serious proportions, approaching 12 % of the value of "cotton manufactures" in the United States in 1909, a further 5½ % represented cotton yarns purchased by establishments within the industry and therefore duplicated in the aggregate. The proportions were about the same for Massachusetts as for the entire country.

The following table shows how far spinning and weaving take place in the same establishment in the United States, New England, and Lancashire (England).

Distribution of cotton mills between spinning and weaving in the United States and in New England, and in Lancashire, England.

	Spinning and weaving mills			Spinning mills		Weaving mills	
	No. of mills	% of total spindles	% of total looms	No. of mills	% of total spindles	No. of mills	% of total looms
			United States				
1919	632	79	97	409	21	180	3
1904	590	83	97	295	17	169	3
1899	502	84	96	274	16	168	3
			New England				
1919	346	83	99	66	17	34	1
1904	308	87	99	53	13	20	1
1899	332	87	99	76	13	17	1
			Lancashire				
1911	236	20·5	33·7	595	79·5	859	66·3

There is no apparent tendency for mills to specialise in weaving, but the demand for cotton yarns in allied industries has encouraged the growth of mills specialising upon spinning, so that yarns produced for sale accounted for more than 20 % of the value of the product of the industry in 1919. The figures for Lancashire indicate clearly the separation of weaving and spinning in England.

As in England, dyeing and finishing are a separate branch of the industry carried on very largely in special establishments, so that the bulk of the cloth produced is first marketed in the grey or unbleached condition. In consequence there is an active market for grey cotton goods which gives a basis for valuation of the products of the "cotton goods" industry without including the diverse and intractable finishing processes. Out of 189 Massachusetts mills included in the cotton goods industry at the census of 1914, only forty-eight were reported as dyeing, bleaching, or printing their own goods, while ten did such work for others. Over 90 % of the cloth was treated in independent industries in 1899, while in the same year nearly 70 % of the prepared yarn was treated in the mills themselves.

I shall make frequent use of returns relating to cotton manufactures made at the decennial federal censuses of 1840 to 1890, the quinquennial censuses 1899 to 1919, and the Massachusetts state censuses of 1845, 1855, 1865, 1875, 1885 and 1895. It will be convenient at this point to say something about the general significance of these returns. Much scorn has been poured upon the United States censuses of manufactures, especially the early ones, by Mr S. N. D. North and other critics. The objections fall under three heads:

(*a*) Incomplete enumeration.

(*b*) Duplication of returns, intermediate products being added to the value of the final products of particular industries and counted in the grand total for manufacturing industries.

(*c*) Changes in classification and definition of industries rendering successive returns incomparable.

These criticisms each have considerable force when applied to the census as a whole, but there are particular industries in which the errors they involve are small. The enumeration of cotton mills, especially in Massachusetts, has been fairly satisfactory from the start. Throughout, "cotton manufactures" has included establishments "engaged in the spinning or weaving of raw cotton together with those which convert the waste cotton into the commercial product. The tables do not cover the operation of any establishments for the manufacture of hosiery or knit goods, nor any of those principally engaged in making elastic fabrics or cotton cordage or twines. Moreover all mills in which mixed textiles are produced are excluded ". The census name for this industry is "Cotton Goods, including Cotton Small Wares"; prior to the census of 1899, no distinction was made between cotton goods and cotton small wares (i.e. establishments manufacturing narrow fabrics such as tapes, webbing and mill binding, braids, shoe and corset laces, and similar goods); separate figures are available for small wares from 1899, but for most purposes they are combined with cotton goods under the head of "cotton manufactures", so as to secure comparability with the early statistics. In any case they form but a small proportion of the product of the industry; e.g. in 1909 "cotton goods" contributed 97·9 % of the total value of the product of the "cotton manufactures" industry.

It has been the practice of the federal census to include all establishments primarily engaged in the manufacture of cotton goods provided the annual value of their output of cotton goods exceeded $500. Prior to the Civil War a few cotton mills may have been excluded on this count, but the output of nearly all the mills has been above this limit; as the census office developed better technique, more establishments manufacturing cotton and other goods have doubtless made their contribution to the cotton goods industry. Dyeing, bleaching and finishing have throughout been excluded from the cotton manufactures except in so far as mills engaged primarily in spinning and weaving also do some dyeing, bleaching, or finishing.

The Massachusetts state census classification "cotton goods" agrees roughly with the federal class of "cotton manufactures"; Colonel C. D. Wright had much to do with the administration of both censuses during the latter half of the nineteenth century and was himself familiar with the cotton manufacturing industry. In 1885 the state census classification was brought into line with the federal system, while the returns for the cotton goods industry in 1875 are fairly comparable. At this census returns of wages were made for the first time in the state census, and I have used them together with the federal returns to estimate the proportion of the receipts of the industry going to labour at quinquennial intervals from 1870. The chief difference between the federal and state classification is in the treatment of establishments manufacturing cotton together with goods which were included in a miscellaneous group by the Massachusetts office until 1895; moreover the state census included all establishments regardless of output, so that the returns exceed the federal returns up to 1875. Print works, dye-works and bleacheries were excluded from the cotton goods industry from the first. Colonel Wright claims that the statistics for the industries considered (of which cotton goods was the most important in Massachusetts) are "practically complete", even in 1845, 1855 and 1865, so I have included them in the general table of statistics relating to the growth of the cotton manufactures in Massachusetts.

Duplication of returns *within* the cotton goods industry is not serious for purposes of comparison. Throughout the period weavers of piece goods have been accustomed to spin their own yarn; the growth of establishments manufacturing small wares, threads and fancy goods from purchased yarns has increased the duplication of materials in the value of cotton manufactures, but the item is still small. The value of cotton yarns and cotton waste purchased in the United States for use as materials in cotton manufactures did not reach 10 % of the value of the product even in 1919, in 1909 it was just over 6 %. An allowance of 5 % of the value of the materials will cover duplication of materials within the cotton manufactures industry of Massachusetts from 1840 to 1914. The production of cotton yarn for sale to other industries (hosiery, knit goods, etc.) is more troublesome than duplication for my purposes; this item already exceeded 10 % of the value of cotton manufactures in Massachusetts and the United States in 1909, in 1919 it had risen nearly to 17 % for Massachusetts and 12 % for the United States. There is no duplication on account of the small amount of dyeing and finishing done by cotton manufacturing establishments for other mills, since the census reports only the value added by finishing; again the complication introduced by the dyeing of yarn and the finishing of cloth within the manufacturing establishment is more serious if one wishes to study the manufacture of grey cloth.

A word upon the precise period covered by the census returns will explain some apparent contradictions in the tables of the appendix and the text. The returns made at the decennial censuses, both federal and state, prior to 1900, refer mainly to the business year ending during the census year itself. Since 1900 a federal census of manufactures has been taken every five years and these returns relate principally to the business year ending in the calendar year preceding the year of census. I have usually followed the practice of the census office and referred each set of returns to the year preceding the census, but in one or two tables I have found it convenient to tabulate returns for the season ending in the year stated, in which case I have related the statistics prior to 1900 to the census year itself.

Finally I pass to the analysis of the products of American cotton mills, according to grade. There has been much talk of the growth of a fine goods industry, especially in New England. New Bedford has been manufacturing piece goods of a much finer quality than the average American product since the 'nineties, but the bulk of the cotton goods manufactured in New England is still of medium to coarse grade. Consider the analysis of yarns produced: the table on p. 154 gives the weight of yarn produced in the United States, New England and Massachusetts by grades from 1889 to 1919.

Up to 1890 over 90 % of the yarns spun in Massachusetts were of medium or coarse count, and these two grades still account for about 85 % of the cotton yarn produced in the state. The increase in the proportion of higher counts is significant, but selling price index numbers based upon coarse and medium cloths have a clear title to represent the industry as a whole in this present study.

Cloths for printing or converting accounted for about 30 % of the receipts of the industry before the War, but in 1919 they had fallen to about 20 %. Sheetings and shirtings gave way to southern competition in the two decades 1889–99 and 1899–1909, but the peculiar needs of the industry stimulated this branch and there was a slight recovery from 6 % in 1909 to 8 % in 1919. Increased production of fancy woven fabrics, twills and sateens, cotton flannels, and the finer print cloths,

Coarse, medium and fine yarns spun in the United States, New England and Massachusetts (in millions of pounds)

Year	1889	1899	1904*	1909	1914	1919
Count of Yarn	United States					
No. 20 and under	480	850	804	1014	989	1123
Nos. 21–40	387	540	602	866	1026	1063
No. 41 and over	35	77	124	157	155	161
	New England					
No. 20 and under	208	305	249	290	273	252
Nos. 21–40	332	269	317	461	462	504
No. 41 and over	35	72	101	115	125	114
	Massachusetts					
No. 20 and under	103	164	142	175	152	135
Nos. 21–40	187	236	178	283	276	302
No. 41 and over	19	43	61	65	84	79

Percentage of yarn spun in Massachusetts which was coarse, medium and fine

Coarse, No. 20 and under	33	37	37	34	30	26
Medium, Nos. 21–40	61	53	47	54	54	59
Fine, No. 41 and over	6	10	16	12	16	15

Percentage of total yarn of each grade produced in the United States which was spun in Massachusetts

Coarse, No. 20 and under	21	19	18	17	15	12
Medium, Nos. 21–40	48	44	30	33	27	28
Fine, No. 41 and over	54	56	49	41	54	49

* The statistics for 1904 are abnormal on account of the prolonged Fall River strike, which reduced the production of print cloth in Massachusetts.

lawns and muslins, has raised the average quality (or fineness) of the cotton goods manufactured in Massachusetts, but this tendency has been checked by the growth of the duck and drill trades to meet the demand for strong tyre fabrics, etc. Moreover the rapid increase of yarns produced for sale has materially reduced the relative importance of the other products of the industry. Upon the whole I think this table of piece goods confirms the general conclusion suggested by the counts of yarn spun in Massachusetts. In spite of the undoubted increase in the production of lawns and muslins, twills, sateens, napped fabrics, corduroys, and velvets, the industry is still dominated by goods of medium to coarse quality, viz. printing cloths made from medium yarns, sheetings and shirtings, duck and drill, ginghams, ticking, denims and stripes. This group of fabrics accounted for about 50 % of the value of the product of the industry in Massachusetts in 1889, 42½ % in 1909 and 36½ % in 1919. Print cloths and sheetings are still among the largest classes of cotton goods made in the state, being second only to tyre duck. The census classification of cotton goods, however, is better adapted to analysis of the composite demand for cotton textiles than to determination of the relative amount of the different grades of cloth produced. For there are coarse, medium and fine qualities of each class of goods distinguished in the table, and the relative increase of, say, the finer plain cloths for printing and converting may easily be the most significant change in a decade. Judged by English standards the bulk of American products, even of the better quality, are of medium to coarse grade, as is indicated by the analysis of yarns spun.

To conclude this lengthy introduction: "The cotton goods industry is one of the oldest and most typical factory industries in the United States. In 1909 it ranked third among the industries of the country in the number of wage earners, being exceeded only by the lumber industry, and the foundry and machine shop industry, and seventh in value of products and in value added by manufacture ". Throughout the fabrics have been manufactured mainly from medium and coarse yarns, and although the progress of the industry has been accompanied by increasing diversification of the product, the heavy sheeting, the regular print cloth and kindred fabrics have been the staple manufacture since the industry was established upon a commercial scale. The New England section forms a natural unit for study; the local markets for raw cotton and cloth have been in close touch with the central market in New York, so that the course of prices quoted at New York for these commodities is a good index of the changes in the cost of cotton to the New England manufacturers and in the prices they obtain for their cloth.

Spasmodic attempts at the beginning of the century made by large amalgamations of capital to obtain monopoly power failed and the industry has remained intensely competitive, while the mobility of labour between the various centres has been a powerful inducement for the manufacturers to keep abreast of the times. The statistical study has been confined to Massachusetts because the general conditions of employment have changed less and the records of wages in this state are more satisfactory than for any other in the Union; the census returns are also more reliable and are available for every five instead of every ten years since 1840. In short the cotton goods industry in Massachusetts is admirably suited to the purpose in view, and I shall proceed to describe how I have calculated index numbers showing the course of real costs of cotton manufacture in Massachusetts from 1850–1910.

§ 2. THE INDEX NUMBERS OF PRICES AND COSTS

I. *Selling price.*

The selling price index is based upon two series of prices:

(*a*) Regular print cloth 28 in. 64 × 64, 7 yd. to the lb.

(*b*) Standard brown sheetings, 36 in. 3 yd. to the lb.

The data have been taken from statistical abstracts of the United States which contain a continuous record of the average annual prices of these fabrics from 1847 to 1920. The prices are net at New York and were computed by the following gentlemen from daily quotations in the market.

1847–92 Mr Joshua Reece, Jr., of the *Daily Commercial Bulletin*, New York.

1893–1911 Mr Alfred B. Shepperson, New York.

1912–20 Mr Carl Geller, of New York.

These fabrics were the standard American cotton piece goods for sixty years before the War of 1914 and they continue to represent the market very closely, although a slightly different print cloth (27 in. 64 × 60, 7·60 yd. to the lb.) has now become the standard in place of the old regular cloth. It has already been argued at some length that medium and coarse goods have predominated among the cotton manufacturers of New England since the middle of the nineteenth century; the regular print cloth represents the medium and the standard sheeting the coarse products. "The yarns which are woven into print cloths of which the calico of commerce is made are for the most part No. 28 for warps and No. 36 for filling. The best standard sheetings and shirtings are spun from nearly the same numbers ",[1] but the sheeting quoted in the statistical abstract is of a somewhat coarser construction (say Nos. 14–28) representing changes in the prices of duck, drill, etc., as well as brown sheetings.

The selling price index has been calculated by expressing the annual average prices of regular print cloth and standard sheetings as a percentage of the prices in 1913, and taking the mean. The *Aldrich Report*[2] provides a useful check upon these index numbers from 1847–91 and the U.S. Bureau of Labour Statistics wholesale prices series serves the same purpose from 1890 onwards.

The data in these reports refer for the most part to special brands of cloth made by particular firms and enjoying some protection from the reputation and established business connections of their manufacturers; moreover quarterly quotations only are available for the Aldrich series while the annual relative prices of the Bureau of Labour are the average of twelve monthly quotations. I therefore chose to rely upon the two New York market series for my index numbers, using this second body of data to confirm my results.

In Table I of the *Aldrich Report* (Part I, pp. 37, 38) Professor Falkner expressed as percentages of 1860 the January quotations for the eight cotton goods series going back to 1847. Comparison with the statistical abstract series (reduced to the base 1860 = 100) shows that the relative price of standard brown sheetings represents closely the general movements of coarse goods such as sheetings, shirtings, drillings, denims and tickings from 1847–91; while the prices of prints and print cloths move in close sympathy with the regular print cloth: the average of Professor

---

[1] *Eleventh United States Series* 1890—*Manufactures*, Pt III, p. 183.
[2] *Report* from Senate Committee on Finance upon "Wholesale Prices, Wages and Transportation", March 3rd, 1893.

Relative wholesale prices of cotton textiles 1860–90

Base 1860 = 100

Date	Falkner's series 8–27 articles January quotations	Mitchell's series based upon 8 articles quarterly prices	Index numbers based upon regular print cloth standard sheeting
1860	100	100	100
1861	95	98	105
1862	128	161	195
1863	254	292	336
1864	321	462	502
1865	468	411	402
1866	337	320	267
1867	242	227	185
1868	156	181	168
1869	167	174	166
1870	160	159	146
1871	136	146	151
1872	141	151	153
1873	139	140	135
1874	124	124	114
1875	110	112	107
1876	100	93	86
1877	91	87	87
1878	84	79	74
1879	75	79	80
1880	90	90	89
1881	87	—	83
1882	88	—	81
1883	84	—	78
1884	77	—	71
1885	72	—	66
1886	69	—	68
1887	72	—	70
1888	75	—	75
1889	75	—	74
1890	72	—	70
1891	71	—	65

Base 1913 = 100

Date	United States Bureau of Labour Statistics cotton goods	Index numbers
1913	100	100
1914	—	93
1915	—	84
1916	122	117
1917	176	184
1918	264	306
1919	257	279
1920	329	292
1921	159	—
1922	172	—
1923	199	—
1924	195	—
1925	181	—

Falkner's eight price relatives for 1847 is 99 while my selling price index number expressed as a percentage of the 1860 index number is 103. For the period 1860-80 Professor Wesley C. Mitchell[1] calculated an index number for cotton textiles based upon these eight series, but using the four available quotations in each year. Professor Falkner himself (*Aldrich Report*, Part I, pp. 72-4 and p. 82) computed an index number for cotton textiles 1860-91 based upon January quotations only and introducing additional series as they became available until he had twenty-seven instead of eight articles for the last ten years. In the table opposite I have reduced my selling price index numbers to the base 1860 = 100 and brought them into comparison with the cotton textile series of Falkner and Mitchell.

As one would expect the index numbers based upon market quotations of standard cloths are more sensitive than those based upon the prices asked by particular manufacturers, but the general agreement of the three series, calculated in different ways from different data, is remarkable and proves beyond question the title of the regular print cloth and the standard sheeting to serve as a price index for American cotton textiles over the period 1847-91. From 1890-1913 the U.S. Bureau of Labour Statistics' wholesale price series gives relative prices for about twenty cotton goods which demonstrate the representative character of my selling price index. The bureau has recently calculated an index number for cotton goods based upon these series of relative prices.

In the table I have brought this index number into comparison with mine for the years 1913-20. Considering the magnitude of the price changes involved and the diversity of goods (comprising yarns and finished cloths as well as grey goods) included in the Bureau of Labour Statistics' index number the agreement of the two series is good.

II. *Cost of materials.*

Raw cotton is the only material employed in cotton manufacture in sufficient quantity to call for separate correction: the cost of fuel, chemicals, etc., is considered under "other expenses".

---

[1] *Gold, Prices and Wages*, p. 278.

The index numbers of cost of raw cotton have been computed from the average annual price of middling upland cotton net at New York, as recorded in the tables of the statistical abstract referred to in I. This series calls for no comment; the "ons and offs" for other grades of cotton fluctuate slightly from time to time, but it is well recognised that middling upland represents the course of the American cotton market very closely; the grade has also been well defined throughout the period.

III. Efficiency wages.

In seeking a measure of changes in the rate at which the cotton manufacturer has paid for the efforts of his employees, we are again forced to fall back upon the assumption that the representative worker has put about the same amount of effort into a full week's work throughout the period under review, except in so far as allowance can be made for recent "uneconomical" reductions in the weekly hours of work. This assumption is probably not far from the truth, for the New England mills have been fed with cheap unskilled immigrant labour. By 1845 the stream of immigrants was already large and it continued until 1914: during the 'fifties the Irish began to displace the Yankees, in the 'seventies the French-Canadians appeared in large numbers, and by the 'nineties the invasion of Southern Europeans was in spate.[1] The hours and conditions of work in Massachusetts cotton mills have been fairly uniform and the successive reductions of hours widespread. If one may generalise from the four Massachusetts firms making returns in the *Aldrich Report*, it appears that the practice varied considerably from firm to firm before 1870. Establishment No. 40 worked eighty-four hours per week during the 'forties but reduced to seventy-two hours in January 1852; on the other hand

[1] M. T. Copeland, *The Cotton Manufacturing Industry*, pp. 13, 118. On p. 114 Professor Copeland points out that "the demands imposed by technical changes have called for more male labour. The machinery has become heavier and is run at a higher speed, thus requiring greater muscular exertion and causing a more intense nervous strain on the operatives". As will be seen later, allowance can be made for the partial displacement of women by men; while the additional strain placed upon the operatives by the faster machinery serves to offset the deterioration of the average quality of the workers resulting from the successive invasions of immigrants.

Establishment 43, making ginghams, already worked a regular sixty-six and a half hours, a five-and-a-half day week, in the late 'forties and reduced to sixty-six in January 1854. There appears to have been a fairly general reduction of about 8 % at the beginning of the next decade (1861, 1862) while all establishments reporting were on a sixty-six hour week by the end of the 'sixties; the gingham firm working five and a half and the others six full days in the week. Since 1870 the more important changes have taken place simultaneously in all Massachusetts firms, the working week being largely determined by the minimum hours permitted by law for women and minors. The successive reductions were as follows:

66–60 hours per week as from January 1st, 1875
60–58   ,,   ,,   ,,   July 1st, 1892
58–56   ,,   ,,   ,,   January 1st, 1910
56–54   ,,   ,,   ,,   January 1st, 1912
54–48   ,,   ,,   ,,   January 1st, 1919

A few special classes of workers, e.g. watchmen and boiler-tenders, have had their peculiar hours while (at least in recent years) card strippers and tenders appear to have worked about half an hour extra.

Fortunately one can get some *rough* indications as to the effects of these changes upon the personal efficiency of the operators[1]; by dividing the Fall River weavers' piece rate into the full-time weekly earnings we get a fairly good measure of weekly output in adjacent years. Care is necessary in interpretation for the Fall River weavers' piece rates, although the basis of wage agreements in that district is not the average weaver's piece rates for Massachusetts, while they do not necessarily represent

---

[1] The figures used in this argument are taken from Dr S. E. Howard's *The Movement of Wages in the Cotton Manufacturing Industry of New England since 1860*, p. 17, Table I, column 5. Annual average weaving rate at Fall River 1881–1918. pp. 66, 67, Table XII. Full-time weekly earnings of (*a*) Frame spinners: female. (*b*) Weavers: male; female.
N.B. Howard's figures for full-time earnings in 1910, 1911 and 1912 are based upon the *average* of the figures obtained by the U.S. Bureau of Labour Statistics from different sets of establishments. It would be possible to obtain figures for identical sets of establishments but the results would not differ appreciably.

spinners' piece rates even in Fall River; still I believe the figures for changes in weekly output which follow are significant for my present purpose:

(a) Reduction from sixty to fifty-eight hours per week became effective July 1st, 1892.

	Weekly output	
	1891	1893
Frame spinners (female)	28·2	28·7
Weavers: Female	37·4	38·1
Male	42·4	42·2

Thus the weekly output of female spinners and weavers rose 2 % between 1891 and 1893 while the output of male weavers fell ½ %. A part of the rise of the former may be attributed to the 5 % increase in piece rate, but it is at least clear that the employers were getting as much work done on an average in the fifty-eight as in the sixty hour week.

(b) Reduction of hours from fifty-eight to fifty-six per week became effective January 1st, 1910.

Piece rates remained unchanged in 1909, 1910 and 1911, so that half-time earnings may be assumed proportionate to output. Frame spinners' (female) weekly earnings rose from $7.20 in 1909 to $7.32 in 1910 and to $7.36 in 1911—say an increase of 2 % in weekly output.

Female weavers' weekly earnings fell from $8.73 in 1909 to $8.44 in 1910 and to $8.27 in 1911—an apparent fall of 2¾ % in weekly output, but since the hourly earnings of female weavers also fell in 1911 it is reasonable to assume that disturbing factors other than the change in hours are at work and to neglect this item.

Male weavers' weekly earnings fell from $9.36 in 1909 to $9.12 in 1910 and rose to $9.16 in 1911—say a fall in weekly output of 2 %. One gets a similar fall of about 2 % in the weekly earnings of male card strippers and loom fixers.

Supposing the erratic movements of the female weavers' weekly earnings to be due to extraneous forces (their hourly earnings rose slightly in 1910 only to fall 2 % in 1911), it appears that the weekly output of male workers fell about 2 %, while that of female workers rose 2 %, with no significant resultant change in weekly output, since there are approximately as many women as men employed in the industry.

(c) Reduction from fifty-six to fifty-four hours per week, effective from January 1st, 1912.

Piece rates rose 10 % between 1911 and 1912.

	Weekly output		Decrease
	1911	1912	(%)
Frame spinners (female)	37·4	36·1	3½
Weavers: Male	46·6	44·8	3½
Female	42·0	41·6	1

We have already seen that there is reason to suspect that the earnings reported for female weavers in 1911 were low; neglecting this series, we find that a reduction of just under 4 % in hours worked was accompanied in this case by an almost proportionate fall in weekly output.

These calculations have taken into account only direct changes in the effectiveness of the worker, but it seems reasonable to conclude that reductions in hours of work in the Massachusetts cotton industry have been largely offset by proportionate increase in the personal efficiency of the workers; but the change from a fifty-six hour week to a fifty-four in 1912 and from a fifty-four to a forty-eight in 1919 were probably accompanied by an almost proportionate decline in weekly output per worker.

From 1845–1911, inclusive, changes in full-time weekly earnings will serve as an index of changes in the cost of labour to the manufacturer; but from 1912 onward hourly earnings seem to be a better measure of labour costs. The search for an index of efficiency wages is thus reduced to the computation of the relative full-time weekly earnings of cotton operatives in Massachusetts.

It is now well recognised that limitations of data and technique make the choice between different index numbers purporting to measure the same thing turn largely upon the use to which one puts them. Throughout the present study, therefore, it is well to remember the object in view as outlined in Part I. In particular my index numbers of changes in wages are used to reduce manufacturers' aggregate wage bills in any given year to the amount they would have been had they employed a similar quality and quantity of labour at the wage rates prevailing in the base year. Hence it is all important that the several series of relative wage rates from which the index numbers are constructed be computed from quotations which refer throughout to workers who are similar in respect of the amount and quality of the effort put into their work (i.e. are engaged upon work which calls for the same order of intelligence, the same degree of application, and involves the same nervous and physical strain). But, having series of comparable relative wages, the weights used in combining them into a single series to represent changes in the "cost of labour" should vary as the composition of the labour force actually employed changes from year to year; index numbers which reflect changes in the wages of a stable body of workers are only satisfactory for our purpose if that body is equally representative of the industrial group throughout the period studied. Finally the occupational series should be weighted according (a) to the number of workers they represent in each year, (b) the relative wages of workers in the different occupations in the base year.

Fortunately the various occupational series move in the same general direction, while the relative number employed in the different occupations has not changed greatly during the period under consideration. The most important change is the increase in the proportion of male to female operatives.[1] In round numbers the ratio of male to female in the New England cotton manufacturing industry increased from 1 : 2 at the opening of our period to 1 : 1 by the turn of the century (computed from census returns). "With the expansion of the industry men have obtained a larger share of the work in departments where women are employed",[2] but one would expect the *efficiency* wages of men and women to be approximately equal in such

---

[1] As will be seen later the *Aldrich Report* data enables one to allow for changes in the composition of the labour force prior to 1890. The decline in the proportion of children and young persons took place before 1890 in Massachusetts, but the number of men employed continued to rise relative to women.

[2] M. T. Copeland, *The Cotton Manufacturing Industry*, p. 113.

occupations, or at least to move parallel; thus a series of relatives based upon the wages of either sex should, in theory, represent the occupations.

In practice, therefore, it is found that the different methods of weighting which might reasonably be employed give index numbers which rarely show significant differences. Where possible, allowance has been made for changes in the number of workers represented by the several occupational series, but after 1890 the data are not available, so that constant weights based upon occupational census returns have been used; since the unweighted and weighted index numbers are almost identical for the period 1890–1914 the error involved must be negligible. In every case workers have been treated as of equal importance for purposes of weighting regardless of wide differences in wages; again the error involved is probably small.

There follows a tedious analysis of the material available for the index of relative full-time earnings of Massachusetts cotton operatives, and the methods I have adopted. The discussion falls naturally into two divisions:

A. 1845–91; B. 1890–1914.

The trusting reader may skip these pages and, accepting my results, proceed to IV, p. 189.

A. *The period 1845–91.*

A large collection of data relating to wages in manufacturing industries was made in 1892 by the U.S. Bureau of Labour for the Senate Committee which prepared the famous *Aldrich Report upon Wholesale Prices, Wages, and Transportation*. The data cover a period of fifty-two years and give average wage rates for the leading types of manual labourers employed in certain manufacturing establishments in January and July of each year, together with the number and sex of the workers represented by each wage quotation: they were published in Parts II, III and IV of the *Report*.[1] Though badly manipulated by Professor

[1] For a summary of criticisms see *History of the Greenbacks*, pp. 280–2, and references there given. Professor Mitchell, like other critics (e.g. Dr A. L. Bowley, *E.J.* vol. v, pp. 369–83), objects to the way Professor Falkner

Roland P. Falkner and inadequate for the purpose of measuring general changes in wages, the material was carefully collected and may be used confidently if properly interpreted. Four establishments manufacturing cotton goods in Massachusetts are included in Table XII of the *Aldrich Report*:

Est. 38 returns cover the period 1851–91
Est. 39   ,,   ,,   ,,   1842–91
Est. 40   ,,   ,,   ,,   1840–91
Est. 43   ,,   ,,   ,,   1848–91[1]

Mr Joseph D. Weeks also made a large collection of data relating to wages in manufacturing industries during the early part of our period, but many of the series only give quotations every ten years while no information is given as to the number or sex of the workers represented by the quotations. This material was published in volume xx of the *Tenth Census of the United States* 1880, without any attempt at analysis. So far as Massachusetts cotton manufacture is concerned there are two establishments giving wage rates for the leading occupations annually from 1850–80 and one from 1853–80, while the Merrimack Manufacturing Company, Lowell, Massachusetts, gives quotations for 1824, 1840, 1850, 1860, 1870 and 1880. Professor Wesley C. Mitchell[2] compared tables of relative wages 1860–80 based upon the *Aldrich* and *Weeks Reports* and showed that, when treated by the same statistical methods, the results for the same industries in the same geographical area were in very close agreement. In particular he compiled tables of unweighted relative wages in the cotton textiles industry of the eastern states, and found that "on the whole the correspondence between the deciles as well as medians is closer than one could expect from two sets of data collected independently" (p. 217).

used the data but has a high opinion of the material itself. The wage material for the cotton industry in Massachusetts is in point of fact among the best groups in the exhibits. See also *Gold, Prices and Wages*, pp. 169–74.

[1] Establishment 43 was returned as manufacturing "ginghams", a variety of cotton goods, and was on that account excluded from Falkner's relative wages of workers in "cotton textiles" and allowed the doubtful privilege of industrial isolation.

[2] *Gold, Prices and Wages*, chap. iv, section 3.

The third collection of data relating to the wages of Massachusetts cotton operatives during this early period is that made by Colonel C. D. Wright at the Massachusetts Bureau of Statistics; it falls naturally into three groups:

(a) Data taken from certain manufacturers' pay rolls and first published in C. D. Wright's article upon the Factory System, *Tenth Census of the United States* 1880, vol. II. Returns of average gross weekly wages, classified according to occupation, and sex are given for six Massachusetts cotton mills:

Est. 1	making returns for	1840, 1850, 1860, 1870, 1875, 1880[1]	
Est. 3	,, ,,	1848, 1850, 1860, 1870, 1875, 1880	
Est. 6	,, ,,	1860, 1870, 1875, 1880	
Ests. 2, 4, 5	,, ,,	1870, 1875, 1880	

In addition a table on p. 45 represents average daily wages of cotton mill workers for thirty-eight New England establishments in the year 1843, distinguishing between the sexes and giving separate averages for the six principal departments. A few quotations are also given for earlier years.

Part of these data was republished in the *Annual Report of Massachusetts Statistics of Labour* 1885, Part IV, pp. 423–7, in the form of average gross weekly wages by occupations and sex, but no indication is given of the establishments from which the data are taken. Comparison with the census article, however, shows that the figures for 1843 (and probably 1838 also) were obtained by multiplying the average daily wages from the thirty-eight New England establishments[2] by six, and therefore refer not simply to Massachusetts but to New England as a whole. Again the figures for 1840 are taken solely from Establishment 1 Massachusetts of the census article, while those for 1848 are from Establishment 3 alone. For 1850 the figures are also largely taken from Establishments 1 and 3, while for 1860 Establishment 6 is added.

---

[1] *Loc. cit.* pp. 46, 47.
[2] *Tenth United States Census* 1881, vol. II, folio 577.

It is clear that general averages based upon such data are apt to be utterly meaningless.

(b) Enquiries were made periodically by agents of the Massachusetts Bureau of Statistics concerning the wages of workers engaged in manufacture in the principal towns and cities of the state. These investigations were fairly wide in their scope even in the earlier years (the proportion of cotton operatives covered was never less than 25 %), but the averages based upon these returns by the Bureau are misleading for various reasons.

(1) The information was collected chiefly from employees.

(2) The returns refer largely to adult male workers and children, the numerically important class of women and young persons being about 6 % of those making returns in 1860, 26 % in 1872, 7 % in 1881, whereas, according to the census returns, more than half the cotton operatives in the state fall into this class.

(3) No attempt was made to weight the different occupations or sexes according to their relative importance but a simple average was taken of all the returns available.

This group of enquiries covers the years 1860, 1872, 1874, 1875, 1878 and 1881.

(c) In 1883 and 1891, special investigations were made by the Massachusetts Bureau of Statistics,[1] the source of information being in these cases "the pay rolls of great manufacturing establishments" (vide Report 1884, p. 138). In the case of cotton manufacture a large proportion of the operatives was covered in each case, and in the opinion of the Bureau the results for 1883 and 1891 are comparable.

The census returns for 1875 and 1880 also fall in this group, since they were taken from manufacturers' pay rolls and worked up into averages for the different occupations and for the industry. From 1885 onwards, however, the census returns were published in the form of frequency tables not distinguishing the

---

[1] A similar enquiry was made in 1897 but the data, though published (vide Report for 1897), were not reduced to averages or any other convenient form.

sex or occupation of the workers but only their distribution according to wage groups in each industry.

It is clear that the construction of comparable series of relative wages from this heterogeneous mass of returns would be impossible. The most one can hope for is that they may prove useful as a check upon the *Aldrich Report*. In vol. xv of *Massachusetts Statistics of Labour* 1884, Part III,[1] Colonel Wright brought together the available material for the period 1860–83 in the form of general averages for each industry and also for men, women, young persons, and children engaged therein. In the case of cotton manufacture the averages for all operatives are almost meaningless since they are unweighted arithmetic means and the proportion of women making returns varied greatly, being approximately 4 % in 1860; 22 % in 1872; 60 % in 1875; 4 % in 1881; 64 % in 1883, whereas at least half the workers in Massachusetts cotton mills during this period were women. I think, however, that a comparison of the general averages for each sex separately may profitably be made. In the period 1840–60 the difficulties increase a thousandfold. I have done the best I can with the available data calculating an average gross weekly wage for each sex in the six principal departments of the cotton mill and then taking the arithmetic mean of these six quotations to obtain the average weekly wages of males and of females employed in the industry. The result is:

Average gross weekly wages of Massachusetts cotton operatives computed from figures in *Annual Report of Massachusetts Statistics of Labour* 1885, Pt IV, pp. 426–7

Date	Males	Females
1840	$6.45	$3.02*
1850	$6.98	$3.62
1860	$6.80	$3.35

* Average of returns for 1838, 1840, 1843.

The corresponding figures for 1860 computed from the figures used for the period 1860–83 (see above) were:

Date	Males	Females
1860	$7.25	$4.34

[1] Republished as Part III of the *Annual Report of the Massachusetts Statistics of Labour* 1885.

I have therefore raised the figures for 1840 and 1850 into proportion; whence the final series:

Average gross weekly wages of male and female cotton operatives in Massachusetts 1840–83

Date	Males	Females	Source, etc.
1840	$6·88	$3.91	*Massachusetts Statistics of Labour*
1850	$7.44	$4.56	1885, Pt IV, pp.426–7, originally from a few establishments in New England, chiefly Massachusetts. 1840 = average of 1838, 1840, 1843
1860	$7.25	$4.34	*Ibid.* 1885, Pt III, or *ibid.* 1884,
1872	$10.64	$6.55	Pt III. Sources, pp. 319–20: Tabular results, pp. 348–9. Originally from enquiry of employees
1875	$10.51	$6.89	*Ibid.* but originally from census of Massachusetts
1878	$8.72	$4.45	*Ibid.* but originally from enquiry
1881	$8.89	$6.52	of employees
1883	$9.44	$5.90	*Ibid.* but originally taken by the Bureau from pay rolls

Note. (1) Although separating the sexes has removed the most serious objection to this comparison, the early returns are too high relative to the later because "heads of families" are unduly represented.

(2) The figures for 1872 and 1875 have been converted from the gold into paper standard so that all the quotations are in terms of the local currency.

This brief survey of the available material will make it clear that the *Aldrich Report* contains the data most suited to my present purpose. Fortunately Professor Wesley C. Mitchell[1] has worked up the material contained in Table XII of the *Aldrich Report* for the period 1860–80 while Dr S. E. Howard[2] has extended Professor Mitchell's tables of arithmetic means of relative wages in cotton textiles (including ginghams) up to 1891. I have myself carried these index numbers back to 1845 following Professor Mitchell's methods so far as the data will allow. The procedure is described fully in *Gold, Prices and Wages*, chap. iv, section 1 (*a*) and (*b*), pp. 92–7. "Sets of wage-quotations covering the years 1860–80 and showing the pay received by persons of one sex, employed at one kind of work in one

[1] *Gold, Prices and Wages*, chap. iv, Section 1.
[2] *The Movement of Wages in the Cotton Manufacturing Industry of New England since* 1860, pp. 56–61.

establishment" were extracted from the *Aldrich Report*, Table XII, and reduced to percentages of the wage paid in January 1860; each set of wage quotations then constituted a "series" of relative wages. In computing arithmetic means of relative wages for the industry each series was weighted according to the numbers of employees returned as receiving that wage at the date in question. Professor Mitchell included all series which were reasonably complete (occasional breaks in series such as bobbin men, bond boys, etc., probably means that the number of such hands employed fell temporarily to zero and should not exclude the series from the tables of arithmetic means), and I have followed his example in carrying the index numbers for the industry back to 1845.[1] Dr Howard excluded series representing workers who are not "in a narrow sense textile operatives", as beltmen, blacksmiths, boilermen, carpenters, machinists, masons, oilers, watchmen, scrubbers, sweepers and yard hands; overseers in the mill departments were also excluded on the ground that they are not "operatives" in the commonly accepted sense. Now the wages of all these workers are items of labour cost in the manufacturer's account and should, therefore, have a place in the index numbers which I use for eliminating changes in the cost of labour. Dr Howard's index numbers consequently show too great a rise of wages between 1880 and 1891 but, as we shall see later, there is a compensating error.

The scope of the data used in the construction of the final index number of full-time weekly earnings 1845-91 is shown in the table on p. 172. The Aldrich returns are for daily wages, but as there was no change in the number of days worked per week in any of the establishments they serve equally well for weekly wage rates.

Dr Howard[2] compared arithmetic means and medians for 1880 of the 135 series used by Professor Mitchell with means and medians of the seventy-four series chosen by him, and found that there was so little difference that a junction between the two sets of index numbers could be effected by taking the average of the two as index numbers for 1880 and leaving other years untouched.

[1] *Loc. cit.* p. 56.　　　　[2] *Loc. cit.* p. 58.

Conspectus of data employed in construction of index numbers of weekly wages of Massachusetts Cotton operatives 1845–91

Data obtained from *Aldrich Report*, Table XII, pp. 549–892

Period	No. of establishments	No. of wage series Males	Fe-males	Both sexes	No. of wage earners represented at the beginning and end of the period Males	Females	Both sexes
1845–51	2	33	12	45	101–125	97–103	198– 228
1851–60	4	73	23	96	347–513	648–510	995–1023
1860–80	4	103	32	135	622–918	561–900	1183–1818
1880–91	4	47	27	74	—	—	1419–1883

N.B. (1) The average number of wage earners represented 1860–80 = 1423.

(2) The base wage for the individual series of relative wages is in each case the wage paid in January 1860 or the nearest available quotation.

The same method of splicing suffices to join the index numbers for the period 1851–60 to those for 1860–80. By a curious chance the average for 1851 of the forty-five series used for the period 1845–51 is also within one point of the average of the ninety-six series used in the years 1851–60, so that the two series may be used as if continuous; this is not so with the separate index numbers for males and females.

For some reason which is not quite clear Professor Mitchell included two piece-rate series in his index numbers of average wages of workers in cotton textiles, namely those for female weavers in Establishment 40.[1] Since these two series are heavily weighted I have thought it necessary to apply a correction for the difference between female weavers' time and piece rates of wages relative to 1860. I therefore compared the weighted average of these two piece-rate series with all the available series of relative full-time earnings of female weavers in Massachusetts 1860–80, namely:

1. *The Aldrich Report.*

   (*a*) Est. 39 Mass. p. 700 (p. 460 in *Gold, Prices and Wages*).

   (*b*) Est. 43 Mass. p. 887 (p. 470 in *Gold, Prices and Wages*).

[1] *Vide Gold, Prices and Wages*, p. 466 and references to *Aldrich Report* there given.

2. *The Weeks Report.*

    (*a*) Mass. Chicopee Falls, p. 347 (p. 574 in *Gold, Prices and Wages*).

    (*b*) Mass. unknown, p. 348.

3. *C. D. Wright's "Factory System", Tenth Census,* vol. ii.

Decennial wage rates of cotton operatives in certain Establishments, Mass. Establishments 1, 3 and 6 give figures for female weavers' average full-time earnings in 1860, 1870 and 1880.

4. *Graded Wages* 1830–91—*Massachusetts Statistics of Labour* 1898.

The female weavers' series, medium grade, in Massachusetts 1840–91 is useful but needs careful handling.

After a careful comparison of these data I came to the conclusion that the series from *Aldrich Report*, Establishment 39, shows an unusually rapid rise of female weavers' wages between 1860–80. The series for Establishment 43, ginghams, is probably somewhat low, while the weighted average of the two piece-rate series from Establishment 40 stood at 176 in 1880 as compared with 174 for the best series from the *Weeks Report*, i.e. 2 (*a*), Chicopee Falls, given on p. 574 of the Appendix to *Gold, Prices and Wages*. Clearly, therefore, the inclusion of these two piece-rate series introduces no great error as between the year 1860 and the year 1880; but with the intervening period the case is different. All the data available indicate a rapid rise in female weavers' full-time earnings up to a maximum in or about 1873 followed by a decline to 1880. The piece-rates series, on the other hand, show an almost continuous even rise of relative wages from 1860–80. I have therefore thought it worth while to substitute the best series of female weavers' full-time earnings from the *Weeks Report* (p. 574 of *Gold, Prices and Wages*) for the two piece-rate series used by Mitchell, and to correct the arithmetic means of relative wages in cotton textiles by the method of difference. In the absence of other female weavers series for Establishment 40 Dr Howard has also included these two piece-rate series for the period 1880–91, while I have employed one of them in my extension of Mitchell's index numbers to cover the period 1845–60. The errors involved are not, however, serious in these periods of comparatively stable piece rates; in no case would a correction of more than one point be called for in the index numbers for 1845–60, while the error is largely offset between 1880 and 1891 by an opposite error due to Howard's exclusion of overseers, etc. If we take Colonel C. D. Wright's figures for medium average weekly wages of female weavers in 1883 and 1891 to measure the rise of female weavers' full-time earnings during this period, and compare them with the change in piece rates, we find that a correction of approximately four and a half points (i.e. about half a point per annum) should be added to Howard's index numbers for the industry, while an addition of five and a half points should be made to the females' index numbers. Fortunately Professor Mitchell[1] calculated the arithmetic mean of the 135 series for January 1891, and we are able to compare the results with Dr Howard's figures.

It will be seen that Howard's omission of overseers, etc., has raised his index three and a half points between 1880 and 1891 (the two were each 152 in January 1880) relative to Mitchell's,

Arithmetic means of relative wage rates, January 1891

Cotton textiles (including ginghams) base, January 1860 = 100.

	Both sexes	Males	Females
Mitchell's 135 series	167½ (+ 4½ = 172)	156¼	177 (+ 5½ = 182½)
Howard's 74 series	171	158	180

[1] *Gold, Prices and Wages*, p. 173, Table XLVII.

N.B. The "cotton textiles" and "ginghams" averages were combined to get the figures used in the text. The weights were in proportion to the average number of employees represented by the two groups 1860–80.

	Cotton textiles	Ginghams
All employees	1	1
Males	4	3
Females	3	4

This method was also used in computing the index numbers for the separate sexes 1860–80 since Professor Mitchell only calculated arithmetic means for all employees in the combined group.

leaving only one point to be added upon account of the difference between private weavers' time and piece-rate relatives—a correction which is not worth the making. So with the females' index numbers a correction of a quarter point per annum for ten years is not worth making.

Finally the mean of the January and July index numbers has been taken to represent the year, and a continuous series of average relative full-time weekly wages of workers in the manufacture of cotton goods in Massachusetts compiled for the period 1845-91. The following references will enable the reader to find the semi-annual figures since 1860.

1860–80 Semi-annual figures for all employees from *Gold, Prices and Wages*, Table XXXVII, p. 120.

Semi-annual figures for males and females separately obtained from *Gold, Prices and Wages*, Table XXXVIII, p.122, by combining the numbers given for cotton textiles and for ginghams, weighting according to the average number of employees represented by each group, i.e. cotton textiles; ginghams, males 4 : 3, females 3 : 4.

1880–91 Semi-annual figures obtained from *The Movement of Wages in the Cotton Manufacturing Industry of New England since 1860*, Table XI, p. 59.

The results of Professor Mitchell's comparison of the *Weeks* and *Aldrich Reports* have already been indicated; it remains only to bring Colonel C. D. Wright's data into comparison with the index numbers for 1845-91. Since the representation of the sexes varied so markedly in the investigations of the Massachusetts Bureau of Labour, I have made separate comparison of the wages of males and females. These series provide strong confirmation of the general trend of the Aldrich index numbers. When one remembers that the "general averages" for males in 1840, 1850 and 1860, are based largely upon the earnings of "heads of families", and that men were fighting their way against women into the spinning department during this period, the chief divergences between the series based upon the *Aldrich Report* and those based upon the Massachusetts Statistics of Labour are explained, while the general agreement of the series of women's earnings is found to be remarkable.

B. *The period* 1890–1914.

The *Nineteenth Annual Report of the Commissioner of Labour* 1904, contained data relating to wages in each of the years 1890–1903, and the series there begun have been continued in the bulletins of the United States Bureau of Labour and its successor the United States Bureau of Labour Statistics. These wage quotations have been obtained by agents of the Bureau from the pay rolls of important establishments in the different industries and states. Average full-time hourly earnings and average hours worked per week in the several occupations were computed from pay rolls covering one or two weeks (or more where the employees are paid upon a longer basis) in the year, so chosen as to represent normal conditions in the establishment for each year. The Bureau generally calculated the product of these two and published it as average full-time weekly earnings.[1] If the hourly earnings given by the Bureau may be taken to represent the average for the year, then we have quotations for full-time weekly earnings "in the principal distinctive occupations in the leading industries...in all sections of the country" in those years for which the Bureau collected data, i.e. for cotton manufacture every year from 1890–1914, thence every alternate year.

Dr Stanley E. Howard[2] has computed series of relative full-time weekly earnings in the five occupations of cotton operatives for which continuous data are available from 1890—namely:

Card strippers and carding machine feeders—male (255)
Frame spinners—female ... ... (1739)
Loom fixers—male ... ... (670)
Weavers—male ... ... (2844)
Weavers—female ... ... (4096)

[1] In the earlier years allowance was made in the computations of average hours worked per week for short time excluding more than ten months out of the twelve, but in the later bulletins hours worked in a full week are given; in the case of. cotton manufacture these hours are for the most part the maximum hours allowed by state laws for women and minors so that it is possible to make allowance for the fact that changes in hours sometimes took effect in the middle of the year. Dr Howard accordingly revised the Bureau's figures before using them as quotations for average full-time weekly earnings. *The Movement of Wages in the Cotton Manufacturing Industry of New England since* 1860, p. 64.

[2] *The Movement of Wages in the Cotton Manufacturing Industry of New England since* 1860, chap. iv, Table XII.

The figures in brackets indicate the number of employees represented by each occupation in 1916. Thus the five series account for nearly half the workers engaged in the twenty establishments making returns (9604 out of 22,068) which among them employed over 20 % of the cotton mill workers of the state (22,068 as compared with a total of 108,807 at the census of 1915).

Thus Dr Howard's index numbers of cotton operatives' wages in Massachusetts 1890–1916 is based upon wage quotations covering *directly* 10 % of the operatives in 1916, whereas I estimate that they only covered 5 % of the operatives in 1890–1903.

Examination of the material relating to Massachusetts cotton operatives contained in the various bulletins of the United States Bureau of Labour Statistics shows that thirteen occupational series are available from 1907 onwards, while in the current series of bulletins (covering alternate years from 1916) over twenty occupational series are given. Unfortunately the summaries refer either to the United States as a whole or to large geographical divisions, while the carefully constructed chain index numbers compiled by the Bureau refer to the entire country. For my purpose I have decided to use index numbers based upon Dr Howard's five continuous series rather than undertake the laborious task of constructing the best possible index numbers from the original tables of the bulletins. The error involved is not, I think, very great for two reasons:

(*a*) A general "parallelism" is discernible in the movements of the different occupational series.

(*b*) The omission of series for mule spinners and male frame spinners is perhaps the most serious neglect, but

(i) Although male spinners' wages have fluctuated rather more than female frame spinners' full-time earnings, yet the evidence suggests that this series has a strong title to represent the entire spinning department during this period.

(ii) The largest relative movements of wages of the different groups of spinners is the rise of male frame spinners' wages relative to female and the bulk of this movement took place in the period 1890-1906, so that there are no data available to correct for this error. Between 1907-14 the wages of mule spinners and male and female frame spinners move in close sympathy. The extent of their relative movements in Massachusetts 1890-1907 is indicated and a partial explanation suggested.

I have therefore taken Dr Howard's five series of relative weekly wages (*vide* chap. iv) and weighted them according to census returns of numbers employed in the kindred departments,[1] to obtain an index for the industry. I have also carried the index numbers forward to 1924. The Bureau provides data for "splicing" each time they change the sources (establishments) of their information and their index numbers for the industry are constructed by the chain method. Dr Howard is apparently of the opinion that these changes have not been of great importance in the case of Massachusetts cotton manufacture, for wherever two different wage quotations are given for the same year he has taken the average. In practice I doubt if the error on this account is significant. I have looked over the data and find very little difference between average hourly wages based upon the different sets of establishments in any one year, certain it is that the error arising from the fact that returns are only for one or two weeks in the year is generally greater.

---

[1] The weights have been assigned roughly as follows:

Card strippers and tenders	Semi-skilled workers up to the carding department.
Female frame spinners	Semi-skilled workers in the spinning department.
Weavers, male	Male semi-skilled workers in the weaving department.
Weavers, female	Female semi-skilled workers in the weaving department.
Loom fixers	Loom fixers and other high skilled workers including second hands and overseers.

N.B. For a detailed description of the processes of manufacture of cotton goods and the nature of the various occupations, *vide Bulletin* 239 of the U.S. Bureau of Labour Statistics, pp. 140-205, published April 1918.

The fact that the weighted average of these five occupational series does not differ appreciably from the unweighted average between 1890 and 1914 suggests that the wage changes indicated were general for the industry. Further support is given by a comparison of the United States Bureau of Labour Statistics index numbers of wages in the principal cotton textile occupations (*vide Bulletin* 128).

These figures show that the relative movement of the three spinners series took place largely before 1907, as was the case in Massachusetts; and that the wages of card strippers and tenders rose more rapidly than those of drawing frame tenders (who are in the same department) between 1910 and 1918. On the other hand, there is another large group of workers (openers, pickers, etc.) whose wages probably rose still more markedly during that period, so that the card strippers and tenders may be taken to represent the opening, picking and carding department.

Massachusetts has enjoyed a miniature census of manufactures annually since 1889, and the Bureau of Statistics has published a frequency table showing the distribution of cotton operatives in the different weekly wage groups. The "class interval" has been fairly large:

$1.00 for low and medium ranges of wages;
$2.00 for medium high ranges of wages;
$5.00 for high ranges of wages;

but by interpolation I have obtained values for the median wages in each year from 1889–1920, and have reduced these to percentages of the median wage in 1890. This series of medians provides strong confirmation of the representative character of the wage index numbers for the industry. I have tabulated them alongside the relative wages for the different groups and for the industry: the general agreement between the two different kinds of average is remarkable. The rather more rapid rise of the medians between 1911–18 may be attributed to the increase in the wages of the less skilled relative to the more highly skilled labour during that period:

Relative weekly wages of cotton operatives in Massachusetts 1890–1916[1]

Base wage average 1890-9	Card tenders and strippers Male	Frame spinners Female	Loom fixers Male	Weavers Male	Weavers Female	Weighted average[2] All employees	Weighted average[2] Males	Weighted average[2] Females	M N stat of la
	$6.187	$5.408	$10.668	$7.885	$7.151				$
Date									
1890	96·8	101·1	103·4	103·0	99·6	101	102	100	
1891	100·4	99·1	101·2	102·2	99·4	100	102	99	
1892	100·9	99·5	99·4	102·1	100·4	101	101	100	
1893	102·0	106·3	104·0	107·3	106·7	106	106	107	
1894	99·9	95·6	98·2	97·3	97·8	97	98	97	
1895	99·7	97·8	93·6	93·1	96·2	96	95	97	
1896	101·8	103·7	101·8	101·3	101·5	102	102	102	
1897	101·5	103·0	101·7	100·7	100·0	101	101	101	
1898	100·7	98·2	99·9	99·3	101·5	100	100	101	
1899	96·3	95·6	96·7	93·7	96·9	96	95	96	
1900	110·9	111·7	110·2	109·3	110·6	111	110	111	
1901	111·2	110·0	110·5	110·1	111·2	111	110	111	
1902	111·2	110·2	111·3	112·7	111·2	111	112	111	
1903	113·0	113·2	115·1	118·0	114·4	115	116	114	
*1904	112·0	110·2	115·9	116·9	115·8	114	116	114	
1905	112·2	113·2	117·7	121·1	119·8	117	119	118	
*1906	120·6	130·9	124·9	127·5	126·1	127	126	128	
*1907	135·1	149·2	138·8	139·9	137·2	141	139	141	
1908	124·3	141·8	131·5	135·6	132·6	136	135	136	
1909	118·3	133·1	122·2	118·7	122·1	124	119	126	
*1910	116·2	135·3	120·3	115·6	118·0	122	117	124	
*1911	116·5	136·9	121·0	116·2	115·6	122	117	119	
1912	125·4	144·6	131·2	123·0	126·0	131	123	132	
1913	130·0	148·9	132·0	124·5	125·6	133	127	133	
1914	131·7	149·8	133·7	127·3	126·8	134	129	134	
*1916	165·0	183·0	159·0	154·0	155·0	164	157	164	
1918	267·0	274·0	231·0	224·0	228·0	243	254	243	
*1920	462·0	448·0	384·0	364·0	368·0	399	388	395	
1922	344·0	343·0	280·0	282·0	279·0	303	294	300	
1924	386·0	388·0	317·0	330·0	328·0	349	339	348	

N.B. In the years marked * a splice was effected between returns from different s of establishments by taking the average.

[1] S. E. Howard, *The Movement of Wages in the Cotton Manufacturing Industry of New England since 1860*, pp. 66, 67.

[2] The occupational series are weighted differently in the averages for the separate sexes than in the average for all employees, see pp. 183–8. The weights used are:

	All employees	Males	Females
Card tenders (male)	1	1	0
Frame spinners (female)	3	0	1
Loom fixers (male)	1	1	0
Weavers (male)	3	3	0
Weavers (female)	3	0	2

Average relative full-time weekly earnings in cotton manufacture in Massachusetts 1845-1914

Base January 1860 = 100

Date	All employees	Males	Females	Date	All employees	Males	Females
1845	90	80	97	1880	*154	139	170
1846	92	83	98	1881	149	135	161
1847	94	85	99	1882	157	145	167
1848	95	83	105	1883	158	141	172
1849	95	84	103	1884	155	140	166
1850	95	86	101	1885	150	136	159
1851	*95	86	100	1886	153	139	163
1852	92	84	96	1887	160	151	167
1853	94	84	100	1888	164	153	171
1854	93	95	93	1889	169	153	180
1855	97	99	96	1890	*171	157	181
1856	101	102	100	1891	*172	157	181
1857	101	102	101	1892	172	156	182
1858	102	100	103	1893	181	163	195
1859	101	100	103	1894	165	151	177
1860[1]	*100	100	101	1895	164	146	177
1861	101	98	103	1896	174	157	186
1862	102	99	105	1897	172	156	184
1863	108	105	110	1898	171	154	184
1864	120	123	116	1899	164	146	175
1865	142	142	137	1900	190	170	202
1866	167	161	171	1901	190	170	202
1867	174	166	181	1902	190	173	202
1868	170	164	176	1903	196	179	208
1869	174	166	181	1904	195	179	208
1870	175	167	183	1905	200	183	215
1871	188	173	200	1906	217	194	233
1872	195	180	208	1907	241	214	257
1873	192	177	209	1908	232	208	248
1874	180	168	193	1909	212	183	229
1875	166	156	175	1910	208	180	226
1876	159	149	168	1911	208	180	217
1877	151	141	157	1912	224	190	240
1878	153	140	164	1913	227	196	242
1879	148	134	162	1914	229	199	244

N.B. In the years marked * a splice was effected between different series and in these years the compromise figure adopted may differ *one* point either way from the number for either series.

[1] Note that the figures for 1860–80 do not agree with those used by Dr Howard in his Table XIX, (*a*) because, despite his objections to the procedure, he copied Mitchell's series of cotton textiles *not* including ginghams. My series is based on the cotton textiles including ginghams. (*b*) I have corrected for the error due to the inclusion of two piece-rate series in Mitchell's (Howard's) numbers.

Piecing together the various series and reducing all to the base 1860 = 100, we finally obtain the index numbers of average full-time weekly earnings of workers employed in the manufacture of cotton goods in Massachusetts from 1845 to 1914 shown in the table on p. 181.

Sources

(a) All employees 1845–91—*Aldrich Report*
(b) Males 1890–1914—United States Bureau
(c) Females of Labour Statistics

After 1914 United States Bureau of Labour Statistics' data are only available for alternate years; in continuing the index numbers I have, therefore, used the medians of Massachusetts annual census returns as a basis for interpolation.

Average relative weekly earnings in Massachusetts cotton manufacture 1914–24

Base January 1860 = 100

Date	All employees	Males	Females
1914	229	199	244
1915	(231)	—	—
1916	280	242	298
1917	(338)	—	—
1918	415	392	442
1919	(580)	—	—
1920	681	600	719
1921	(557)	—	—
1922	517	453	546
1923	—	—	—
1924	596	523	634

When the relative full-time earnings of Massachusetts cotton operatives are compared with the corresponding index numbers for the United States computed by the Bureau of Labour Statistics from 1890, the most noticeable features are, first, the rapid rise of cotton operatives' wages in the country as a whole relative to the Massachusetts level between 1905–12; second, that the wages of Massachusetts workers in all departments rose considerably more between 1913 and 1924 than the average for the country.[1]

[1] Since 1913 the Massachusetts Bureau of Statistics has computed an index number of average yearly earnings of cotton operatives, based upon the

Prior to 1912 the index numbers of full-time earnings serve as a measure of changes in the cost of labour to the manufacturer but from 1912 a correction is necessary for changes in hours which gives the following results:

Cost of labour

As % of 1860

1912	232	1919	(667)
1913	236	1920	795
1914	238	1921	(650)
1915	(241)	1922	604
1916	290	1923	—
1917	(350)	1924	695
1918	430		

These figures are obtained from the index numbers of full-time weekly earnings by multiplying by 56/54 from 1912–18 and 56/48 from 1920–4. The figures for 1915, 1917, 1919, and 1921, are interpolated by using the median of Massachusetts annual census returns.

Note upon weighting from occupational census returns of the wage index of 1890–1925.

The decennial federal census of the United States provides an industrial grouping "cotton mill operatives" which remained

annual census of manufactures. It is interesting to compare this series with index numbers of full-time earnings reduced to percentages of 1913:

Date	Massachusetts Bureau of Statistics, average yearly earnings	Index numbers of full-time weekly earnings
1913	100	100
1914	97	101
1915	101	102
1916	118	123
1917	141	149
1918	177	183
1919	195	256
1920	252	300
1921	198	245

N.B. The more rapid rise of my index numbers is due (1) to the fact that my numbers represent the relative wages of workers of a given skill and occupation, whereas the Bureau's are averages of all employees regardless of changes in their average quality, (2) to changes in the regularity of employment reflected in the Bureau's numbers but not in mine.

substantially the same from 1870–1900, while the returns for 1910 were grouped under both the old and the new classification and showed so little difference that we may take the aggregates to be continuous. The chief difference is that under the new classification it is not possible to distinguish foremen, bosses, or overseers employed in cotton mills from those engaged in other industries, while all loom fixers and repairers are likewise grouped under one head. By omitting the foremen and including all the loom fixers in the total for cotton operatives we obtain aggregates comparable with the earlier census group of that name.

Number of cotton mill operatives in the United States census returns 1870–1920

	1870	1880	1890	1900	1910 (a)	1910 (b)	1910 (c)	1920
Both sexes	111,606	169,771	173,142	252,391	331,631	329,683	331,209	394,730
Males	47,208	78,292	80,177	125,788	185,341	184,462	184,774	228,873
Females	64,398	91,479	92,965	126,603	146,290	145,221	146,435	165,857

N.B. (1) The figures for 1870 to 1900 inclusive are taken from a comparison made in Table IV of the *Special Report on Occupations* at the twelfth census, 1900.

(2) The series 1910 (a) will be found in Table XV, p. 56 of the *Occupations Report* at the thirteenth census, 1910, vol. IV, where the returns were grouped after the manner of the 1900 census.

The series 1910 (b), 1910 (c) and 1920 were obtained by adding the returns of "labourers" and "semi-skilled" workers employed in cotton mills. 1910 (b) are the figures derived from the thirteenth census, vol. IV, while 1910 (c) are corrected figures given in the *Occupations Report* at the fourteenth census in comparison with the returns for 1920. Since the "semi-skilled" group was not subdivided further at the fourteenth census it has not been possible to trace the error back to a particular group of workers; but whether we compare 1910 (a) and (b) or 1910 (a) and (c) it is clear that the difference is negligible being always less than 1 %.

Previous to 1905 the Massachusetts census occupational returns were classified on the same plan as the annual census of manufacturers, so that cotton operatives fall in a group with all people employed upon the manufacture of cotton goods including small wares. In 1905 the division "cotton mill operatives" was formed after the federal plan, but with fifteen sub-classes. In 1915 the new federal census classification was adopted. It has already been shown that the aggregates of "cotton mill operatives" distinguished under the 1900 and 1910 classifications are comparable for the United States; we may therefore conclude that they are comparable for Massachusetts, giving a series as follows:

Number of cotton mill operatives in Massachusetts
1900–1920

	1900	1905	1910	1915	1920
Both sexes	76,813	89,457	102,373	108,867	113,423
Males	38,889	45,240	54,435	57,845	60,498
Females	37,924	44,217	47,938	51,022	52,925

N.B. The federal census figures (i.e. 1900, 1910, 1920) cover all persons over ten years of age which, in practice, includes all persons of all ages employed in Massachusetts mills as in the Massachusetts returns for 1905. The 1915 returns, however, are for persons "14 years and over" which means that these figures should be raised somewhat. In the Massachusetts census of 1905, 2466 males and 2794 females were returned as being "under 15 years of age" and employed in cotton mills, making 5260 persons of both sexes or nearly 6 % of the total cotton mill operatives. Probably by far the greater part of these 5000 young persons were between the ages of fourteen and fifteen years, so that the omission of the age group 10–13 years probably makes no appreciable difference to the returns for 1915.

In the classification of 1910 the numerous occupations which are distinguished by different titles in different localities have been grouped under ten headings, attention being paid both to the department of the mill in which the operatives are employed and to status of the occupation with respect to pay, skill, etc.

Class 275. *Labourers* (not otherwise classified)—cotton mills, includes all general labourers of the unskilled class wherever employed in the mill, e.g. truckers, sweepers and scrubbers fall in this group. They are largely time workers.

Weaving department, including warp preparation.

Class 310. *Loom fixers*—includes loom fixers and repairers employed in all textile mills, also fixers employed in rubber factories. They are time workers of a dependable character. Weaving "second hands" are chosen from loom fixers.

Class 405. *Beamers, warpers, slashers*—covers the group of fairly skilled and strong workers engaged in the preparation of the warp after spooling. They are largely time workers.

Class 435. *Winders, reelers, spoolers*—a heterogeneous group of nimble and active workers of no great skill engaged upon the rewinding of yarn from caps and bobbins on to spools, reels, quills, etc., which are more convenient for working and weaving. They are paid by the piece.

Class 430. *Weavers*—a more highly skilled group including weavers, braiders and tenders, drillers and pattern makers. Weavers form a very large part of this group. The basis of payment is piece rate for weavers with due attention to quality.

Carding department.

Class 415. *Carders, combers, lappers*—a group of workers requiring little skill but constant attention to simple duties, tending machines in the carding department proper. They are paid either time or piece but usually on a time basis. Card strippers (i.e. the heavy dirty work of cleaning the card, etc.) are not included in this group but are placed in Class 440.

Class 420. *Drawers, rovers, twisters*—covers a large group of operatives possessing some little special skill engaged in tending the various "drawing" machines used in the stage between carding and spinning. These workers are usually paid by the piece, though time work is quite common. Doffing the "fly frames" involves an awkward twisting of the body but gets lighter as one proceeds from the stubbing frame to jack frame. Piece work predominates in this department.

Spinning department.

Class 425. *Spinners*—a well-defined class of skilled workers who are paid by the piece. No further description is needed save to add that frame, jenny, mule, ring and thread spinners are here represented.

Class 410. *Bobbin-boys, doffers, carriers*—a heterogeneous class of workers, mostly boys, engaged in the spinning and weaving departments Filling and carrying calls for no skill but doffers acquire considerable skill, while band-boy (grouped here) is often the stepping stone from doffer to section hand. Time work predominates.

Class 440. Takes the residue of cotton operatives save that foremen are grouped elsewhere. Here we find card grinders and strippers, drawers-in, warp-tyers, etc., etc. Reference to the index of occupations published with the thirteenth census will remove any remaining doubts as to the classification.

Occupations of cotton operatives in Massachusetts

Titles	1905			Class	Titles	Sex	1910	1915	1920
	Males	Females	Total						
Labourers	1,528	—	1,528	275	Labourers (N.O.C.)	T.	6,710	6,742	10,069
						M.	6,055	6,521	8,686
						F.	655	221	1,383
Foremen	2,743	11	2,754						
Loom fixers	2,418	4	2,422	310	Loom fixers	T.	4,341	4,477	4,874
						M.	4,341	4,469	4,874
						F.	—	8	—
Warpers	216	945	1,161	405	Beamers, warpers, slashers	T.	2,617	2,849	
						M.	1,516	1,584	
						F.	1,101	1,265	
Doffers	2,655	817	3,472	410	Bobbin-boys, doffers, carriers	T.	4,415	4,138	
						M.	3,487	3,143	
						F.	928	995	
Card room operatives	4,054	1,571	5,625	415	Carders, combers, lappers	T.	5,329	5,384	
						M.	3,474	3,701	
						F.	1,855	1,683	
Speeders	548	3,780	4,328	420	Drawers, rovers, twisters	T.	7,413	8,280	
						M.	2,318	2,642	
						F.	5,095	5,638	
Spinners	5,562	7,759	13,321	425	Spinners	T.	12,946	15,299	
						M.	5,240	5,790	
						F.	7,706	9,509	
Weavers	14,506	16,119	30,625	430	Weavers	T.	34,607	32,843	
						M.	17,513	17,032	
						F.	17,094	15,811	
Winders	115	1,870	1,985	435	Winders, reelers, spoolers	T.	7,839	8,447	
Spoolers	229	4,448	4,677			M.	834	615	
						F.	7,005	7,832	
Drawers-in	183	1,448	1,631	440	Other semi-skilled occupations	T.	16,156	20,408	
Cloth room operatives	759	1,652	2,411			M.	9,657	12,348	
Other cotton mill operatives	9,654	3,793	13,447			F.	6,499	8,060	
Aggregate	45,170	44,217	89,387	—	Aggregate	T.	102,373	108,867	113,423
						M.	54,435	57,845	60,498
						F.	47,938	51,022	52,925

1920 column (Classes 405–440): Semi-skilled operatives not classified further. Total 98,480; Males 46,938; Females 51,542.

N.B. (1) Apprentices are separately classified but this does not affect the cotton industry.
(2) Loom fixers 1910–20 include those engaged in all textile mills or rubber factories; also loom repairers.

We are now in a position to discuss the weighting of the occupational wages series available for Massachusetts cotton operatives from 1890 onward.

(a) The card tenders (male) series may be taken to represent Class 415. The proportions of total operatives covered by this group were:

	1910 (%)	1915 (%)	1920
Both sexes	5·2	5·0	—
Males	3·4	3·4	—
Females	1·8	1·6	—

(b) The frame spinners (female) series to represent Class 425, viz.:

	1905 (%)	1910 (%)	1915 (%)
Both sexes	14·9	12·7	14·1
Males	6·2	5·1	5·3
Females	8·7	7·6	8·8

(c) The weavers (male and female) series may be assigned weights according to Class 430, viz.:

	1905 (%)	1910 (%)	1915 (%)
Both sexes	34·3	33·8	30·2
Males	16·2	17·1	15·7
Females	18·1	16·7	14·5

(d) The loom fixers series may perhaps be taken to represent foremen and overseers also in the absence of specific information about them:

	1905 (%)	1910 (%)	1915 (%)	1920 (%)
Loom fixers	2·7	4·2	4·1	4·3
Foremen, etc.	3·1	—	—	—

N.B. Included all loom fixers after 1905.

In calculating a wage index for all cotton operatives I therefore propose to weight in the ratio:

Card tenders (male)	1
Frame spinners (female)	3
Loom fixers (male)	1
Weavers: male	3
female	3

For a male wage index the weights would be the same:

Card tenders 1, Loom fixers 1, Weavers (male) 3;

but for a female wage index one would combine in the ratio:

Frame spinners 1, Weavers (female) 2.

IV. *The weighting of the different items of expense.*

(*a*) *Labour*. The ratios between the census returns of "amount paid in wages" and "value of products" show the share of the receipts of the cotton manufacturers paid to labour at frequent intervals; and, as spinning and weaving are largely conducted by the same firm, these receipts approximate closely to the un-duplicated value of the cotton goods produced. Hence one obtains figures for the average labour cost of manufacture of cotton piece goods (in census years), expressed as a percentage of the selling price of the goods. If the cotton goods produced in Massachusetts were all of the type represented by the composite bundle of print cloth and sheeting which constitutes the selling price index, or if they were related in a definite and constant fashion to this bundle, then these percentages might be used directly to weight the corrections made to this selling price index on account of changes in wages. Unfortunately regular print cloth and standard brown sheeting are not the only products of the Massachusetts cotton mills; moreover the development of the fine goods trade at New Bedford has so changed the industry that it is necessary to enquire further before using the census returns even to estimate *changes* in the weights appropriate to labour in correcting the selling price index. The finer the product the higher the grade of cotton required, the greater the labour cost per unit of product, and the larger the overheads. It is possible that the three items of expense expanded in such proportions as the character of the product changed that the percentage of the receipts of the industry going to labour (in wages) was unaffected by the change. Fortunately the character of the industry varies considerably from city to city and state to state in New England, so that one can discover how far the percentage of receipts paid in wages varies with the type of goods manufactured.

Census data are separately available for each of the New England states, showing the percentage of the selling value of the final product represented by materials, wages and salaries. The three series are available back to 1849, 1859 and 1899 respectively. The conclusions to be drawn from examination of this material are as follows:

(1) Prior to 1914 an allowance of 2 % of the value of the products will cover the variations in the percentage of receipts going to labour from state to state in any one year, with a few exceptions. For 1914, 1919 and 1923 the range of fluctuation is about 5 %. Moreover when salaries and wages are added the variation from state to state is still further reduced.

(2) The percentage of receipts going to pay wages in Massachusetts is always a little (but not much) below the average for the group of states except in 1923 when it equals the average.

(3) The average share of the product going to pay wages in New England has oscillated between about 20 % and 30 %.

In short the analysis suggests that labour gets nearly the same share of the receipts, *ceteris paribus*, in New England establishments whether they are producing coarse or fine goods, and this is confirmed by a comparison of the percentage paid in wages in Fall River, New Bedford, Lowell, and Lawrence—four Massachusetts cities which manufacture very different piece goods. The *Massachusetts Labour Bulletin* for January 1898 gives a summary of census returns relating to these four cities for the years 1890–7 (annual state censuses of manufactures), from which I have computed the following table:

Percentage of value of product paid in wages in certain Massachusetts establishments manufacturing cotton goods, 1890, 1895, 1897[1]

	1890	1895	1897	No. of establishments covered (average)
Fall River	26·0	29·8	32·4	34
New Bedford	25·8	27·5	31·1	9
Lowell	22·5	28·0	26·9	6
Lawrence	31·3	35·3	35·3	5

The *Bulletin* also analyses the financial condition of these establishments during this period.[2] Fluctuations in the relative

---

[1] *Massachusetts Labour Bulletin for* 1898, p. 11.
[2] *Ibid.* pp. 22–8.

prosperity of the different cities explains a large part of the variation in the percentage of receipts going to labour in 1890 and 1897, but in 1895 the financial conditions of the firms in the different cities were much alike, so that the percentage of the receipts paid to labour may fairly be compared. In that year (1895) labour's share of the product in New Bedford was rather more than 1 % below its share in Fall River, while Lowell fell between the two cities in this respect. Lawrence showed a much higher proportion of wages owing to the custom of dyeing, bleaching, and finishing the cloth at the mill which is practised in that city.

I conclude finally that the proportion of receipts paid in wages tends to be higher in establishments manufacturing coarse cotton goods than in mills producing the finer fabrics, but the difference is so small that no great error is committed in using the census returns for cotton manufacture in Massachusetts to estimate the labour cost of manufacturing regular print cloth and brown sheetings.

The selling price index numbers (base 1913 = 100) may be regarded as measuring the price in dollars of 13 yards of regular print cloth and 6·2 yards of standard brown sheeting. This composite product will hereafter be called the "bundle". The ratios of wages to product at the various federal and state censuses give the labour cost of manufacture of this bundle of cloth in 1859, 1869, 1874, 1879, 1884, 1889, 1894, 1899, 1904, 1909, 1914 and 1919. Thence figures for the labour cost of 1913 wage rates are obtained by means of the index numbers of efficiency wages and, by interpolations, annual index numbers are obtained for the physical volume of labour (measured at 1913 wage rates) required to manufacture the said bundle of cloth each year from 1859 to 1919. Prior to 1859 there were no census returns of wages, but in the *Proceedings of the New England Cotton Manufacturers' Association*, vol. XXI, p. 10, a careful comparison is made between the cost of manufacturing sheetings and drillings of standard type in 1838 and in 1876. The comparison is based upon an analysis of the costs of two of the best known mills in New England—the Jackson Company, Nashua, New Hampshire, manufacturing "Indian Head" standard sheetings and the Booth cotton mills producing standard drillings. From these comparisons I estimate that a bundle of cloth requiring forty units of labour in manufacturing in 1876 would have required about ninety units of labour in 1838, but the index number of labour cost of manufacture at 1913 wage rates of the bundle of cloth constituting the selling price index is approximately forty: the corresponding number for 1838 is therefore about ninety and the missing index numbers for 1847 to 1859 may be computed by interpolation.

In this way figures are obtained which approximate closely to the average labour cost of manufacture of the bundle of cloth at 1913 wage rates in each year from 1847 to 1919 and thence, by means of the index numbers of efficiency wages, figures for the actual labour cost of the bundle. These are tabulated in Appendix IV, Table I, columns 6 and 5 respectively.

(b) *Raw cotton.* There has been little change in the quantity of cotton consumed in the manufacture of a given piece of cloth since the middle of the nineteenth century. Improvements in machinery have effected some saving, and one of the important arguments for shorter working hours is the reduction of waste, but the aggregate economy has been small compared with the amount of cotton consumed. Constant weighting of the corrections for changes in the price of raw cotton therefore involves no great error. I have simply estimated the cost of cotton consumed in the manufacture of the bundle of cloth in 1913, reduced the selling price of middling upland to this base, and used the resulting index numbers to represent the cost of cotton required in each year from 1847 to 1920.

The calculation is as follows:

13 yards of print cloth weighing 7 yards to pound, weight	1·86 pounds
6·2 yards of sheeting weighing 3 yards to pound, weight	2·07 ,,
Net loss of weight during manufacture of cloth (i.e. waste-weight added in sizing)	10 %
Therefore cotton consumed in manufacture of bundle of cloth	4·32 pounds
But price of middling upland cotton in 1913	$.128 per pound
Therefore cost of cotton in "bundle" in 1913	$5.525
Therefore cost of raw cotton required to manufacture $100 of print cloth and sheeting in 1913	$55.00

The index numbers of selling price of middling upland have therefore been calculated to the base 1913 = 55

(c) *Other expenses.* There remains a margin between the selling price index number and cost of labour and cotton, which varies from about 40 % at the beginning to about 20 % at the close of our period, also fluctuating violently from year to year with the trade cycle. This margin has to pay for all items of expenditure other than wages and raw cotton, including materials other than cotton, freight, taxes, interest, depreciation and insurance, salaries of officials and clerks, and a normal profit to business ability.[1] No one of these items is of sufficient importance to call for separate correction, but in the aggregate changes in the supply prices of these factors are considerable, raising the index number of real cost twelve points between 1913 and 1850. The only recourse is to correct this margin by one index number of general prices chosen so as to include these items so far as possible, or, alternatively, items which are known to fluctuate in sympathy. From 1875 Mr Carl Snyder's index of the general price level[2] is the best available because it includes wages, rents and other items of the type which constitute the margin of "other expenses" in cotton manufacture; moreover the index is a stable one, being well constructed from good constituents. For the period 1847 to 1875 the only suitable index numbers are based upon the data of the *Aldrich Report.* Professor Falkner did not make the best possible use of this material in calculating the index numbers of wholesale prices published in the report, but Professor Mitchell has calculated, from the same data, quarterly index numbers for the period 1860–80; I have used the average of his quarterly index numbers for each year from 1860 to 1875. This covers the greenback period satisfactorily and, in the absence of a better, I have used Professor Falkner's unweighted index number for the first thirteen years, i.e. 1847–60.[3] Piecing together these three lengths by the common

---

[1] According to the *Annual Report of Massachusetts Statistics of Labour* 1890, Pt IV, materials other than cotton absorbed about 6 % of the receipts of the industry in 1884–5, freight took about 2 %, salaries 1½ %, taxes 1½ %, interest and depreciation 10 %.

[2] *Journal of the American Statistical Association*, June 1924. Note that the use of Mr Snyder's index for the present purpose in no way commits me to Mr Snyder's "deflation" theory or practice.

[3] Compare *U.S. Bureau of Labour Statistics Bulletin*, 284, p. 158.

splice and expressing all as a percentage of 1913 gives the required index of general prices 1847–1920, viz.:

1847–1860. Professor Falkner, *Aldrich Report*, Part I, p. 93, "all articles simply averaged".

1860–1875. Professor Mitchell, *Gold, Prices and Wages*, p. 59, based upon the *Aldrich Report*.

1875–1924. Mr Carl Snyder, *Journal of the American Statistical Association*, June 1924.

Instead of applying a constant weight to the correction of "other expenses" as in the study of British industries, I have calculated the margin (i.e. excess of selling price index number over the sum of the index numbers for cost of labour and raw cotton) each year, and thence computed its value at the 1913 price level, *vide* Appendix IV, Table I, columns 5 and 6 respectively.

There is considerable evidence that the distribution of expenses resulting from the calculations described above is close to the facts.

1. *Massachusetts Labour Bulletin*, No. 45, January 1907, analyses the distribution of the receipts of 149 Massachusetts cotton mills as returned at the census of 1904, and the results show:

cash wages 25·05 %; raw materials 61·75 %; other expenses (including dividends) 13·20 %.

The distribution for 1904 shown in Appendix IV, Table I, is: labour 25·0 %; raw cotton 56·7 %, 18·2 %.

The difference of 5 % between the total raw materials and the raw cotton is a reasonable allowance for fuel,[1] sizings, and materials other than cotton.

2. *Massachusetts Labour Statistics* 1890, Part IV, presents figures showing the distribution of aggregate receipts of certain industries among the factors of production at the census of 1885. The procedure and terminology calls for no comment, save that

---

[1] The cost of fuel used in cotton manufacture in Massachusetts in 1890 was 1·87 % of the value of the product: *vide Massachusetts Labour Bulletin*, January 1898, p. 7. Materials other than raw cotton accounted for 4·2 % of the value of product at the census of 1909.

the rent item entered as an "expense" includes only rent paid out of the business to another party; while *no* interest charge is allowed in costs. The following is a summary of the results (*vide* pp. 304–5) for the cotton goods industry.

Relation of cost to selling price in 137 establishments in Massachusetts

Classification	% of selling price
Stock used (i.e. materials)	59·39
Salaries	1·46
Wages	27·61
Rent	0·07
Taxes	1·70
Insurance	0·34
Freight	2·33
New equipment	0·86
Repairs	1·84
Other expenses	0·14
Excess of selling price over costs of production	4·26
Total	100·00

The excess of selling price over cost of production is equivalent to 2·25 % upon the capital invested, i.e. all capital employed in the business, and is further analysed:

Classification	% of selling price
Interest (5 % upon cash and credit capital)	4·04
Depreciation (10 % upon value of machinery, implements and tools)	6·13
Allowance for selling expenses and losses by bad debts (5 % of selling price)	5·00
Net loss	− 10·91
Total	4·26

In the census year (1884–5) fifty out of the one hundred and thirty-seven firms failed to make a net profit as defined by the Massachusetts Bureau of Statistics. The net loss is equivalent to 5·77 % upon capital invested.

I have reproduced this analysis because, whatever quarrel one may have with the procedure, it gives one some idea of the relative importance of the items classed as "other expenses" in my analysis. In the following table the above results are brought into direct comparison with my estimates for 1884.

Analysis of selling price of cotton manufactures in Massachusetts 1884

Massachusetts Bureau of Labour Statistics		Estimate used in the text	
Classification	% of selling price	Classification	% of selling price
Materials	59·39	Raw cotton	52·6
Wages	27·61	Wages	27·6
Other expenses	13·00	Other expenses	19·8
Total	100·00	Total	100·00

Again the only significant difference is an allowance of 5·8 % for materials other than cotton. At the federal censuses of 1880 and 1890, materials other than cotton accounted for 6·8 % and 5·7 % respectively of the value of products, so that it is clear that this comparison confirms my estimate for both raw cotton and wages.

3. The *Weeks Report upon Wages in Cotton Manufacture* (Tenth Census 1880, vol. xx, Statistics of Wages, pp. 327–67) contains information concerning labour costs of manufacture appended to the tables of wage returns from the several establishments. Comparison with these returns suggests that my estimate is perhaps a little low, although the ratio of wages to selling price fluctuates so violently from firm to firm in any given year that it is difficult to generalise from the few comparable returns available. At least the evidence is strong that my estimates, if low, are within one or two points of the truth, even before the Civil War.

I conclude finally that the distribution of the expenses of manufacture of grey cotton cloth shown in Appendix iv is in close accord with the facts for the entire period 1847–1920: the items "labour" and "cotton" are probably both rather underweighted in the early years, but not sufficiently to introduce any serious error into the index numbers of real cost.

V. *The calculation of the index numbers of real cost.*

The description of the sources and derivation of the statistics contained in Table I of Appendix IV is now complete. The product of these labours is the following series of annual index numbers, each continuous from 1847–1920:

(1) The selling price index (1 print cloth, 1 sheeting) Appendix IV, Table I, column 1; base 1913 = 100.

(2) The cost of raw cotton consumed in this bundle of cloth Appendix IV, Table I, column 2; base 1913 = 55.

(3) The cost of the labour consumed in manufacturing this bundle:

(*a*) at the current wage rates, column 3;

(*b*) at the wages current in 1913, column 4.

(4) The margin left above the cost of cotton and labour to cover all other expenses:

(*a*) the actual margin, i.e. at current prices, column 5;

(*b*) the margin valued at the prices of 1913, column 6.

From these series the required corrected selling price index numbers are easily calculated as follows:

The index of selling price of grey cloth corrected for changes in the supply prices of labour, materials and other expenses—Appendix IV, Table II, column 3—is obtained by adding to the selling price index numbers the algebraic sum of the differentials between the cost of labour and cotton at the 1913 prices and their cost at the prices current in the year to which the index number refers, together with a third differential on account of other expenses, namely, the difference between the value of the margin at the 1913 and at the current prices.

Having the required annual index numbers, it remains only to estimate their trend, which is done by taking a seven years' moving average and placing the results opposite the middle year, i.e. the fourth, since the period of the cyclical fluctuations shown by the annual index numbers was not more than seven years at any time between 1847 and 1920. To accommodate gentlemen who turn pale at the idea of deflating by means of an index of general prices I have computed seven years' moving averages of all three selling price indexes, which give the following series:

(1) The trend of the selling price of grey cotton cloth 1850–1910, Appendix IV, Table II, column 2, i.e. index numbers of *Money Costs*.

(2) Ditto corrected for changes in the supply prices of labour, materials and all other items of expenses, Appendix IV, Table II, column 4, i.e. the index of *Real Costs*.

It was explained in Part I that the index numbers of real cost measure changes in the quantity of resources consumed in the manufacture of a unit of the product, the different kinds of resources being weighted according to their prices in the base year (in this case 1913). To test the effect of changing the base year I have recalculated the index numbers of real cost, using precisely the same bundle of cloth as selling price index and the same data as to expenses, but correcting for differentials between the various items of current expense and their value at the prices prevailing in 1860 instead of in 1913. This gives the last two columns of Table II in Appendix IV, namely:

(1) Index of selling price of grey cotton cloth (1 print cloth and 1 sheeting) corrected for labour, materials and other expenses, the items being weighted according to their values in 1860—Appendix IV, Table II, column 5.

(2) Seven years' moving average of the same, i.e. index of the real cost of manufacture of grey cotton cloth in Massachusetts, 1850–1910, in terms of resources, the different items being weighted according to their prices in 1860.

For convenience I have expressed these index numbers as a percentage of 1913, although their "base year" is really 1860.

Comparison of the two indexes of real costs shows that they fluctuate in very close sympathy, the ratio charts of the annual numbers out of the seven years' moving averages showing a striking similarity; but the 1860 series shows real costs in 1850 only 62 % above 1913, while the 1913 series shows real costs in 1850 to have been 83 % above 1913. This is the result one would have expected, *a priori*, for the price of raw cotton in 1860 was 86 % of its price in 1913, whereas efficiency wages in 1860 were less than 43 % of the 1913 rates. A large part of the improvement effected in the industry during this period represents economy of labour, while there has been but little saving of cotton: in the series based upon 1860 cotton receives a higher weight relative to labour than in the 1913 series, consequently the latter shows somewhat greater fall of real costs than the former. This result is of general importance, for wages rose during the period 1850–1910 relatively to the supply prices of the other factors of production in nearly every important British or American industry, so that index numbers of real costs computed for any industry in these two countries, first upon a base near the end of the period and second on a base near the beginning of the period, would bear the same sort of relation the one to the other as the indexes of real cost of cotton manufacture to the base 1860 and 1913 respectively. In short, the choice of a base year near the end of the period *exaggerates* the fall of real costs in British and American industries between 1850 and 1910, but the error is small and on the right side for my purpose, and so I shall proceed to use the series based upon 1913.

VI. *Errors in the derivation of the index of real costs.*

(a) *Prices.* The index numbers of selling prices of grey cloth probably reflect changes in the average annual prices obtained by Massachusetts manufacturers for regular print cloth and standard sheetings within 5 %; during the Civil War and the years immediately following, the data of the *Aldrich Report* (which contain price series for cotton fabrics collected in Boston as well as in New York) suggest that cloth prices in Boston were somewhat higher than in New York, but the differences never exceed 5 % and, taking the period as a whole, relative prices are almost the same for both cities. Similar remarks apply to the raw cotton series based upon the price of middling upland cotton at New York. It is more difficult to appraise the value of the efficiency wage series and the index of general prices. However, in view of the stability and uniformity of labour conditions in the Massachusetts mills and the care with which the original data were collected, I estimate that an allowance of

5 % is adequate to cover all errors in the wage series prior to 1914, and that a similar allowance is an adequate margin for error in the general price index.

If it so happened that the errors in these constituent price series lay in one direction in a particular year, then the index number of real costs for that year might be out as much as 10 % (5 % for the selling price index and 5 % for the wages, cotton and general price series together, since their weights together make up the selling price index) but this is an unlikely occurrence. In practice it is improbable that the net error in the index of real costs due to faults in the constituent price series exceeds 5 %, while 3 % may be a sufficient allowance.

(b) *Weighting*. The accuracy with which the expenses of manufacture have been distributed among the various items of manufacture has already been discussed at some length and need only be summarised here:

(1) The item labour, i.e. wages, is probably rather under-weighted in the early years, but the error does not exceed 5 % (i.e. one point in the index of labour cost).

(2) The item raw material (cotton) is also underweighted in the first part of the period, but the error is small, for it has been customary since the middle of the nineteenth century for books on cost accounting to allow 15 % or 16 % waste of cotton during manufacture, whereas in Massachusetts to-day an allowance of 12 % or 13 % is still necessary; the difference of 3 % represents the economy in the use of cotton effected during our period. Again 5 % is probably adequate to cover all errors in the weighting of raw cotton.

(3) The margin left to cover other expenses is, of course, increased by underweighting labour and raw materials but this diminishes rather than increases the net error involved—for there has been a rough parallelism between the movements of wages, cotton and general prices. The prices of cotton and of labour (relative to 1913) diverged very considerably from general prices in the early part of the period, but diverged in opposite directions. Thus, if both series be underweighted, the errors will partially offset one another: in any particular year the error in the index number of real costs due to equal and similar errors

in the weighting of raw cotton and of labour will be proportionate to the algebraic sum of the relative movement of the index numbers (to the base 1913 = 100) of price of raw cotton and general prices and of labour and general prices. Neglecting the Civil War and the years immediately following, this algebraic sum was greatest in 1855 and 1870 of all the years from 1847 to 1914; for other reasons the percentage of error in the index number of real costs is rather greater in 1855 than in 1870, so I shall calculate it for the former year.

The net effect upon the index number of real costs in 1855 of underweighting labour 5 % would be to *lower* the index about one and a half points, while a similar underweighting of the correction for cotton would *raise* the index nearly half a point. The net error in the index of real cost due to underweighting cotton and labour 5 % is a loss of one point out of 185, i.e. little more than $\frac{1}{2}$ %.

In conclusion I think one may safely say that errors in the index of real costs due to inaccurate weighting do not exceed 1 %, while the net error attributable to faulty price series is probably not greater than 3 %; allowing 1 % for untraced errors, it appears that my index numbers of real costs represent changes in the average quantity of resources required to manufacture a unit of the composite product (print cloth and brown sheeting) within 5 %, even in the early years, while the error rapidly diminishes as the base year (1913) is approached. These I call "statistical errors"; there remain questions of interpretation—how far the composite product represents the entire industry of Massachusetts and of New England and what is the effect of weighting the different factors of production according to their prices in the base year. It is difficult to express these influences in quantitative terms, but evidence was put forward in the Introduction to the effect that the composite product may be taken as highly representative of the industry, while index numbers calculated to the base 1860 show a fall of 38 % in real costs between 1850 and 1910 as compared with the drop of 46 % indicated by the series based on 1913.[1] I shall return to the question of interpretation in the concluding pages of this part.

[1] Cf. Appendix IV, Table II, columns 4 and 6.

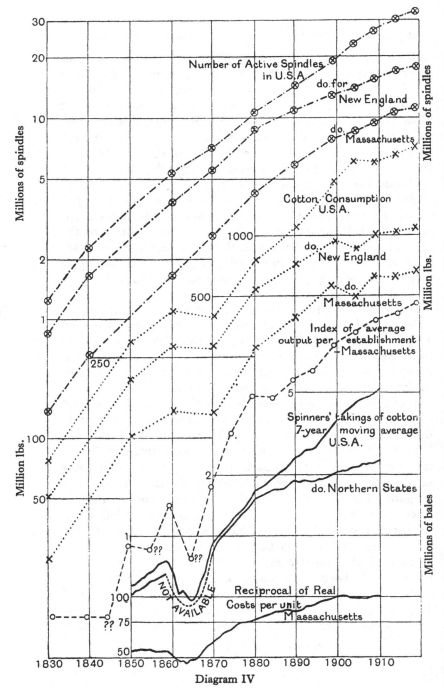

Diagram IV

Number of Active Spindles in U.S.A., New England, and Massachusetts, 1830–1920. Cotton Consumption for same period and areas. Spinners' takings of cotton, U.S.A. and Northern States, 1850–1910. Average output per establishment and reciprocal of real costs in Massachusetts, 1850–1910.

§ 3. THE SIZE OF THE INDUSTRY AND OF THE FIRMS ENGAGED THEREIN

[*Vide* Diagram IV]

I. *The industry as a whole.*

The choice of a suitable index of size with which to correlate the cost series presents difficult problems both in economic theory and in statistical technique. The cost series measure directly changes in the efficiency of the Massachusetts industry only; though they probably reflect closely conditions in New England as a whole, they have no title to represent the development of the industry in the southern states. One would expect economies which result from intimate contact with neighbouring establishments (dubbed by economists "localisation") to be correlated most closely with the expansion of manufacture of grey cotton cloth in Massachusetts, to be less intimately connected with the development in New England, and to show very little sympathy with the southern growth. On the other hand, one would expect economies resulting from the further division of labour made possible by the expansion of the market to be correlated with changes in the output of the country and, to a less extent, with the expansion of the world market. Clearly no single comparison is sufficient. The statistical difficulties arise mainly from the limited data available and the conflicting claims of "cotton consumed" and "spindles active" to serve as an index of size. In the Introduction it was argued that the spindle is a satisfactory measure of the comparative quantities of resources engaged in cotton manufacture in different districts at a given stage of industrial development, but when it is used to measure changes in the size of an industry over long periods allowance must be made first for speeding up of the machinery, second for cheapening of the machinery, etc., so that a representative mill of, say, twenty thousand spindles represents a smaller amount of capital measured in terms of labour and waiting as the industry progresses. These two tendencies work in opposite directions and the second objection is valid against the use of cotton consumed as index of size, so that for long periods as for short the number of active producing spindles (or better the number of "spindle hours") remains the best single index of size of a cotton manufacturing industry which consists largely of establishments engaged upon the spinning *and* weaving of cotton goods. Unfortunately, prior to 1905, there are no reliable records of spindles engaged annually in the United States or in the several geographic divisions. The only satisfactory continuous figures available are for cotton consumed in the United States. In practice, therefore, one has to make use of both spindles active and cotton consumed as indexes of changes in the size of the industry.

[N.B. The statistics refer to spindles in cotton mills which were in operation at the same time during the census year. Prior to 1899 doubling and twisting spindles, also spindles engaged in the manufacture of cotton small wares, are included. From 1899 producing spindles operating in mills manufacturing cotton piece goods only are included.]

1. *Cotton consumed—trend.* (*a*) In United States—seven years' moving average of annual figures for actual consumption taken from the annual census bulletins upon the supply and distribution of cotton in the United States.[1] (Figures include linters.)

(*b*) Cotton consumed in New England—decennial estimates of trend calculated from census returns by multiplying by the ratio of the seven years' moving average of cotton consumed in the United States to the actual amount of cotton consumed in the United States in the census year. This is a device for correcting for cyclical fluctuations upon the assumption that they are common to the northern and southern states.

(*c*) Cotton consumed in Massachusetts—quinquennial estimates of trend calculated from state and federal census returns in the same manner as the estimates for New England.

I have made an arbitrary addition of ten million pounds to the

[1] *United States Bureau of the Census Bulletin* 160, Cotton Production and Distribution—seasons of 1925-6, p. 49 (which see for original sources). The statistics of consumption were compiled from a variety of sources:

1790–1894—from publications of the Department of Agriculture.
1895–1903—from reports of Latham, Alexander and Company.
1904–1925—Census figures.

In the chart the statistics are shifted forward one year so as to relate to the year of consumption instead of to the year of marketing of the crop.

figure for 1904 to allow for the six months strike at Fall River. The estimate of ten million is based upon the census of 1900.

2. *Spinners' takings by mills in the Northern States.* Although subject to changes in mill stocks, spinners' takings are a guide to actual consumption. Lacking better information, I have computed a seven years' moving average of Shepperson's series[1] for cotton taken by northern mills. It is a more sensitive index of the expansion and contraction of the northern industry than any of the series so far discussed, since annual figures are available and, used in conjunction with the above series, it throws a good deal of light upon the relation between declining costs and the expansion of the industry.

II. *Size of Establishments.*

The data relating to the size of the manufacturing unit in American cotton textiles are much more satisfactory than the meagre information available for English cotton manufacture, but there is the same paucity of information regarding the unit of financial control. The unit of economic enterprise employed by the United States census bureau corresponds closely to the manufacturing unit in this industry; it is defined by the census as follows:

As a rule the term "establishment" represents a single plant or factory, but in some cases it represents two or more plants which were operated under a common ownership or for which one set of books of account was kept. If, however, the plants constituting an establishment as thus defined were not all located within the same city, county, or state, separate reports were secured in order that the figures for each plant might be included in the statistics for the city, county, or state in which it was located.[2]

Since 1904 the census bureau has published tables showing the frequency distribution of the establishments in the industry according (a) to the average number of wage earners, (b) to the value of products, while for 1909 and 1919 the classification

---

[1] *Vide Shepperson's Cotton Facts.* The data are given in running bales counting round as half bales: the average net weight of the bales of cotton produced in the United States of America varied from 430 to 490 lb. during this period, but these figures are higher than the average weight of bales consumed, which however has probably shown a similar upward trend.

[2] *Census of Manufactures,* 1919.

according to average number of wage earners is available by states. Both methods of comparison reveal a high concentration of establishments about the modal size, with little change in the character of the distribution. As early as 1904 85 % of the cotton manufacturing establishments of the United States reported products valued between $20,000 and $1,000,000 per annum, and these establishments accounted for 56 % of the total product of the industry. In the same year 99·8 % of the output of the industry was manufactured in establishments reporting an annual product greater than $20,000. Clearly there are very few really small establishments engaged in the manufacture of cotton goods. Owing to price changes the classification by value of products is of little value in comparing the sizes of pre- and post-War establishments, so we must turn to the classification by number of wage earners employed. The table presents a summary of the available data:

Size of establishments by average number of wage earners, United States and Massachusetts

Wage earners (inclusive)	Year	United States			Massachusetts	
		1919	1914	1909	1919	1909
0–5	Establishments	56	47	40	4	5
	Wage earners	177	125	116	15	2
6–20	Establishments	143	100	102	28	1
	Wage earners	1,842	1,197	1,302	370	13
21–50	Establishments	163	153	181	27	1
	Wage earners	5,682	5,494	6,534	874	48
51–100	Establishments	220	217	224	24	2
	Wage earners	16,403	16,332	16,317	1,744	1,43
101–250	Establishments	438	375	360	22	2
	Wage earners	71,743	61,502	58,942	3,611	3,51
251–500	Establishments	228	213	213	35	2
	Wage earners	81,371	74,840	76,793	13,192	11,18
501–1000	Establishments	157	144	127	49	4
	Wage earners	108,658	99,099	88,745	34,065	29,01
Over 1000	Establishments	91	79	77	42	3
	Wage earners	160,976	134,815	130,131	70,279	63,11
Total	Establishments	1,496	1,328	1,324	231	18
	Wage earners	446,852	393,404	378,880	124,150	108,91

Perhaps the most striking feature of this table is the similarity of the distributions at the successive censuses. The figures for the country as a whole show perhaps a slight tendency towards concentration about the modal size, but no such tendency is discernible in Massachusetts. Moreover, there is no marked tendency for the number of very large establishments to increase faster than other classes. The largest number of establishments in any one group falls in the same class each year, namely 101 to 250 wage earners for the United States and 501 to 1000 wage earners for Massachusetts. If the distribution has changed as slowly during the period 1850–1900, for which we have no frequency tables, as in the last twenty years, then the simple average has a strong claim to represent changes in the scale of production within this industry. In point of fact, the rapid development of small mills in the southern states did lower the average size of establishments in the country as a whole between 1880 and 1900, and altered the character of the distribution of firms according to size for the country as a whole, but index numbers based upon the average size of establishments operating in Massachusetts are free from this disturbing influence and the general character of the distribution in this state has probably changed little.

III. *Size of the unit of control.*

Writing in 1912 Dr M. T. Copeland[1] discussed the progress of industrial combination in cotton manufactures. At that time a few "local mergers" had been effected but, with the single exception of the American Thread Company, the few attempts made to secure monopoly power by amalgamations had failed miserably. On the other hand "a distinct tendency toward integration...of several establishments, perhaps producing different grades, under a single management, with a single selling agency and with its own finishing plant" was already apparent. The movement began about 1900, assumed importance about 1906–12, and has continued to develop. It is, of course, impossible to say what economies have been effected by such integration; there may have been a considerable saving of expense upon buying and selling, but the exceedingly slow growth of the movement suggests that the net economies to be reaped are not very large.

[1] *The Cotton Manufacturing Industry*, chap. ix.

Dr Thorp's study[1] of the data collected at the census of 1919 relating to the practice of operating a number of establishments from a central office, throws some light upon the extent to which industrial combination has proceeded. Unfortunately the figures given relate to the textile industry as a whole and therefore include woollen manufactures, hosiery and knit goods, etc., as well as the cotton goods industry; still they suffice to show that the practice of central office control, though important, covers only a small part of the industry. In 1919 only 10 % of all textile establishments were in central office groups; of these central offices over 60 % operated only one or two establishments, while nearly 92 % operated less than five establishments from a single office; over 75 % of the central office groups confined their operations to the textile industry, while nearly 96 % operated within one or two industrial groups.

There is no accessible statistical evidence concerning the development of extensive units of financial control *via* the more subtle means of interlocking directorates, etc., but the cotton manufacturing industry of the United States was frequently quoted as an example of a large industry which remained practically untouched by the "trust movement" before the War, and there is no reason to doubt the accuracy of the descriptions for post-War conditions. With the development of company law the organisation of the cotton mills changed from the large private firm or partnership to the corporation, but remaihed intensely competitive. In 1885 111 out of the 165 cotton manufacturing establishments in Massachusetts were already corporations; by 1914 98 % of the establishments in Massachusetts had adopted the corporate form of organisation.[2]

---

[1] *United States Census Monograph*, III, chaps. vii, viii.
[2] State and federal census figures respectively.

§4. PROVISIONAL CONCLUSIONS

On the whole the annual index numbers of real price (i.e. selling price corrected for labour, materials, and value of money) fluctuate with the selling price of grey cloth, but less violently; the amplitude and frequency of these oscillations, however, are much greater than was the case for British cotton manufacture during the same period. In some of the cycles there is a discernible tendency for real prices to reach maxima a little before and minima a little after selling prices, thus confirming the tendency noted in the British study, but in other years the two series are closely synchronised. The only continuous figures relating to output available are for annual consumption of cotton in the United States and the cyclical oscillations of this series are masked by the rapid upward trend for the greater part of the period; on the whole, output fluctuates in close sympathy with the selling price of cloth.

It also appears that fluctuations in the selling prices of cloth in America and Britain are fairly closely correlated, though the oscillations of the former are rather more violent and the maxima and minima of the British series sometimes differ by a year from the corresponding turning points in the American prices.

There is very little sympathy between the movements of the real prices of cloth in England and America until toward the close of the nineteenth century; the cycles from 1899–1914, however, were almost synchronised in the two countries.

These points are stimulating to one interested in the trade cycle, but it is necessary to remember that the annual index numbers of real price represent cost in terms of resources *plus* a fluctuating margin of quasi-rent and that the costs refer to goods *produced* in the year to which the price refers and not to goods *sold* in that year. However, the points noted above are particularly interesting, because they are just what one would expect *a priori* from the dominant influence of the price of raw cotton upon the price of cloth and from the entry of American manufactures into British cloth markets towards the close of the last century.

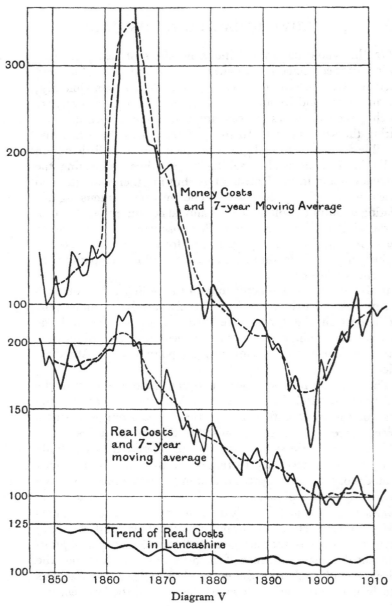

Diagram V

Money Costs in the Massachusetts Cotton Industry 1850–1910.
Real Costs in Massachusetts and Lancashire.

It is, however, with the trend of prices, costs and output rather than their movements from year to year that this study is concerned. Before entering upon a discussion of the relations between these trends it may be well to present a summary recapitulation of the statistical material to be used in the discussion:

1. *Money costs.*[1] The seven years' centred moving average of the annual index numbers of selling price of regular print cloth and standard brown sheeting.

2. *Real costs.*[2] The seven years' centred moving average of the annual index numbers of selling price of grey cotton cloth corrected for changes in the price of labour and raw cotton, and general prices, i.e. the index numbers of real costs measure changes in the quantity of resources required to produce a unit of grey cotton cloth, the resources being valued at their prices in 1913.

3. *Size of the industry.*[3] The rate of increase of active producing spindles in Massachusetts cotton mills, as indicated by the quinquennial figures, is the principal measure of the rate of expansion of the industry since the Civil War; but the seven years' moving average of cotton consumed annually in the United States and the general trend of cotton consumed in Massachusetts mills as shown by the census figures have been used to supplement the returns of active spindles. Supplementary evidence as to changes in the "size" of the industry is also provided by the seven years' moving average of cotton taken by spinners in the northern states, the general trend of cotton consumed in New England and the federal census returns of spindles active in New England and in the United States.

4. *Size of the representative firm.*[4] The index numbers of average output per establishment engaged in cotton manufacture in Massachusetts at the quinquennial censuses form the best single index of the growth of the manufacturing unit, but index numbers are also available for the average number of wage earners and active spindles per establishment in Massachusetts and in the United States.

5. *Efficiency.* For the convenience of direct comparison I have plotted the reciprocals of the index numbers of real cost of cotton manufacture in Massachusetts upon the same ratio chart as the various series relating to the size of the industry.

---

[1] Appendix IV, Table II.
[3] Appendix IV, Table III.

[2] Appendix IV, Table II.
[4] Appendix IV, Table IV.

At the beginning of our period (1850) real costs were falling at the rate of $\frac{4}{5}$ % per annum, but the Civil War lowered the efficiency of the industry and the index numbers of real costs rose from 185 in 1850 to 209 in 1862, whence they fell almost continuously to a minimum of 99 in 1900, only to rise slightly to about 102 in 1901-7 and finally settle at 101[1] in 1908-10. Meantime money costs rose very rapidly from 112 in 1850 to a maximum of 367 in 1865, then fell continuously to a minimum of 67 in 1896 to 1898 and rose finally to 99 in 1910. The price of cotton followed a similar course, but the amplitude of the fluctuations was much greater. General prices and wages of course rose abnormally during the Greenback inflation, but gold wages and prices showed a general upward trend throughout the period.

As in the study of the British industry, the most striking feature of the curve of real costs is the success with which price fluctuations have been eliminated and changes in the physical quantity of resources employed per unit of product revealed. British prices and money costs followed a similar course to American, but the index numbers of real cost agree only in reaching the minimum for the period in 1900 and rising slightly in the first decade of the present century. For the rest the efficiency of the Massachusetts industry increased nearly four times as much as that of Lancashire between 1850 and 1900: the bulk of the improvement in Lancashire took place between 1856 and 1867 when the American industry was suffering from the disturbance of the Civil War. From 1870 to 1900 the real cost of manufacture fell very gently but steadily in Lancashire, while in Massachusetts it fell rapidly but at a diminishing rate.[2]

---

[1] The progress of the industry did not suffice to halve the real cost of manufacture of grey cotton cloth in sixty years, despite the fact that the quantity of labour employed per unit of product in 1910 was only one-third of the quantity required in 1850.

[2] It is interesting to observe that the temporary rise of real costs in Lancashire between 1886 and 1890 was accompanied by a similar check to the fall of real costs in Massachusetts. During these years prices of cloth and cotton, wages and output increased rapidly in both countries, so that the temporary rise of the index numbers of real cost may be attributed in part to abnormal profits, in part to reduced efficiency under the strain of prolonged prosperity.

Clearly the movements of real costs indicated cannot be explained by price changes. How far have they been associated with changes in the size of the industry?

Period	Rate of fall of real costs (% per annum)	Rate of expansion of the industry (% per annum)	Elasticity of return
1850–4	⅘	4*	5
1865–8	5½	7†	1¼
1869–74	4⅓	8‡	2
1874–6	5	5*	1
1876–80	1	2†	2
1880–5	2	4†	2
1885–90	—	2½†	—
1889–94	1½	3½‡	2½
1900–5	—	1⅞†	—
1905–10	—	2½†	—

* Trend of cotton consumed in the United States.
† Spindles active in Massachusetts.
‡ Spindles active and trend of cotton consumed in Massachusetts.

The figures for elasticity of return have been computed upon the assumption that the entire fall of real cost is attributable to the expansion of the industry. This, in fact, is not the case in so far as improvements were effected by changes in technique (machinery, hours of labour, etc.) which would in any case have taken place with the progress of society. The values given for the elasticity of return therefore fix only the upper limits for the tendency to increasing return. It is of course impossible to draw a sharp line between changes which are and changes which are not the result of the expansion of the industry, but the development of cotton manufacture in New England between 1850 and 1910 was remarkably free from external influences calculated to modify the index numbers of real cost. The principles underlying the machinery employed in modern cotton mills were already known before 1850 and similar machines were in common use before the Civil War. To quote Mr Edward Stanwood, "all of Arkwright's patents, which included improvements in carding, drawing, roving and spinning, were thrown open in 1785. In the same year Dr Cartwright invented the power loom and thus completed the group of fundamental inventions of which all modern spinning and weaving machinery is but an adaptation and a series of improvements ". The last fifty years of the eighteenth century had discovered to us the principles of modern spinning and weaving, the first half of the nineteenth showed us how to prepare the cotton for spinning and how to finish the cloth. The scutching machine was invented in 1800 by Mr Snodgrass of Glasgow, the lap machine in 1814 by Mr John Crichton of Manchester, the revolving flat card in 1834, and finally "the combing machine was first exhibited by its inventor, Mr Josue Heilman, of Mulhouse, at the Paris Exposition, in 1851 ".[1] Thus the technical progress of the industry between 1850 and 1910 consisted largely in the perfection and more general introduction of machines already known in 1850. This process involves thousands of minor inventions, but they are of the type which may reasonably be associated with the growth of the industry; the self-centring spindle and the automatic loom introduced in 1885 and 1895 respectively are the only inventions of the period which can lay claim to the title "substantive"; even these were the anticipated result of efforts deliberately devoted to their achievement, and only awaited the time when it seemed economical to make the necessary outlay.

Again the cotton manufacturing industry of New England has not been "hampered" by militant labour movements, and the legislation restricting hours of work, etc., has probably had little effect upon the efficiency of the industry as measured by real costs. Finally, the products of the industry remained substantially the same in character during the sixty years under consideration. It is reasonable, therefore, to assume that the relations between the size and efficiency of the industry during this period approximate closely to the normal.

To return after this digression to the values for the elasticity of return shown in the table. The rate of fall of real costs between 1865 and 1868, as measured by the seven years' moving average of the real price index numbers, is influenced by the War figures and is therefore too high. The true value for the

---

[1] For the whole of this summary see the article by Mr Edward Stanwood in the *United States Census of Manufactures* 1900, vol. IX, pp. 43, 44. Mr Stanwood also sketches the development of cotton textile machinery up to 1900.

elasticity of return during this period is probably nearer 2 than 1¼. If this correction be accepted it appears that the elasticity of return was approximately 2 during the thirty-five years 1865–1900, the only breaks being in 1874–6 when real costs fell fourteen points in three years and in 1886–90 when there was a temporary check to the fall of real costs.[1] In short, an increase of 2 % in the size of the industry was generally accompanied by a fall of 1 % in the real cost of manufacture. If this is a measure of the net economies to be expected as the markets for the products of such industries (i.e. resembling cotton manufacture in New England (1865–1900) in their nature and stage of development) expand, it is a most interesting figure, giving us an idea of the strength of the tendency to increasing returns in a typical complex factory industry.

It is difficult to probe into the detailed relation between changes in costs and the expansion of the industry, for the only continuous measures of changes in size available are the seven years' moving averages of cotton consumed in the United States and of cotton taken by spinners in the northern states. In so far, however, as these series move in the same direction as would the seven years' moving average of cotton consumed in Massachusetts, they throw interesting light upon the relation between the efficiency of the industry and the physical volume of production (i.e. the normal output or average of seven years). It appears from comparison of the curve of real costs with the curve of active spindles in Massachusetts (quinquennial census figures) that a check to the fall of real costs is accompanied *pari passu* by a check to the expansion of plants as shown by the increase in the number of spindles (and looms) in operation. On the other hand, all the evidence suggests that the check to the normal output of the industry (as measured by the trend of cotton consumed) lags behind the check to the fall of real costs, e.g. the rate of fall of real costs fell to 1 % per annum in 1876–80,

---

[1] About 1874–6 all prices, including money wages, were falling very rapidly, yet output increased steadily. It is possible that manufacturers had to accept an abnormally low profit under these conditions and that this in turn stimulated economy. Both circumstances would tend to accelerate the fall in the index of real cost. Cf. footnote 2 on p. 212 where a similar explanation of the temporary check in 1886–90 is put forward.

but the corresponding check to normal output occurred about five years later.

Improvements in efficiency were again checked and real costs rose a little in 1887-9, but the corresponding check to normal output was delayed until 1890 to 1894. Finally, real costs rose in 1901 and 1902, yet the corresponding fall of output in Massachusetts came in 1903 and 1904. One is tempted to generalise, arguing that a check to the expansion of plant slows up the rate of improvement of the industry, which, in turn, leads to the loss of markets which would have been open if the rate of improvement had been maintained, but it is difficult to be sure that the small fluctuations observed are not due to elements of quasi-rent which have not been eliminated by taking a seven years' moving average, e.g. in 1889 when real costs rose sharply to a maximum, the seven years' moving averages of cotton consumed in the United States and of cotton taken by spinners also touched maxima. Indeed, some of the detailed relations of the curve of real costs to the trend of cotton consumed are best explained upon the assumption that, with a given organisation of the industry in respect to plant, etc., efficiency varies inversely as the volume of production within the limits of the fluctuations of the seven years' moving average of cotton consumed.[1]

The index numbers relating to the average size of establishments provide interesting comparisons. Allowance must be made for the fact that some censuses (e.g. 1899 and 1909) were taken in years of boom and others (e.g. 1884 and 1904) in years of depression, so that the index numbers of wage earners and output per establishment (and to a slight extent active spindles per establishment) based upon the census returns fluctuate about the trend. Still the broad indications are clear: between 1840-5 and 1910-14 the average number of wage earners per establishment increased about eight or nine times, the number of spindles per establishment multiplied twenty times, or more than twice as fast as the number of wage earners, while the physical volume of production per establishment increased thirty times. Taking the period as a whole, therefore, the rates of increase of workers : plant : output are approximately as 1 : 2 : 3. This relation

[1] Cf. p. 215, n. 1 above.

between spindles and output is a much more satisfactory guide to changes in the efficiency[1] of cotton textile machinery than the quantity of cotton consumed per spindle given by the census. The figures for output (physical volume of production) are computed by multiplying the number of wage earners by their effectiveness in the manufacture of a constant quality of cloth (regular print cloth and standard brown sheetings), and are therefore free from complications due to changes in the fineness of the goods produced. It is true that mills spinning and weaving coarse goods require *ceteris paribus* more opening, carding and weaving machinery than fine mills, but, on the other hand, the finer mills are likely to be equipped with every modern convenience and with better machinery for finishing and packing; the number of spindles, therefore, though not a perfect guide in this respect, is a fairly good measure of the capital equipment of an establishment. Expressed as a percentage of the ratio for 1879, output per spindle in Massachusetts was about 80 at the beginning of our period (1840–55) but rose to 90 before the Civil War; during the war it fell to 50 and did not fully recover until about 1875; cyclical fluctuations make the ratio high in 1879 and low in 1884, but in 1890 to 1895 it was about 95 and had risen to 110 in 1909–14; in 1919 it was 143. The quantity of cotton consumed per spindle, on the other hand, reached a maximum in 1900 and has tended to decline during the last twenty years.[2]

The index numbers of output per establishment are infrequent and subject to considerable variations according to the prosperity of the industry in the census years, so that it is impossible to discover how far the fall of real costs indicated by my index numbers was due to internal and how far to external economies. The evidence suggests, however, that Dr Marshall was correct in his view that the size of the representative firm tends to increase *pari passu* with the expansion of the industry. Over the

---

[1] Efficiency is here strained somewhat to indicate the ratio between quantity of machinery or plant and the physical volume of the product; perhaps the word effectiveness, used later in the text, would be better for the purpose.

[2] Cf. articles in the successive censuses of manufacture, especially: 1900, vol. IX, pp. 48–50; 1905, Pt III, pp. 43, 44; 1909, vol. X, pp. 58–9.

whole period there has been a strong tendency for the size of the manufacturing unit to increase, but the rapidity of this expansion has varied in sympathy with changes in the rate of growth of the industry.

Dr M. T. Copeland[1] discusses the technical developments of American cotton manufacture between 1860 and 1912 in great detail; he also describes the changes taking place in the organisation both of manufacture and marketing during this period. As there is nothing abnormal[2] in the story I shall conclude with a comparison of the results obtained in this study with those obtained for the Lancashire cotton industry. The most obvious and most important feature of this comparison is brought out clearly in the chart, where the two curves of real costs 1850–1910 are plotted together. Both are remarkably smooth, being free from the influence of price changes, but the American curve has an average downward slope five times as steep as the British from 1870 to 1900. The values for the elasticity of returns in the two countries, however, fall much closer together: in the decades 1850–60 and 1870–80 the elasticity of return in the Lancashire cotton industry (as calculated from the rate of fall of real costs) was 5, in Massachusetts 5 and 2 respectively. The corresponding figures for the decade 1890–1900 were Lancashire 2, Massachusetts 2⅓. It appears that, in general, one cannot expect a fall of more than ½ % in real costs to result from 1 % increase in the size of cotton manufacturing industries even in modern industrialised communities, i.e. the rate of return increases only half as fast as the industry expands.

---

[1] *The Cotton Manufacturing Industry*, chap. iv.

[2] One point mentioned by Copeland (*loc. cit.* chap. ix) is perhaps of interest; all the attempts to secure monopoly profits by combination occurred during the decade 1900–10 when real costs were steady after reaching a minimum in 1900.

PART VI

THE AMERICAN PIG IRON
INDUSTRY 1883–1925

§ 1. INTRODUCTION

THE technical revolution in the manufacture of pig iron in the United States, which was initiated by the introduction of anthracite coal as a fuel about 1840, was succeeded by equally fundamental changes in the smelting process with the substitution of coke (made from bituminous coal) for anthracite.[1] In 1883 the quantity of pig iron made with bituminous coal (or coke) exceeded one-half of the total production of the United States, and iron made from anthracite and charcoal has continued to decline in relative importance since that date.[2] One may say broadly that the principles of modern American blast-furnace practice had already been widely introduced in 1883; the quantity of anthracite and charcoal iron produced remained much the same until the financial crisis of 1907, but the expansion of the industry since 1880 has been due entirely to the development of coke smelting and the prices of coke-made iron have dominated the market. In short, those substantive inventions (e.g. the hot and cold high pressure air blast, the use of waste gases to heat boilers, etc.) which made modern smelting practice possible, had already become public property[3] when the period chosen for study opens, so that subsequent economies may be attributed largely to the normal growth of the industry.

[1] Cf. *Tenth United States Census* 1880—Manufactures: Iron and Steel, by J. M. Swank. Part II of this Report is devoted to the history of the industry and pp. 113–19 are devoted to the transient growth of anthracite smelting and the development of the modern coke process.

[2] *Annual Statistical Report of the American Iron and Steel Institute for* 1925, p. 9, gives the production of pig iron by fuels 1860–1925. Compare also *Twelfth United States Census*, vol. x, p. 42, where the changes in the relative importance of the different fuels are analysed in some detail.

[3] Cf. *Tenth United States Census* 1880—Manufactures: Iron and Steel, by J. M. Swank, pp. 131–2.

There are important differences, rising from conditions peculiar to the particular localities, in blast-furnace practice in the several regions of the United States,[1] but all the markets for pig iron, ore and fuel are closely connected and are dominated respectively by the prices quoted for pig iron at Pittsburgh, Lake Superior ores, f.o.b. Lake Erie dock, Connellsville coke, f.o.b. cars at the coking furnaces of the Connellsville region of Pennsylvania. Moreover Illinois, Pennsylvania and Ohio (three states lying close together in the region lying between Lake Superior and the east coast) accounted for nearly 70 % of the pig iron produced in the United States even in 1880, and their share exceeded 75 % by 1900.[2] Money wages differ appreciably in the different regions, but the important changes have affected all alike, so that it is possible to treat the production of pig iron in the United States as a single industry.

The progress of horizontal and vertical integration in the iron and steel industry since the beginning of the century invalidates the prices of steel and iron rails, etc., as a measure of competitive value (and therefore cost of production), but the attempts of the United States Steel Corporation to control pig iron prices have failed, the number of independent producers being too large to permit of effective monopoly.[3] Moreover sufficient pig iron is still sold in the open market to give a basis for valuation of the total product. In 1904 only 60 % of the pig iron made was

[1] *Twelfth United States Census* 1900, vol. x, pp. 20–21, where the facilities of the different states for the production of pig iron are analysed and the sources from which their deficiencies are made good indicated.

[2] *Twelfth United States Census*, vol. x, pp. 36, 37. Cf. also pp. 6 and 7 where the value of the iron and steel products of the different regions is analysed.

[3] Cf. *Eleventh Special Report of the United States Bureau of Labour Statistics* (1904) *upon the Regulation and Restriction of Output,* chap. iii, Iron and Steel, p. 235: "There have been formed at different times several pig iron associations which have in the course of time disappeared, the Southern Pig Iron Association being the most recent of this list. The Pig Iron Association of the Mahoning and Shenango valleys, a combination of independent furnaces which sell their product to the United States Steel Corporation, is effectively maintained with a common selling agency. Recently this association decided to shut down all furnaces for a period of 30 days in order to prevent the accumulation of stock." This is the strongest statement of monopoly price fixing of pig iron practice I have found. As we shall see later the policy enjoyed only transient success and that under abnormal conditions.

consumed in works owned by the company producing it; by 1914 the proportion had risen almost to 67 % and in 1919 to 71 %.[1] A substantial proportion of the fuel and ore used is also produced by firms independent of the smelting companies, so that significant market prices are also obtainable for the principal materials consumed in the manufacture of pig iron. Finally, the United States Census of Manufactures has published separate statistics for the blast-furnace branch of the iron and steel industry.[2] At the census of 1880 the resources engaged in mining and allied occupations in connection with blast furnaces were unintentionally included in the blast-furnace returns, so that comparison of subsequent census figures with the returns for 1880 is difficult. In 1919 the ferro-alloys, which had previously been grouped with pig iron under the general title of blast-furnace products, were assigned to a separate group, but the value of the ferro-alloys produced in 1919 was less than 1 % of the value of the pig iron produced, so the pig-iron statistics are left almost unaffected by the change.[3]

In short the smelting of iron ore in the United States constitutes one process in the manufacturing operations of many large integrated concerns, but the data available permit a study of this process as a separate industry. Moreover, the connections between the several important pig iron producing regions in the United States are so intimate that the country is the most suitable geographical unit for statistical investigations.

I proceed, therefore, to describe the calculation of index numbers showing changes in the real costs of smelting iron ore in the United States between 1885 and 1910. As in the other studies I have carried the calculations through the War period and brought them up to date where possible, but the index numbers obtained require very careful interpretation after 1914.

---

[1] *Fourteenth United States Census* 1920, vol. x, p. 316.
[2] There is no duplication in the returns for blast furnaces taken as a separate industry, but double counting introduces serious errors into the aggregate for the iron and steel industry. Cf. *Twelfth United States Census*, vol. x, p. 21.
[3] The present biennial census (1921, 1923, ...) has returned to the practice of including the ferro-alloys with ordinary pig iron.

§ 2. THE INDEX NUMBERS OF PRICES AND COSTS

I. *Selling price.*

The selling-price index[1] is based upon the price of the composite pig iron "devised by the *American Metal Market and Daily Iron and Steel Report* to show at a glance the bulk movement of all pig iron" sold in America: it is made up as follows:

1 ton Bessemer, valley ⎫ i.e. Pittsburgh prices
2 tons basic, valley ⎭
1 ton No. 2 foundry, valley
1 ton No. 2X foundry, Philadelphia
1 ton No. 2X foundry, Buffalo
1 ton No. 2 foundry, Cleveland
1 ton No. 2 foundry, Chicago
2 tons No. 2 southern foundry, Cincinnati

Total 10 tons

The annual average price of this composite since 1890 is given in current issues of *Metal Statistics*, an annual statistical abstract published by the American metal market. It will be noticed that six out of the eight constituent prices are for foundry irons, since the bulk of the iron sold in the open market is of that kind; nevertheless the index reflects changes in the value of pig iron used for making steel as well as forge and foundry, since the different sorts are often produced in the same establishment and furnaces can readily be adapted to deliver different sorts of pig iron.

Many of the constituent prices of the metal market composite are not available prior to 1890, so the price index has been extended by use of the simpler average:

1 ton Bessemer at Pittsburgh
1 ton Gray Forge, lake ore, at Pittsburgh
1 ton Gray Forge at Philadelphia

The statistical abstract of the United States contains records of the average annual prices of these items based upon the weekly quotations published in *The Iron Age*. However, the Bessemer series does not begin until 1886, and I have been unable to find figures for 1883–6 elsewhere. I have therefore computed

---

[1] Appendix v, Table I, columns 1, 2.

for each of the years 1883-6 the average of the quotations for Bessemer pig iron per gross ton, four months delivery, at Pittsburgh given in *The Iron Age* the first week of each calendar month, and used these to complete the series in the statistical abstract.

In 1890-2 the average prices per ton of pig iron computed from the two composites were as follows:

	Average of 8 items	Average of 3 items
1890	$17.00	$16.82
1891	$14.82	$14·84
1892	$13.48	$13·57

I have therefore joined the two series in 1891 by taking the mean of the two averages as the index price for 1891, and expressing the entire series 1883-1925 as a percentage of the average price of the metal-market composite in 1913.

II. *Materials.*

(a) *Fuel.*[1] *Metal Statistics* records the average price of Connellsville coke annually from 1880. The table is compiled by the local business paper, the *Connellsville Courier*, and the prices, it is claimed, are representative of the Connellsville and Lower Connellsville region; they are quoted f.o.b. at the ovens per net ton of 2000 pounds and refer to all grades of coke shipped from the region during the year. There are considerable differences between the prices of the various grades[2] (e.g. foundry coke costs about $1.00 more per ton than furnace coke), but there have been no appreciable changes in the average quality of the coke produced in the Connellsville region, so that the series may safely be used to measure changes in the cost of fuel to American ironmasters.[3]

---

[1] Appendix v, Table I, columns 3, 4.
[2] During the War the prices of the different kinds of coke fluctuated violently relative one to another, but all followed the same trend. Prices for prompt delivery also fluctuate more violently and are higher than the average prices.
[3] Writing in the *Tenth United States Census* 1880, J. M. Swank estimated that "fully one third of the annual production of pig iron in this country is made with this fuel" (Iron and Steel, p. 132), and the Connellsville region still supplies about the same proportion of the fuel used.

(b) *Ores*.[1] The *Iron Trade Review*, a local business paper of high standing, has for many years supplied the prices of Lake Superior ores recorded in the *Annual Reports of the American Iron and Steel Association*, etc. *Metal Statistics* carries a tabular statement of the annual average prices of the different kinds of ore, so far as available, back to 1885; I have supplemented this series from the early reports of the Iron and Steel Association and thus obtained the following series of average annual prices:

> Old Range ores: Bessemer 1885–
> Non-Bessemer 1883–
> Mesabi Range ores: Bessemer 1894–
> Non-Bessemer 1894–

Prior to 1900 the prices quoted are the average paid for the grades of ore most commonly produced in these regions and we are warned that "Particularly 1894–9 some grades sold at materially higher prices".[2] Early in the present century it became customary to base prices upon standard ores, and since 1905 the standards prevailing have been regulated by the Lake Superior Iron Ore Association. The base first adopted by this association was the one already customary and approximated to the grades of ore commonly mined in this area during the last quarter of the nineteenth century. The natural iron contents of the first standards were approximately:

> | | (%) |
> |---|---|
> | Bessemer ... ... | 56·70 |
> | Non-Bessemer ... ... | 52·80 |

These were changed before the sales for 1907 were made to a natural iron content

> | | (%) |
> |---|---|
> | Bessemer ... ... | 55·0[3] |
> | Non-Bessemer ... ... | 51·5 |

so as to represent the market more closely. Fortunately the *Annual Statistical Report of the American Iron and Steel Asso-*

---

[1] Appendix v, Table I, columns 5, 6, 7.

[2] Cf. *Statistical Report of American Iron and Steel Institute for 1925*, p. 92, which quotes prices for Lake Superior ore, 1893–1926, which are identical with those of the *Metal Statistics* from 1905 onwards, but differ appreciably in some earlier years.

[3] In 1925 the natural iron content of the Bessemer standard was reduced to 51·5 %, i.e. the same as the non-Bessemer.

ciation for 1907 (p. 29) quotes prices for the old standard grades
to correspond to the prices actually fixed for the new base ores:

		Old standard	New standard
Old Range:	Bessemer	$5.15	$5.00
	Non-Bessemer	$4.30	$4.20
Mesabi:	Bessemer	$4.90	$4.75
	Non-Bessemer	$4.10	$4.00

which enables me to effect a splice between the two series. In
the report for 1903[1] it is remarked that there was an effective
agreement between buyers and sellers of Old Range ores from
1895 or 1896 to 1904, but that Mesabi prices were only affected
by this agreement in one or two years. I have, therefore, spliced
Mesabi and Old Range prices in 1894 and based the index
numbers upon Mesabi prices alone from that date.

The series of index numbers thus obtained is probably a good
measure of changes in the supply price of ore of a given quality
to ironmasters, since the great bulk of iron ore consumed in the
United States is drawn from the Lake Superior region, e.g. in
1919 the shipments of lake ore exceeded 48,000,000 tons gross
compared with a total consumption of about 55,000,000 tons of
ore in the United States.[2] In the twenty years, 1883-1903, the
index numbers may be subject to variations due to changes in
the quality of the ore upon which they are based, but the error
is probably small since the average quality of the ore mined in
these ranges did not change greatly while the prices used have
been tabulated for comparative purposes.

III. *Labour*.[3]

As in the British study one is compelled to employ an index
of changes in hourly wages as a measure of changes in the supply
price or cost of labour to the ironmaster. The United States
Bureau of Labour Statistics has published data relating to

---

[1] *Loc. cit.* p. 45.

[2] Cf. *Annual Statistics Report of the American Iron and Steel Institute for*
1925, p. 61, where a tabular statement is made of all ore produced in the
United States annually 1889-1925. In 1889, 51·79 % of all the ore produced
in the country was mined in the Lake Superior district; the proportion rose
rapidly reaching a maximum of 85·94 % in 1919.

[3] Appendix v, Table I, column 8.

earnings in the "principal distinctive wage working occupations" of the iron smelting industry for one representative pay period in each year since 1890, except 1916, 1918, 1921, 1923 and 1925. From 1890 to 1907 the blast furnace occupations covered are five—cinder snappers, hot blast men, keepers, keepers-helpers and top-fillers.[1] *Bulletin* No. 77, July 1908, p. 130, presents an index number of the relative wages per hour of blast furnacemen, 1890–1907, computed by the chain method in order to utilise all the data from the varying number of establishments making returns. Even in 1890, however, data were obtained from sixteen to eighteen establishments and by 1907 the number had risen from twenty-five to twenty-six, so that the group of plants making returns may be regarded as representative after that date and the chain method discarded. The later bulletins distinguish about a dozen principal blast furnace occupations, and in the most recent *Bulletin* (p. 4) the average earnings per hour of workers in these principal occupations are reduced to percentages of the average for 1913. By splicing these two series I obtain the desired index of changes in the average hourly wages of workers in the principal blast furnace occupations since 1890. It is true that the index numbers refer to a changing group of workers, but the relative importance of the different occupations has not changed very much so that this error is small.

There are no comprehensive data in accessible form relating to the wages of blast furnacemen previous to 1890. The *Aldrich Report*[2] has one series for foremen and one for journeymen in a single establishment, 1850–91, and the various State Bureaux of Labour have wage material scattered through their annual reports, but it is discontinuous and inadequate. Fortunately "what the puddler receives in earnings affords a basis from which to rate the wages of every branch of labour engaged in the production of iron".[3] In his book *The Iron Age*, second edition, pp. 498–9, Mr J. M. Swank states that the prices paid for boiling

[1] For a description of the various occupations of workers in the iron and steel industry see *Bulletin* No. 218, Glossary of Occupations, pp. 467–526; the blast furnace department is dealt with on pp. 467–75.

[2] *Report* from Senate Committee on Finance upon "Wholesale Prices, Wages, and Transportation", March 3, 1893, Part I, p. 150.

[3] *Annual Report of Ohio Bureau of Labour Statistics*, 1892, p. 117.

(puddling) iron at Pittsburgh and Philadelphia were adjusted by a uniform scale from 1881 to 1892 save for a slight agreed change in the rate of fluctuation on the Pittsburgh scale. "The Pittsburgh schedule prevails", says Mr Swank, "in the western part of the United States and the Philadelphia schedule is fairly representative of the wages paid in the eastern mills." Moreover the two scales moved in close sympathy between 1880 and 1890, and the work involved in puddling iron did not change appreciably, so that the prices paid for boiling iron at Pittsburgh may be used as an index of changes in the efficiency wages of blast furnacemen from 1880-90. From 1880 to 1892 this price was $5.50 per ton except for a short period in 1885-7. The average price paid in 1886 was $5.00 per ton, and in 1885 and 1887 $5.25.[1] The wage changes indicated are confirmed by the scattered information in the state labour reports. By extending the index numbers of average hourly wages based upon the bulletins of the United States Bureau of Labour Statistics according to the price paid for boiling iron at Pittsburgh I obtain a continuous index number of the efficiency wages of blast furnacemen from 1883.

IV. *The Weighting of the factors.*

The United States census reports enable one to compute the proportion of the receipts of the industry going to pay for the different factors of production in 1889, 1899, 1904, 1909, 1914 and 1919. I have weighted the coke series according to the amount spent upon all fuels and the ore series by the cost of all iron ores, scrap iron, mill cinder, scale, slag, etc., while I have included in labour costs the amounts returned as salaries as well as wages since the two were not fully separated at the earlier censuses, and are in any case closely allied. I have estimated the weight appropriate to labour in 1885 from the returns of wages paid and value of products made by 121 blast furnace establishments in Pennsylvania as reported in the *Annual Labour Statistics* of that state for 1885 (about half the pig iron made in the country about that time was smelted in Pennsylvania and the ratio of wages to selling price was much the same as the

---

[1] *Annual Report of Ohio Bureau of Labour Statistics*, 1892, p. 162.

average for the country). Finally I have based my weights upon the returns for the entire industry (coke, anthracite, and charcoal) in spite of the fact that separate statistics are available for furnaces operating upon mineral fuel in the earlier census reports. However, I have brought the weights appropriate to this branch into comparison with the weights actually used in the tables which follow. It will be observed that the differences are slight, and as Connellsville coke is used as an index of changes in the price of all fuels, my procedure is justified.

There follows a detailed statement of the weights assigned to the different price series in obtaining the index numbers of real cost:

(a) *Labour—the efficiency wage series.* Weighted according to the proportion of receipts going to pay salaries and wages, viz.:

Date	% of selling price, i.e. % of value of products at the census[1]	Wages and salaries per 6½ tons of pig iron, i.e. the amount in the selling price index	
		At current wages	At 1913 wage rates
1885	13·0	13·7	18·5
1889	11·2 (11·0)	11·9	15·4
1899	10·0 (10·0)	11·2	14·7
1904	8·0	8·4	10·1
1909	9·1	8·0	7·9
1919	11·0	21·4	8·5
1921	10·0	—	—
1923	7·1	—	—
1925	—	—	—

Hence by interpolation figures are obtained for the cost of labour at 1913 wage rates required to produce the 6½ tons of pig iron contained in the selling price index in each year from 1883 to 1925 as shown in Appendix V, Table II, column 6, and thence the cost at current wage rates (column 5) is obtained by multiplying by the wages index numbers.

(b) *Coke—Connellsville courier prices.* Weighted according to cost of all fuel used, whether in smelting or for raising steam.

---

[1] The figures in brackets refer to the production of pig iron from mineral fuel only—see *Twelfth United States Census*, 1900, vol. X, pp. 43–5.

Date	% of selling price[1]	Cost of quantity used per 6¼ tons of pig iron	
		At current prices	At 1913 prices
1879	24·6 (23·8)	40·8	67·2
1889	26·0 (24·8)	27·6	61·3
1899	21·4 (20·7)	24·0	35·3
1904	27·0	23·5	39·8
1909	27·7	29·0	42·7
1914	27·9	25·4	37·4
1919	29·7	57·6	36·2

The gaps have been filled by interpolation as in the case of labour, *vide* Appendix v, Table II, columns 3 and 4. Note that a part of the fall in the weight given to coke between 1889 and 1899 is due to a change in the method of valuation. Prior to 1899 all materials were valued at the furnace and thus all freight was included but since that date only a part of the freight has been counted in cost of coke and ore.

(c) *Ore—Lake Superior prices.* Weighted according to the cost of all ore, scrap, cinder, scale and slag consumed in the furnaces.

Date	% of selling price[2]	Cost of ore in 6¼ tons of pig iron	
		At current prices	At 1913 prices
1889	45·8 (47·8)	48·6	48·1
1899	33·7 (34·7)	37·8	47·6*
1904	45·2	39·3	52·5*
1909	49·4	51·9	50·4
1914	49·6	43·6	51·9
1919	44·5	86·4	55·4

* In these years the price of ore changed so rapidly that it was necessary to use the mean of the prices for the year quoted and the next year in order to cover the census period more accurately.

Ore prices fluctuate so violently and the quantity of ore used has changed so little that I have thought it best to use a constant weight; assuming that the cost at 1913 prices equals approximately 50 throughout the period, I have, therefore, reduced the selling price of ore to the base 1913 = 50[3] and used this as an index of changes in the cost of ore consumed in the production

[1] Brackets refer to the mineral fuel branch of the industry.
[2] Brackets refer to the mineral fuel branch of the industry.
[3] Appendix v, Table II, column 2.

of the $6\frac{1}{2}$ tons of pig iron constituting the selling price index. $50.00 of lake ore at 1913 prices would weigh $13\frac{1}{4}$ tons and contain about 7 tons of iron so that my estimate allows for 7 % waste in smelting.

(d) *Other expenses.* As in the cotton study I have used Mr Carl Snyder's index of general prices as applicable to the margin left over the expense of labour and materials.[1] This margin averages about 15 % of turnover of which some 5 % is required to meet other expenses in the accountant's sense of the term and 10 % to cover normal gross profit.[2] The returns of total capital invested in the industry are more satisfactory for iron and steel than for many other industries. It appears that capital is turned over on an average from one to one and a half times a year,[3] which makes an interesting comparison with Sir Hugh Bell's estimate of once a year for the British heavy iron and steel industries.

V. *The calculation of the index numbers of real cost.*

I have now completed the history of Appendix v, Table II. The index numbers of real price have been derived from the selling price index numbers by adding the algebraic sum of the differentials between the cost of the various factors at the

---

[1] Appendix v, Table I, column 9, and Table II, columns 7, 8.

[2] The amounts returned for expenses (i.e. broadly manufacturer's current outlay) were analysed in the *Thirteenth United States Census*, 1910, vol. x, p. 213 as follows:

% of total reported expenses of blast furnaces represented by

Date	Salaries	Wages	Materials	Miscellaneous expenses
1909	1·8	6·8	88·4	3·0
1904	1·4	9·0	85·0	4·6
1899	1·4	11·6	82·3	4·7

" Miscellaneous expenses comprise the amount paid for rent of works, power and heat, local taxes, rent of offices, interest, insurance, internal revenue tax and stamps, ordinary repairs to buildings and machinery, advertising, contract work, and sundry expenses of all kinds not elsewhere reported." *Twelfth United States Census*, 1900, vol. x, p. 4.

[3] The actual rates of turnover at the censuses 1880 to 1920 were:

1879	1·00	1904	1·02
1889	1·08	1909	1·25
1899	1·35	1914	1·45
		1919	1·01

prices prevailing in 1913 and their cost at the prices current in the year to which the index number refers. Having obtained the annual index numbers of real price I have estimated their trend by taking a five years' moving average; these centred moving averages I call the index numbers of real cost.

Appendix v, Table III, columns 1–4, therefore presents the following series of index numbers:

(1) The selling price of composite pig iron:
    (*a*) Annual averages 1883–1920.
    (*b*) Five years' moving average 1885–1918.

(2) The same corrected for changes in the supply price of fuel, ore, and labour and other expenses:
    (*a*) Annual averages 1883–1915 (i.e. real price of pig iron).
    (*b*) Five years' moving average 1885–1913 (i.e. real cost of pig iron).

VI. *Statistical errors in the index numbers of real cost.*

(*a*) *Prices.* There is nothing to guide one in estimating the accuracy of the price series used in computing the index numbers of real cost. However, the series for pig iron, coke and ore are taken from the largest markets in the country and refer directly to the varieties commonly used, while the wage investigations of the United States Bureau of Labour Statistics have been carefully conducted with the purpose of obtaining a record of the trend of wages in the country as a whole. The cost of other fuels (anthracite, charcoal, etc.) may have varied considerably relative to coke prices but the latter undoubtedly form a good measure of changes in the average cost of fuel to ironmasters. Upon the whole an allowance of 5 % for error in each constituent price series seems adequate. If superimposed these errors would vitiate the index of real costs by 10 %, but the net error in the index of real costs due to faulty price series is probably not greater than 3 % or 4 % even in the early years.

(*b*) *Weighting.* Comparison with the special reports covering the production of pig iron from mineral fuel at the earlier census (1880–1900) suggests that my distribution of expenses leaves labour slightly overweighted, coke overweighted, and ore under-weighted but in no case do the weights attributed to any factor err by 5 %. Errors in the weighting of these distinctive factors of production cause opposite errors in the margin left to cover other expenses; the net errors in the index numbers of real cost are likely, therefore, to be greatest when the relative movement between the prices of these factors and the general price index used to correct the margin is at the maximum for the period—in this case 1887 having regard to the sense of the errors in weighting. I shall, therefore, estimate the net error in the index numbers of real price for 1887 which would be introduced by an error of 5 % in the weights given to each factor, supposing the weights given to labour and fuel to be too large and the weight given to ore too small.

Overweighting the correction for changes in wages by 5 % would not affect the index number of real price appreciably in 1887.

Overweighting the correction for changes in the price of fuel by 5 % would raise the index number of real price in 1887 about $1\cdot3 - \cdot8 = \cdot5$ points.

Underweighting the correction for changes in the supply price of ore by 5 % would raise the index number of real price in 1887 about $\cdot7 + 1\cdot2 = 2$ points approximately.

The net error in the real price for 1887 due to faulty weighting of corrections is thus $2\frac{1}{2}$ points, i.e. about 2 %.

As in the case of cotton, therefore, we may conclude that the statistical operations result in index numbers of real price 1883-1913, and real cost 1885-1910, which are probably within 5 % or 6 % of their defined values but, as we shall see in the conclusion, elements of quasi-rent make it difficult to interpret these index numbers in terms of the resources consumed in the production of pig iron.

§ 3. THE SIZE OF THE INDUSTRY AND OF THE OPERATING UNITS

I. *The size of the industry.*

The data relating to the growth of the American iron industry are very satisfactory. The quantity of pig iron produced annually is an excellent measure of output and the American Iron and Steel Institute (and its predecessor the Association) has collected data upon the production of pig iron in the United States annually during the whole of our period; the totals are reproduced in the Appendix v, Table III, column 5, and the five years' centred moving average is entered in column 6. The data contained in Appendix v, Table IV, relating to active and idle blast furnaces in the United States are also collected by the Iron and Steel Institute. Taken together these two series provide an excellent guide to the expansion of the American blast furnace industry.

Size of blast furnace establishments by average number of wage earners in the United States, 1909–19

Wage earners (inclusive)	Year		1909	1914	1919
1–5	Establishments	...	2	3	1
	Wage earners	...	7	12	4
6–20	Establishments	...	9	11	12
	Wage earners	...	118	143	152
21–50	Establishments	...	26	12	15
	Wage earners	...	988	465	544
51–100	Establishments	...	52	40	45
	Wage earners	...	4,094	3,034	3,424
101–250	Establishments	...	74	61	71
	Wage earners	...	11,958	10,016	10,902
251–500	Establishments	...	31	20	31
	Wage earners	...	10,496	6,266	10,313
501–1000	Establishments	...	13	12	17
	Wage earners	...	9,241	8,157	11,842
Over 1000	Establishments	...	1	1	3
	Wage earners	...	1,527	1,263	4,479
Total	Establishments	...	208	160	195
	Wage earners	...	38,429	29,356	41,660

II. *The size of the firms engaged in the industry.*

(*a*) *The manufacturing unit—the establishment.* The separation of the smelting process from the later stages of steel manufacture appears most artificial when one considers the growth of the manufacturing unit. However, most integrated iron and steel works organise their blast furnaces as a separate department, and the census statistics relating to the size of blast furnace establishments are of interest if one remembers that many of the so-called establishments are but single departments of large works.

The table on p. 233 shows the distribution of establishments according to the number of wage earners in 1909, 1914, 1919. As in cotton manufacture the modal size lies between 100 and 250 wage earners. The distribution shows a tendency towards larger establishments, but its general character remains unchanged, the frequency curve having a marked skew to the right.[1]

Dr Willard Thorp has worked up the census material relating to the growth in the average size of blast furnace establishments between 1869 and 1923. This tabular statement is reproduced in Appendix v, Table V, and calls for little comment beyond Dr Thorp's remarks:

In this branch of the iron and steel industry the trend towards concentration has been in existence for 50 years...the outstanding development is the enormous increase in output per establishment, which was at a rate nearly eleven times as great as the rate of increase in number of wage earners per establishment during the same period. The much greater increase in product than in wage earners is the result of the introduction of labour saving machinery, notably the use of pig casting machines in place of sand casting, and improvements in general charging devices and in ore-handling machines for stocking and charging.[2]

It will be noticed that the rate of increase of output per establishment, though rapid, has been diminishing since 1890 and fell with great rapidity after 1910. If the abnormal expansion

---

[1] The census has also classified establishments according to value of products since 1909. Before the War over 85 % of the pig iron produced in the United States was smelted in establishments reporting an annual turnover in excess of one million dollars on account of their blast furnace departments alone. In 1919 this class made 97 % of the pig iron produced in the country.

[2] "The Integration of Industrial Operation"—*Census Monograph*, iii, p. 59.

of production in 1914–18 be neglected it appears that, broadly speaking, output per establishment increased at a rather greater rate than the total quantity of pig iron produced between 1880 and 1920, but that the growth of the manufacturing unit was accelerated or checked by the corresponding changes in the rate of expansion of the industry.

(*b*) *The size of the unit of control.* It would require a special study to trace out the ramifications of interlocking directorates and other financial ties between the different companies engaged in the iron and steel industry.[1] However, I have already argued that the United States Steel Corporation and other combines have been unable so far to control the market price of pig iron as they did the price of steel rails for many years. The following table taken from the census of manufactures shows the extent to which blast furnaces are situated in establishments producing pig iron as an intermediate rather than final product of the plant.

Pig iron production for consumption 1919, 1914, 1909, 1904

	% of total			
	1919	1914	1909	1904
Establishments	100·0	100·0	100·0	100·0
Producing for consumption	44·5	40·0	27·4	27·4
Producing for sale	55·5	60·0	72·6	72·6
Pig iron production	100·0	100·0	100·0	100·0
For consumption in works of company producing	71·0	66·6	61·8	59·7
Consumed by steel works and rolling mills during the year	69·3	65·4	59·5	—
Balance for foundries, etc.	1·7	1·2	2·3	—
For sale	29·0	33·4	38·2	40·3
Purchased by steel works and rolling mills during the year	9·0	9·5	14·9	13·6
Balance for foundries, etc.	20·0	23·9	23·3	26·7

It appears that more than one-third of the pig iron annually produced was sold in the market before the War; at the beginning

---

[1] Mr William G. Gray writing in the *Twelfth United States Census*, 1900, vol. x, p. 8, states that many consolidations took place between 1890 and 1900, and in 1900 fourteen companies owned or operated 136 blast furnaces controlling 54 % of the total capacity of the country.

of our period (1883) the proportion sold probably exceeded one-half.

Finally Dr Thorp has investigated the development of "central office groups" in iron and steel manufacture (among other industries). In 1919 8 % of the establishments in the industrial group "iron and steel and their products" were in central-office combinations; the average number of establishments per central-office group was 3·44 but the three largest groups each controlled between 26 and 50 establishments[1]; while there is no reason to suspect that great monopoly power is being exercised in pig iron production it is clear that the vertical integration of the iron and steel industry is proceeding rapidly and the separation of the smelting from the converting of iron is becoming highly artificial.

§4. PROVISIONAL CONCLUSIONS

The data as to output and costs are plotted on Diagram VI. The scale of this diagram, it will be seen, is smaller than that of preceding diagrams.

The form of the constituent price series prevents one from drawing conclusions concerning changes in the real price of pig iron during the trade cycle from the movements of the annual index numbers of selling price corrected for changes in the supply prices of the factors of production. One can only remark (a) that the corrected price appears to be a better index of the prosperity of the industry than the uncorrected selling price, (b) that the real price of pig iron frequently reaches a minimum in depression before the selling price because the prices of ore, coke, etc., anticipate the market for pig iron, and (c) that the period of the trade cycle in this industry varies from about three years to six years, five years being the most frequent between 1883 and 1913, (d) there is a rough correspondence between the

---

[1] *Census Monograph*, III, Part II, the figures are taken from Tables XLIII, XLV, and XLVI on pp. 107, 113, and 114 respectively, but the iron and steel industry is frequently referred to in illustration of the main thesis of the second part of the book.

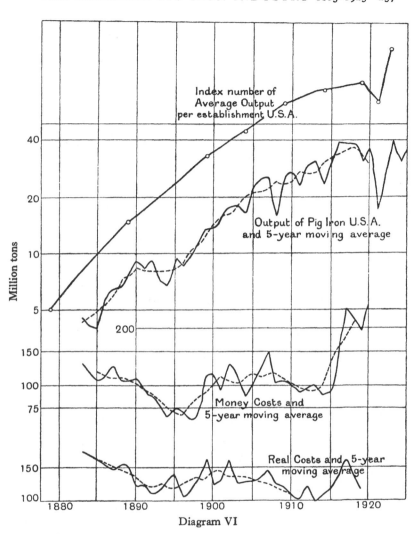

Diagram VI

Money Costs and Real Costs of Pig Iron in U.S.A., 1883–1913.
Total output 1883–1925, and average output per Establishment
at Census dates 1879–1923.

movements of British and American pig iron prices but considerable difference in detail, e.g. both countries experienced peak prices in 1890, 1900, 1907 and 1913, and low prices in 1904, 1911 and 1914, but the period of the trade cycle in the British iron industry (or at least the north-east section thereof) varied from six to ten years compared with America's three to seven, moreover the highest price before the depression of the 'nineties occurred in America in 1887, in England not until 1890, while the price of pig iron in England reached a maximum for the period in 1900, in America in 1907. Upon the whole the ten years' moving average seems to be the best measure of the trend of English prices and output while the five years' moving average gives the best fit for the corresponding American series. However, changes in the period of the cyclical fluctuations of the annual American index numbers cause the five years' moving average to fluctuate somewhat about the trend.

Turning to the discussion of trends, the main purpose of this study, we find that the index numbers of real cost cannot safely be used between 1890 and 1907 because the prolonged depression of the early 'nineties, followed by abnormally high prices in 1899–1900 and 1902–3, introduces elements of negative and positive quasi-rent which modify even a ten years' moving average considerably.

At the opening of our period both real and money costs had been falling steadily for more than a decade while the industry had been expanding rapidly. Real costs continued to fall and output to expand rapidly until 1890. Between 1890 and 1896, however, the quantity of pig iron produced in the United States oscillated about 8 million tons per annum while the five years' average lay between 8 and 8·3 million tons per annum from 1891 to 1895 inclusive. The index numbers of real cost fell rapidly after 1890 to a minimum in 1894 but rose between 1895 and 1900 at an average rate of 3 % per annum, whence they fell slowly (average rate about 2 % per annum) but at an increasing rate until 1907. Between 1907 and 1912 efficiency increased rapidly and real costs fell about 3½ % per annum, but rose of course during the War. Meantime the quantity of pig iron produced in the United States was increasing rapidly but at a diminishing rate (the general trend was upwards at an average rate of 13 % per annum between 1895 and 1900, 9 % per annum between 1900 and 1905, 3½ % per annum between 1907 and 1912). It is impossible to tell how far the fluctuations in the index numbers of real cost during the last decade of the nineteenth and the early years of the twentieth century were due to changes in efficiency and how far to fluctuating quasi-rents; certainly a large part of the slump between 1890 and 1897 must be attributed to negative or low profits, for the cost of labour, coke, and ore absorbed, on the average, more than 95 % of the receipts of the industry during this period, leaving a margin of less than 5 % for all other expenses including profits compared with a margin exceeding 15 % in the previous five years. During the five years, 1898–1902, on the other hand, the margin left for other expenses averaged over 30 % of the receipts of the industry, which looks very much like abnormally high profits. Clearly the story lying behind these figures is somewhat as follows: for twenty years previous to 1890 production had been showing a rapid upward trend and the market had expanded to take the greatly increased output at a profit to the manu-facturer. Investment in plant was therefore proceeding apace in the anticipation that the market would continue to expand; old furnaces were torn down or abandoned and more efficient stacks of much greater capacity were constructed. In the early 'nineties ironmasters, equipped for a huge increase in output, were over-taken by a big fall in the demand schedule for their products. The depression was so severe that all obsolete plant was soon abandoned and the less efficient of the new ventures were also squeezed out, so that the efficiency of the industry probably did increase considerably. However, investors were not getting a normal return to their efforts so the index numbers record too great a fall in real costs. The revival of demand in the decade 1895 to 1905 found investors shy of embodying their wealth in new blast furnaces however imposing they might be, so that those enterprises which had weathered the slump enjoyed large quasi-rents and their owners abnormally high profits. Again, released from the pressure of adversity the industry probably declined somewhat in efficiency, all the existing plant being put into full operation and pressed until marginal prime costs rose to the high current price of pig iron—but it is impossible to say how far the rise in the index of real costs between 1895 and 1900 is due to a decline in the efficiency of the industry and how far to abnormal profits. It seems probable that important elements of quasi-rent vitiate the index numbers of real cost until 1905 or 1906, but the fall between 1907 and 1912 almost certainly reflects the increasing efficiency of the industry free from abnormal influences.

This thesis is supported by the data relating to furnaces active and idle in the United States during this period.[1] The percentage of furnaces actually in blast at the end of each year, 1880–92, oscillated between 40 % and 70 %, but it fell to 26 % in 1893 and did not rise above 52 % until 1899. From 1899 to 1906 the proportion of furnaces active averaged over 70 %, then fell to a normal level ranging between 36 % and 72 % for the next ten years. It is difficult to attach a precise meaning to the figures for total number of furnaces because they are complicated by the irregular abandonment of obsolete furnaces and periodic rebuilding of those retained in operation. Moreover the average capacity·of the furnaces constructed has increased continuously. Still, such as they are, the figures bear out my thesis. From 1880 to 1892 the number of furnaces in the industry decreased slowly, but the capacity of the plant increased owing to the substitutions of larger stacks for the obsolete furnaces. In 1882 there were 602 furnaces reported and in 1892, 564, a decrease of 38 in ten years, but the number fell by 46 in 1893 and by the end of 1895 was down to 468. In spite of the recovery of prices in 1899 the number of furnaces continued to decline until the end of 1901 when 406 furnaces were reported. A net addition of 23 furnaces was made during the next five years and by 1910 the numbers had risen to 473.

I conclude that the index numbers of real cost are only reliable as a measure of changes in the average quantity of resources consumed per ton of pig iron produced during the first five and the last five years of the period 1885–1912 covered

---

[1] Appendix v, Table IV.

by the five years' moving averages of pre-War prices and costs.
For these two periods we have:

Date	Rate of fall of real costs (% per annum)	Rate of expansion of the industry (% per annum)	Elasticity of return
1885–90	5	8½	1$\frac{7}{10}$
1907–12	3½	3½	1

The elasticity of return is here computed upon the assumption
that the entire fall of real costs is attributable to the expansion
of the industry; it therefore exaggerates the tendency to increasing return. In twenty-five years the real cost of manufacture of pig iron in America fell from 160 to 110 or nearly
one-third, while there was practically no net change in the real
cost of manufacture of pig iron in the north-east coast district
of Great Britain.

Upon comparing the curves of real costs of pig iron obtained
for the American and the British Cleveland districts, one is at
once struck by the fact that the prolonged depression of the
early 'nineties and the boom about 1900 left their mark upon
the English curve of real costs as well as the American. From
the low point in the early 'nineties to the high point in the
beginning of the present century the American index of real
cost rose 15 % and the English 7½ %. A larger proportion of
the fluctuation of the English index number probably represents
changes in efficiency than in the case of America. The north-
east coast blast furnaces were just getting into their stride
when the slump came, and they met it without a check to the
rate of increase of their output (as shown by the ten years'
moving average) in spite of a very considerable slump in the
total production of pig iron in Great Britain from 1892 to 1895.
In short, the Cleveland region, being more efficient, was
obtaining a larger share of the pig iron trade of the country.
When the boom came the north-east coast did not increase its
output appreciably but continued to extend its plant slowly,
enjoying meanwhile a high quasi-rent owing to the lower
efficiency of other districts. A part of this advantage was
absorbed by reduction of the working day from twelve to eight
hours, and the change from two to three shifts per day. The

similarity of the two curves of real costs for this period is due to the fact that Cleveland exports large quantities of pig iron, and did at the time send pig iron to America; however, in a depression it can undersell other British districts so that its annual output rarely slumps except as a result of strikes in the mining and transport industries.

Finally it is noteworthy that the elasticity of return was about the same in the American as in the Cleveland pig iron industry during the only period for which a comparison is possible, namely 1907-12, when the ratio of the rate of fall of real costs to the rate of expansion of the industry was unity in both countries.

Note. Technical changes in the smelting of iron in the United States since 1880 differ only in degree from the developments in the art as practised on the north-east coast of England (*vide* Part IV). Mr Meredith B. Givens (late of the U.S. Bureau of Labour Statistics) writes me as follows:

Daily blast furnace output in the United States has shown a steady and spectacular increase since the beginnings of the expansion of the steel industry after the introduction of the Bessemer process. The voracious demands of the steelmakers, and the assimilation of the greater part of pig iron production within great steel plants where the metal is used in molten condition in Bessemer and open hearth departments, have made it imperative that blast furnacemen steadily increase the daily tonnage of iron per stack.

Among the numerous factors bringing about this change, the most important is the *revolution in the size and shape of the furnace* stack itself. Up to the 'eighties, the typical blast furnace was built with the bosh half way up the stack, and the hearth perhaps only half as wide as the bosh. Stacks were shorter, but most significant is the narrow hearth diameter, commonly 10 ft. or less, definitely limiting the output. Since that time there has been a steady evolution in furnace lines, and a tendency to approximate a straight-lined cylindrical stack, with wider and wider sections. Boshes have been lowered and hearths widened until the latter are almost as wide as the boshes. The objective of furnace designers has been to facilitate the most rapid movement of stock through the crucible without interfering with smelting efficiency.

Larger furnaces require a *greater volume of blast*, frequently blown at much higher temperatures than formerly. The blast furnace is usually filled with air about twice per minute. The older horizontal blowing engines are mostly obsolete, and the most modern plants to-day are equipped with compact and reliable turbo-blowers capable of maintaining high blast pressure and requiring little attention.

Co-ordinate with increased furnace size and heavier blast in relation to daily furnace output, is the *improvement in charging* which has characterised recent developments in the industry. The more scientific mixing of ores and alternating of charges has contributed to more regular working, less channelling, and greater volume of iron per day. Perhaps the greatest improvement has been in the quality of the coke used in making iron.

Labour-saving machinery is a commonplace in the blast furnace industry, and except for a few smaller plants, chiefly engaged in the production of merchant iron in the south, every furnace is equipped with a pig-casting machine, skip hoist, bins and larry car; while most have an ore bridge or car dumper. Progress in crew reduction, especially in blast furnace departments in steel works, is probably almost at an end. The remarkable reduction in labour time per day which has come since the War and especially after the introduction of the eight-hour day has been primarily due to more careful labour management or better labour efficiency as evidenced in the elimination of many occupations and the combination of others.

The smelting process is essentially the same to-day as it was one hundred years ago. The changes have been chiefly in the *scale* of operation, and the methods of handling materials. Certainly since the introduction of coke as the blast furnace fuel there has been no major change in the fundamentals of smelting. To-day progress is to be expected chiefly on the operating side, in the direction of greater and greater average daily production per furnace, through the predominance of larger stacks and hard driving.

As a result of these developments the annual production of pig iron per furnace active in the United States increased from about 10,000 tons in 1880 to 30,000 tons in 1890; 60,000 tons in 1900; 130,000 tons in 1910; 150,000 tons in 1925. During the same period the production of iron per furnace in blast on the north-east coast of England doubled, rising from about 25,000 tons in 1880 to about 45,000 tons in 1910 and 50,000 tons in 1925.

It will be noticed that the production of iron per furnace is nearly three times as great in the United States as in Cleveland. This is due largely to the richer ores (average about 55 % Fe in U.S. and 40 % Fe in Cleveland) and larger furnaces employed in America. Even before the War the diameter of the furnace hearth was quite commonly 16 ft. in America, as against 13 ft. in the Cleveland district, and had increased by 1927 to 22 ft. 3 in. (*vide* Paper read before the American Iron and Steel Institute, October 28, 1927, by William A. Forbes of the U.S. Steel Corporation).

With the widening of the hearth the height of the stack has been increased, e.g. a furnace recently built by the Bethlehem Steel Corporation at Sparrow's Point has a total height of 120 ft., the stack being 100 ft.

Between 1883 and 1913 the quantities of labour and fuel consumed per ton of pig iron produced in the United States were approximately halved (Appendix v, Table II, columns 6 and 4); considerable economies were also effected in the consumption of ore.

PART VII

CONCLUSION

§ 1. SUMMARY OF RESULTS

IF my index numbers are to be trusted, it would appear that the cost in terms of resources of constructing buildings in London and of maintaining them in repair fell about 18 % during the latter half of the nineteenth century, while the corresponding fall in the cost of manufacture of unbleached cotton piece goods in Lancashire was 22 %. During the first decade of the present century the efficiency of the cotton industry fell 5 % and that of building only 1 %, so that the net change in the real costs of production between 1850 and 1910 was 17 % in both industries. The available information concerning iron smelting in England does not cover so long a period, but there seems to have been no appreciable net change in the efficiency of the industry in the Cleveland district during the twenty-five years 1885–1910.

At first sight these results are surprising, for the building industry nearly trebled its output between 1850 and 1910, while the cotton industry was three and a third times as great in 1910 as in 1850, and the production of pig iron on the north-east coast of England expanded from 2,500,000 tons in 1890 to 3,500,000 tons in 1910. One is reassured, however, by the results obtained for the corresponding American industries, which show far greater absolute changes in efficiency than the British industries but about the same rates of change relative to the growth in the physical volume of production.

The real cost of manufacturing grey cotton cloth in Massachusetts was 185 in 1850 (as compared with 101 in 1910) and declined during the next decade about ⅓ % per annum. During the Civil War, however, real costs rose, so that the index number for 1865 is 203. From this point the cost of making grey cotton cloth in New England declined steadily though at a diminishing rate, until the index number of real costs reached 99, the minimum for the period, in 1900, only to rise slightly and hover between 101 and 102 during the decade 1900–10.

It is noteworthy that the progress of the Lancashire industry was most rapid in the decade 1855–65 (real costs falling 1 % per annum) when the American industry was disrupted by the Civil War and the dissension which preceded the strife. In the next decade, 1865–75, the New England industry was recovering from the effects of the war and the index of real costs fell nearly seventy points, while the Lancashire figure fell only two points. During this period the mechanical improvements which had accumulated during the previous decade (notably in the self-actor mule which had been generally adopted in England for nearly all counts of yarn by 1867)[1] were introduced into New England and adapted to the local conditions. The real cost of manufacturing grey cotton cloth reached a minimum for the period in 1900 in both Lancashire and Massachusetts, and rose slightly during the next decade despite the adoption of the automatic loom in New England.

Between 1885 and 1910 the real cost of smelting iron in the United States fell fifty points (from 164 in 1885 to 114 in 1910); while the net change in the real cost of making pig iron on the north-east coast of England was a fall of only three points, from 103 (estimated) in 1885 to 100 in 1910. The only noteworthy feature of this development is the slump in railroad construction which caused a prolonged depression in the iron industry, making it difficult to interpret the index numbers for both Britain and America from 1890–1905, owing to the disturbing influence of fluctuating quasi-rent (i.e. variations in the rate of profit) upon the relation between the selling price and the cost of pig iron.[2]

§ 2. HISTORICAL ASPECTS

Perhaps the most interesting feature of the curves of real cost derived from this enquiry is the measure they afford of industrial progress. It cannot be emphasised too much that the index numbers reveal only changes which have taken place in the

[1] *Vide* p. 118. [2] Cf. Part VI, § 4.

physical product of a unit of resources. There may have been changes in the amount of satisfaction derived from the commodity produced, as when the architect combines the walls and windows which the builder constructs for him in a more pleasing and useful fashion, or the dressmaker by skilful design enhances the value of a piece of cloth. Certainly the conversion of pig iron into steel enables it to do far greater service than of old. But these are for the most part unmeasurable changes outside the purview of statistical enquiry.

The cost in human effort of a unit of resources may also have changed. An attempt has been made in the choice of the indexes of efficiency wages, by which to eliminate changes in the cost of labour, to allow for changes in the effort put into an hour's work and for the greater application demanded of the worker as machinery is speeded up. But the data will not allow of any but a very rough correction even for these changes, while psychic changes which cause the worker to experience greater or less dissatisfaction in putting forth the same effort remain entirely uncorrected. Similar remarks apply to the other factors of production. The atmosphere of the years immediately following the War made saving difficult and the real cost of waiting abnormally high on that account. There may, on the contrary, have been a slight fall in the supply price of some services of management as a result of the more progressive ideas on " Labour Questions " now prevalent.

The neglect of these and other such considerations does not vitiate the results of this enquiry, but limits the conclusions which can safely be drawn from them. The methods employed in compiling the indexes of selling prices, and of the supply price of factors, must be kept constantly in mind when interpreting the curves of real cost. When a generous allowance is made for the limitations of the data and technique of Parts II–VI, the results still appear serious for Great Britain.

The nineteenth century was characterised by a progressive diminution in the quantity of resources consumed per unit of product in British manufacturing industries. By the close of the century, however, this movement had spent its force, so that real costs remained almost constant during the first decade of the

twentieth century in at least three of the basic industries of
Great Britain. This change was accompanied by an adverse
movement of the real rate of interchange between British and
foreign goods, so that the real cost to Britain of her imports
(bought largely with goods made with iron, cotton, and coal)
probably increased; the contemporaneous economies effected in
the "finishing" industries being insufficient to offset the combined effect of the adverse movement of the rate of interchange and the rise in the real costs of the materials used in the
"finishing" industries.[1] In consequence of these developments
the *per capita* real income of the United Kingdom showed no
increase between 1900 and 1913, though it had increased steadily
during the nineteenth century.[2] It may be argued that improvements in the hours and conditions of employment in British
industry increased the total welfare of the community, while
leaving its economic welfare unchanged; but it is well to realise,
as a matter of history, that these reforms have *not* increased the
material income of the community. If we would push on still
faster with reforms which increase costs of production in terms
of resources we must be prepared to sacrifice goods to leisure
and political ideals.[3]

---

[1] Cf. Pt I, § 3, IV.

[2] Cf. *Higher Production*, pp. 102–5, where Mr Denis Milner estimates the
changes occurring in the real income per head of population in the United
Kingdom between 1760 and 1913 from the information available concerning
changes in the national income, the price level, and the population during
this period.

[3] Cotton manufacture and iron smelting do not account for a sufficient
proportion of the national dividend of the United States to permit one to
relate the trend of real costs in these industries to changes in the economic
welfare of the nation. The charts contrast the movements of real costs for
corresponding British and American industries; this comparison is discussed
in Pt I, § 3, IV, Pt V, § 4 and Pt VI, § 4. It is only necessary to note here
that the slight rise in the real cost of manufacturing cotton in New England
after 1900 was more than compensated by the development of this industry
in the Southern States.

§3. ELASTICITIES OF RETURN

It is not possible to correlate changes in the real costs of production, as measured by my index numbers, with changes in the size of an industry by the methods commonly employed, for two reasons. First, the available data do not cover a period long enough to include many cycles of Professor Schumpeter's "long wave",[1] if such periodic movements exist. Second, the trend of a corrected selling price index number fails to measure changes in real cost during periods of secular depression in industries, such as iron and steel, which employ large fixed capitals. In the building industry, however, supplementary costs are unimportant relative to prime, and here *a priori* expectations are verified: real costs cease to decline when the industry ceases to expand.[2]

Although the data will not permit me to fit curves of real cost, like ill-fitting garments, to cycles of industrial expansion and contraction, there are portions of the real cost curves which move in close relation to the normal production of the corresponding industries. By assuming that all changes in real cost occurring during these intervals are due to the expansion of the industries concerned, I obtain limiting values for the elasticity of return. I have made no attempt to correct for economic lag, but the error is probably unimportant, since the curves themselves are based upon five, seven and ten years' moving averages; while real costs were declining and output expanding uniformly during the intervals for which I have computed the elasticity of return. Table I presents, in summary form, the results of these computations; they are described and discussed in detail in the concluding sections of the monographs on the several industries, Parts II–VI, and in general terms in Part I, § 2, VI. I shall therefore proceed without further comment to analyse the relation between the size and efficiency of industries.

---

[1] *Economica*, December 1927, p. 288. What is said below (§ 4) will show that I am in sympathy with Professor Schumpeter's theory of innovation in a capitalistic society. I cannot see however that he has succeeded any better than Professor Pigou in explaining the rhythm of the business cycle. No reason is advanced why there should be *periodic* outbursts of innovation. *Ibid.* p. 299.

[2] *Vide* Diagram I; cf. Pt II, § 11, p. 89.

Table I
Conspectus of results obtained in Parts II–VI

Date	Rate of fall of real cost (% per annum)	Rate of expansion of the industry (% per annum)	Ratio $\frac{col.\ 2}{col.\ 1}$, i.e. minimum elasticity of return
The London Building Industry			
1850–60	½	(2)	4
1865–75	⅓	2⅔	8
1890–5	1	3	3
Cotton Manufacture in Lancashire			
1850–60	(1)	(5)	5
1870–80	½	2½	5
1890–1900	½	1	2
1900–5	—	1	—
1905–10	—	3	—
Cotton Manufacture in Massachusetts			
1850–4	⅘	4	5
1869–74	4½	8	2
1874–6	5	5	1
1876–80	1	2	2
1880–5	2	4	2
1885–90	—	2½	—
1889–94	1½	3½	2½
1900–5	—	1⅔	—
1905–10	—	2½	—
Iron Smelting in Cleveland			
1885–90	⅓	—	—
1902–10	1	1	1
Iron Smelting in United States			
1885–90	5	8½	1 7/10
1907–12	3½	3½	1

N.B. Brackets indicate estimates of doubtful value.

§4. CAUSATION

There is a noticeable tendency for changes in output to lag behind changes in the real cost of production.[1] But this sequence of costs and output is in conformity with the thesis that the

[1] Pt II, pp. 97–8 and Pt V, p. 216.

expansion of industries causes their efficiency to increase. It is of course obvious that a reduction in the normal price of a commodity will, after an interval, cause the market to absorb a larger quantity of it, and that a rise in the price regularly demanded by the producers will, again after an interval, reduce the quantity of the commodity purchased. The present study is concerned not with the inertia of market demand but with the forces which determine the prices normally demanded by producers.

In order to elucidate the somewhat complex relationship between the size and the efficiency of industries I shall distinguish a factor of production "inventive ability" which moves, lethargically but surely, in obedience to the principle of substitution, seeking employment in those opportunities where it receives the greatest return like the other factors of production. In accordance with the distinction made in Part I, pp. 15–16, between discovery and invention I do not include the faculties of pure scientists, who seek knowledge, for the sake of knowledge, in the category inventive ability, because it is only indirectly, through the accident of friendship and environmental stimulus, that such men are interested in, say, the theory of stresses and strains in an elastic fluid which is likely to benefit commercial aeronautics, rather than, say, the theory of numbers which is unlikely to yield economic fruit for centuries. The pure scientist shades off gradually into the applied scientist, just as discovery merges with invention, but the distinction is none the less real and important. New discoveries bring catastrophic changes but industrial development consists largely in the application of existing mechanical and economic principles to the solution of particular problems. Whether the problem to be solved deals with the management of personnel, the design of machines, the filing of accounts, or the marketing of the product, trained men of inventive ability may be confidently expected to solve it in orthodox fashion if they work upon it. The energies which these men expend are productive resources and must be economically employed, just like common labour. Business men frequently unite in a single person the functions of the enterpriser and the inventor but the two are analytically distinct, and are coming to be recognised as separable factors of production. In life the energies of able men may be turned, as by adversity,[1] from other employments to invention so that the supply of inventive ability is in fact elastic; but it will facilitate the exposition of my thesis, and in no way affect the argument, if we assume that there is available for all the industries of a community a fixed stock of inventive ability to be distributed among many competing opportunities according to the net benefit of the several employments.

Since industry is organised upon a competitive basis, the stock of inventive ability will be fully employed even in a stationary state, for there is relative growth among the constituent enterprises in the stationary state, though there is no change in the size of the industries. Young, growing enterprises have to employ inventive ability in order to establish their superiority over the decaying establishments which they must displace in order to grow; while existing enterprises can only retain their position in the market by constantly increasing their efficiency. Hence there is an historical decline of real costs in the stationary state, and inventive ability is so distributed that its marginal private net product is equal in all industries. The economies effected in such a state are all *internal* in the sense that they originate in the enterprises which seek them by financing the necessary inventive ability. But improvements, once effected, are imitated sooner or later, and the innovator loses the differential advantage they first gave him over his rivals. If industries were homogeneous in the sense that in each the innovator could enjoy the same proportion of the full (discounted) social net product of his invention, there would be no social disharmony on this account for the marginal private net product of inventive ability would bear the same ratio to its marginal social net product in all industries. There is no *a priori* reason for supposing that modern industry is heterogeneous in this respect, while the fact that technically complicated industries, where innovation involves large investments in precarious experiments, have quite commonly a high proportion of supplementary costs, which form a protective barrier against would-be-imitators, suggests that it is homogeneous. We may, therefore, conclude

[1] Hence the dictum, "Necessity is the mother of invention".

that there is unlikely to be disharmony between the private and the social interest in respect of internal economies.

When we pass from the stationary state to real life we find that the above argument concerning internal economies holds good with minor qualifications. Inventive ability, like capital, flows readily into rapidly expanding industries, where the opportunities of profit are (supposedly) greater, and eschews those which serve a contracting market. Yet this very fact shortens the period during which the innovator may reap the fruits of his invention in expanding industries and extends the period of differential advantage to the innovator in contracting industries. Hence we frequently find that the few up-to-date producers in a decaying industry prosper exceedingly despite the distress of their rivals. On the other hand there is usually greater scope for improvement in expanding than in contracting industries so that a given amount of inventive ability can effect larger economies. For this reason the marginal net product of inventive ability is higher, *ceteris paribus*, in a growing society than in a stationary state. The quantity of inventive ability employed in an industry which is stationary amid expanding neighbours is therefore less than it would be if all were stationary, and the historical decline of real costs consequently slower.

So much for internal economies: in neither the stationary nor the growing state is there any reason to suppose that the private and the social interest are at variance in the matter of internal economies. There remain external economies.

When there is a rise in the normal demand schedule for the products of an industry *all* the producers find further specialisation of men and machines economical. Since the opportunity to effect these economies is presented simultaneously to all the producers, including new entrants, the individual producers enjoy only a momentary advantage over their immediate competitors and but a fleeting differential profit over the producers in other industries. The net effect, therefore, of the expansion of the market is that the work of production is further subdivided (inventors, managers, workmen and machines being specialised to more particular functions), real costs are reduced and their future historical decline is accelerated; while the benefit is diffused rapidly through the entire body of producers (which may be considered identical with the whole body of consumers).[1] Although the benefit of these "external economies", once realised, is rapidly transferred to the consumer, it may take several years to effect the full economy permitted by a given expansion of the market. Whether the further subdivision of labour is effected through a process of proliferation (the multiplication of specialised firms) or trustification (the multiplication of departments within the financial unit), it takes time to train men and adapt machines to new duties. When, however, the reorganisation of the industry is complete all the factors of production (including inventive ability) are rendered more efficient than they were before the expansion, so that the historical decline of real costs continues on a lower level and at a greater rate than before the expansion. The full value of the external economies effected by the expansion of the market is thus made up of two elements:

(i) The present reduction of real costs.

(ii) The discounted value of the future economies which will be brought nearer by the acceleration of the historical decline of real costs.

External influences aside, the rate of fall of real cost tabulated in Table I, column 1, may now be analysed into three elements:

(a) The historical decline of real cost due to internal economies.

(b) The acceleration of this decline due to the expansion of the industry.

(c) The direct fall of real costs due to the external economies of expansion.

It is of course impossible to measure the decline of real cost due to these several elements. Fortunately, there is some evidence that the historical decline of real cost (a) and (b) was negligible compared with the primary fall (c) due to external economies during the period under investigation; for industry generally was expanding so rapidly that an industry which was stationary failed to secure the services of men of inventive ability. If this assumption is valid the ratio between the rate of

[1] It is clear that the argument of this paragraph applies equally to the internal economies discussed in the preceding paragraph, except that the innovator enjoys a differential advantage for a considerable period.

expansion of an industry and the rate of decline of the real cost of production therein gives a direct measure of the elasticity of return in the industry. *Ceteris paribus*, these industries should be encouraged to expand by bounties or other stimuli, inversely proportionate to their elasticities of return. In this connection it is noteworthy that the elasticities of return (Table I) in the corresponding British and American industries appear to have been nearly equal at corresponding periods of their history; while the ratio 3 : 2 : 1 between the elasticities of return in the building, cotton, and iron industries during the period 1890– 1910 places these industries in the order one would expect from the opportunities they offer for the economical subdivision of labour.

It appears therefore that the economies of industrial expansion are all external in the sense that they cannot be exploited by individual producers. They are due entirely to the economical subdivision of labour (including the work of invention) and are realised in the form of (*a*) a direct increase in the present efficiency of the industry, (*b*) an acceleration of the (future) historical decline of real costs.[1]

Against these progressive forces are opposed two stubborn facts: (*a*) The natural resources available to industry are neither unlimited nor indestructible, so that expanding industries have to pay a higher real price for their raw materials. (*b*) The daily task of co-ordinating the functions of large and complex in- dustries is proportionately greater than the work of co-ordination in a smaller, simpler industrial community. This is true of an autocratic society—a point is soon reached in the raising of an army when the number of officers must be increased faster (in proportion) than the number of men—but it is doubly true of a democratic community where producers must satisfy a demand which fluctuates with the desires of individual consumers. As the work of production is subdivided and the consumers are removed further from the ken of the producers it ultimately

---

[1] One may go further and say that, in a given environment, the division of labour is a function of two variables only: the size and the nature of the industry. It is commonly supposed that invention tends to further the subdivision of labour but this is not generally true. It would be safer to argue, in modern conditions, that invention tends to integrate rather than to subdivide labour; witness recent developments in the art of dyeing and in the manufacture of window glass.

becomes increasingly difficult to anticipate the market, despite the fact that the technique implied in the theory of value is available for the large market. More resources are devoted to forecasting, yet unemployment, due to the imperfect co-ordination of production and consumption, steadily increases. Finally there is the consideration that political friction tends to increase with the separation of society into specialised classes.

These consequences of industrial expansion may be justly called "external diseconomies", for their costs are not carried by the industries (or enterprises) which cause them, but are disseminated among the whole body of producers (or consumers) just like the positive economies of expansion. The fear of external diseconomies therefore in no way deters the individual industry or enterprise from expansion, and there is a disharmony between the private and the social interest which corresponds to the disharmony which arises in respect of external economies.

The net effect of expansion upon the efficiency of manu-facturing industries is therefore the resultant of two opposing tendencies: (a) The specialisation of the factors of production renders them individually more efficient, thus increasing the quantity of work which can be done by the same number of hands. (b) The subdivision of labour with the growth of the industry increases the quantity of work required to fabricate a given quantity of manufactures, by making it more difficult to co-ordinate the several parts of the industry.

Writing in 1891 Dr Marshall observed that:

The development of the organism, whether social or physical, involves an increasing subdivision of functions between its separate parts on the one hand, and on the other hand a more intimate con-nection between them.

The doctrine that those organisms which are the most highly developed, in the sense in which we have just used the phrase, are those most likely to survive in the struggle for existence, is itself in process of development. It is not yet completely thought out either in its biological or its economic relations.[1]

Perhaps my study has tended to confirm this doctrine, while emphasising its limitations.

[1] *Principles of Economics*, 1st ed. Book IV, chap. viii, § 1. This paragraph was retained in all the subsequent editions, the reference is the same throughout.

STATISTICAL APPENDICES

APPENDIX I

THE LONDON BUILDING INDUSTRY 1845–1913

A. LAXTON'S PRICES

Tabular statements of prices chargeable in the several trades annually since 1845, as given in Laxton's *Builders' and Contractors' Price Book.*

Index numbers

Date (Base year 1910)	Selling price of brickwork (including concreting and excavating) (1)	Selling price of carpentry and joinery (2)	Carpentry and joinery: cost of labour in same job in successive years (3)	Selling price of masonry (4)	Selling price of tiling and slating (5)	Selling price of painting (6)	Selling price of plastering (7)	Cost of plasterer's materials (8)	Selling price of plumbing (9)
Base	100·0	100·0	100·0	100·0	100·0	100·0	100·0	35·0	100·0
1845	89·3	138·4	33·6	95·4	71·5	62·5	83·5	29·9	100·0
1846	—	—	—	—	—	—	—	—	—
1847	—	—	—	—	—	—	—	—	—
1848	88·1	132·0	33·6	90·6	71·6	62·5	83·5	29·5	107·7
1849	88·1	132·0	33·6	90·6	69·5	62·5	83·5	29·5	90·4
1850	—	—	—	—	—	—	—	—	—
1851	77·5	124·1	33·6	81·1	68·2	58·3	83·5	28·0	96·2
1852	77·4	114·2	33·6	81·1	68·2	58·3	77·1	27·6	96·2
1853	86·2	114·2	33·6	73·1	72·4	58·3	76·5	27·6	116·2
1854	87·2	132·0	33·6	73·1	80·1	66·6	76·5	31·3	116·2
1855	84·8	132·0	33·6	81·1	80·1	66·6	76·5	31·3	125·0
1856	84·8	132·0	33·6	81·1	80·1	66·6	76·5	31·3	132·7
1857	84·8	132·0	33·6	81·1	80·1	66·6	65·6	31·3	132·7
1858	84·8	132·0	33·6	81·1	80·1	75·0	65·6	30·8	132·7
1859	85·0	132·0	35·4	81·1	80·1	75·0	65·6	28·9	132·7
1860	83·8	132·0	35·4	81·1	80·1	75·0	66·4	28·7	132·7
1861	88·7	103·9	35·4	81·1	80·1	75·0	66·7	28·3	132·7

Year	(1)	(2)	(3)	(4)	(5)	(6)	(7)	(8)	(9)
1862	132·7	28·3	66·9	75·0	80·1	81·1	35·4	103·9	88·7
1863	128·8	28·6	68·1	75·0	89·5	81·1	35·4	121·4	88·1
1864	128·8	28·6	68·1	75·0	89·5	81·1	35·8	121·4	88·1
1865	128·8	29·5	72·9	75·0	89·5	81·1	37·9	124·9	88·1
1866	132·7	29·5	75·4	75·0	90·7	86·7	38·0	130·9	91·5
1867	132·7	31·7	82·7	79·2	98·7	93·8	42·0	142·2	101·8
1868	130·8	31·7	82·7	75·0	98·7	92·2	42·0	144·4	101·8
1869	123·1	30·8	82·7	75·0	98·5	90·6	38·9	130·9	91·2
1870	123·1	30·8	82·7	75·0	98·5	90·6	38·8	126·0	91·2
1871	123·1	30·8	82·7	75·0	92·2	90·6	38·5	127·9	91·2
1872	123·1	30·8	82·7	75·0	92·2	90·6	38·4	126·9	91·2
1873	126·9	32·4	93·9	75·0	92·2	95·8	40·6	130·4	100·1
1874	126·9	33·8	95·6	75·0	98·5	101·8	40·3	130·7	103·5
1875	130·8	36·3	94·5	83·3	118·5	90·6	42·6	129·5	96·7
1876	132·7	36·1	94·5	83·3	125·9	90·6	42·3	128·8	101·7
1877	130·8	36·0	95·9	83·3	125·9	90·6	42·1	128·2	101·7
1878	119·2	36·0	95·9	83·3	116·4	90·6	42·0	127·4	105·3
1879	107·7	36·9	95·3	83·3	101·6	90·6	41·7	126·7	105·3
1880	125·0	36·9	93·7	83·3	97·4	90·6	41·5	126·1	105·3
1881	111·5	36·9	93·7	83·3	97·4	90·6	41·3	125·6	101·7
1882	107·7	36·9	83·7	83·3	91·1	90·6	41·0	124·9	98·7
1883	107·7	36·9	83·7	83·3	91·1	90·6	40·9	119·4	93·8
1884	96·2	36·9	93·7	83·3	91·1	90·6	40·6	118·8	93·8
1885	96·2	36·9	93·7	83·3	91·1	90·6	40·4	118·6	91·7
1886	88·5	36·9	93·7	83·3	91·1	90·6	40·2	118·0	89·4
1887	88·5	35·7	93·7	83·3	91·1	90·6	39·9	116·8	87·0
1888	88·5	35·5	93·7	83·3	91·1	90·6	39·7	116·1	87·0
1889	92·3	35·5	93·7	83·3	91·1	90·6	39·6	116·1	98·7
1890	96·2	35·5	93·7	83·3	89·0	90·6	39·3	103·9	98·7
1891	96·2	35·5	93·7	83·3	85·9	90·6	39·1	103·4	91·7
1892	96·2	35·5	93·7	83·3	85·9	90·6	36·6	103·3	91·7
1893	96·2	33·5	83·2	75·0	83·0	90·6	37·6	94·8	88·1
1894	88·5	33·5	83·2	79·2	83·0	90·6	37·6	96·7	89·3
1895	88·5	32·6	83·2	79·2	83·0	90·6	37·6	96·7	91·8
1896	88·5	33·7	83·2	79·2	83·0	90·6	37·6	96·7	91·8
1897	90·4	33·7	85·7	83·3	88·8	90·6	37·6	96·7	93·0
1898	83·3	34·7	85·7	83·3	98·8	90·6	37·6	96·7	95·5
1899	83·3	35·0	104·7	83·3	98·8	90·6	37·6	96·7	103·2

A. LAXTON'S PRICES—continued

Date (Base year 1910)	Selling price of brickwork (including concreting and excavating) (1)	Selling price of carpentry and joinery (2)	Carpentry and joinery: cost of labour in same job in successive years (3)	Selling price of masonry (4)	Selling price of tiling and slating (5)	Selling price of painting (6)	Selling price of plastering (7)	Cost of plasterer's materials (8)	Selling price of plumbing (9)
Base	100·0	100·0	100·0	100·0	100·0	100·0	100·0	35·0	100·0
1900	103·2	96·7	37·6	90·6	98·8	100·0	104·7	35·0	100·0
1901	103·3	104·2	39·9	90·6	99·4	100·0	108·1	35·9	102·9
1902	103·3	104·2	39·9	90·6	99·4	100·0	108·1	35·9	102·9
1903	103·3	104·2	39·9	90·6	99·4	100·0	108·1	35·9	102·9
1904	107·5	104·2	39·9	90·6	104·7	125·0	117·4	35·9	102·9
1905	107·5	105·5	39·6	100·2	105·4	125·0	117·4	35·9	102·9
1906	103·4	105·5	39·6	100·2	110·1	125·0	117·4	34·2	98·1
1907	103·4	105·7	39·9	100·2	110·1	125·0	117·4	34·2	107·1
1908	103·4	105·7	39·9	100·2	110·1	125·0	117·4	34·2	129·8
1909	105·4	105·7	39·9	100·2	110·1	125·0	117·4	34·2	103·8
1910	100·0	100·0	40·0	100·0	100·0	100·0	100·0	35·0	100·0
1911	100·4	99·8	39·9	100·2	100·0	100·0	100·1	35·5	100·0
1912	100·4	99·8	39·9	114·5	100·0	100·0	100·1	35·5	103·0
1913	101·5	104·8	42·9	133·6	100·0	100·0	100·1	37·0	123·1
1914	109·6	106·4	43·9	133·6	100·0	108·3	135·5	37·0	148·1
1915	111·9	110·1	44·4	133·6	100·0	108·3	135·5	40·0	132·7
1916	111·9	110·1	44·4	143·1	107·9	125·0	135·5	42·2	142·3
1917	114·0	171·9	50·0	143·1	107·9	125·0	133·9	52·8	196·2
1918	138·8	220·4	54·0	143·1	107·9	149·9	271·1	67·1	196·2
1919	274·0	335·0	79·5	372·1	200·2	224·9	321·1	94·6	205·8
1920	301·0	369·8	102·2	459·5	224·9	299·9	390·7	101·6	236·5
1921	386·0	423·0	115·8	477·0	344·4	299·9	352·4	112·3	284·0
1922	339·5	267·9	94·3	—	336·9	299·9	219·3	106·6	236·5
1923	—	234·8	76·5	—	260·5	199·9	219·3	93·0	207·7
1924	—	218·4	90·5	—	260·5	199·9	219·3	80·4	236·5
1925	—	218·4	92·0	—	260·5	199·9	219·3	80·4	290·4

Actual wage rates

Date (Base year 1910)	Bricklayer (pence per hour) (10)	Bricklayer's labourer (pence per hour) (11)	Carpenter and joiner (pence per hour) (12)	Mason (pence per hour) (13)	Mason's labourer (pence per hour) (14)	Slater (pence per hour) (15)	Slater's labourer (pence per hour) (16)	Plasterer (pence per hour) (17)	Plasterer's labourer (pence per hour) (18)
Base	13	8½	13	13	8½	13	9	14	8½
1845	7	4½	7¼	7½	4¼	6¾	3¾	7	4¼
1846	—	—	—	—	—	—	—	—	—
1847	—	—	—	—	—	—	—	—	—
1848	7	4½	7¼	7½	4¼	6¾	4¼	7	4¼
1849	7	4½	7¼	7½	4¼	7	4½	7	4¼
1850	—	—	—	—	—	—	—	—	—
1851	7	4½	7¼	7½	4¼	7	4½	7	4¼
1852	7	4½	7¼	7½	4¼	7	4½	7	4¼
1853	7	4½	7¼	7½	4¼	7	4½	7	4¼
1854	7½	4½	7¼	7½	4½	7½	4½	7½	4½
1855	7½	4½	7¼	7½	4½	7½	4½	7½	4½
1856	7½	4½	7¼	7½	4½	7½	4½	7½	4½
1857	7½	4½	7¼	7½	4½	7½	4½	7½	4½
1858	7½	4½	7¼	7½	4½	7½	4½	7½	4½
1859	7½	5	7¼	7½	5	7½	4½	7½	4½
1860	7½	5	7¼	8	5	7½	5	7½	5
1861	7½	5	7¼	8	5	7½	5	7½	5
1862	7½	5	7¼	8	5	7½	5	7½	5
1863	8	5	8	8	5	7½	5	8	5
1864	8	5	8	8	5	7½	5	8	5
1865	8	5	8	8	5	7½	5	8½	5
1866	8½	5½	8½	8½	5	8½	5½	8½	5½
1867	9	5½	9	8½	5	9	5½	8½	5½
1868	9	5½	9	9½	5½	9	5½	9	5½
1869	9½	6	9½	9½	6	9½	6	9½	6
1870	9½	6	9½	9½	6	9½	6	9½	6
1871	9½	6	9½	9½	6	9½	6	9½	6
1872	9½	6	9½	9½	6	9½	6	9½	6
1873	10	6½	10	10	6½	9½	6	10	6½
1874	10½	7	10½	10½	7	9½	6	10½	7

A. LAXTON'S PRICES—*continued*

Date (Base year 1910)	Bricklayer (pence per hour) (10)	Bricklayer's labourer (pence per hour) (11)	Carpenter and joiner (pence per hour) (12)	Mason (pence per hour) (13)	Mason's labourer (pence per hour) (14)	Slater (pence per hour) (15)	Slater's labourer (pence per hour) (16)	Plasterer (pence per hour) (17)	Plasterer's labourer (pence per hour) (18)
Base	13	8½	13	13	8½	13	9	14	8½
1875	10½	7	10½	10½	7	10	6	10½	7
1876	10½	7	10½	10½	7	10½	7	10½	7
1877	10½	7	10½	10½	7	10½	7	10½	7
1878	10½	7	10½	10½	7	10½	7	10½	7
1879	10½	7	10½	10½	7	10½	7	10½	7
1880	10½	7	10½	10½	7	12	7	10½	7
1881	10½	7	10½	10½	7	12	7	10½	7
1882	10½	7	10½	10½	7	12	7	10½	7
1883	10½	7	10½	10½	7	12	7	10½	7
1884	10½	7	10½	10½	7	12	7	10½	7
1885	10½	7	10½	10½	7	12	7	10½	7
1886	10½	7	10½	10½	7	12	7	10½	7
1887	10½	7	10½	10½	7	12	7	10½	7
1888	10½	7	10½	10½	7	12	7	10½	7
1889	10½	7	10½	10½	7	12	7	10½	7
1890	10½	7	10½	10½	7	12	7	10½	7
1891	10½	7	10½	10½	7	12	7	10½	7
1892	10½	7	10½	10½	7	12	7	10½	7
1893	11	7½	11	11	7	12	7	11	7½
1894	11½	7¾	11½	11½	7½	12	7½	11½	7½
1895	11½	7¾	11½	11½	7½	12	7½	11½	7½
1896	11½	7¾	11½	11½	7½	12	7½	11½	7½
1897	12	7¾	12	12	7½	12	7½	12	7½
1898	12	8¼	12	12	8	12	8	12	8
1899	12	8¼	12	12	8	12	8	12	8
1900	12	8¼	12	12	8	12	8	12	8
1901	12	8½	12½	12½	8	12	8	12½	8
1902	12	8½	12½	12½	8	12	8	12½	8
1903	12½	8½	12½	12½	8	12	8	12½	8
1904	12½	8½	12½	12½	8½	13	9	13	8½

Prices of particular materials

Date (Base year 1910)	Stock bricks (shillings per 1000) (19)	Chalk lime (delivery and profit) (shillings per cu. yd.) (20)	Thames sand (delivery and profit) (shillings per cu. yd.) (21)	Portland cement (pence per bushel) (22)	Tiles (delivery and profit) (shillings per 1000) (23)	Countess slates (delivery and profit) (shillings per doz.) (24)	Portland stone (delivery and profit) (pence per cu. ft.) (25)	Deals (£ per Petrograd standard) (26)	Milled lead in sheets (£ per ton) (27)
1905	12½	8½	12½	12½	8½	13	9	13	8½
1906	12½	8½	12½	12½	8½	13	9	13	8½
1907	12½	8½	12½	12½	8½	13	9	13	8½
1908	12½	8½	12½	12½	8½	13	9	13	8½
1909	12½	8½	12½	12½	8½	13	9	13	8½
1910	13	8½	13	13	8½	13	9	14	8½
1911	13	8½	13	14	8½	13	9	14	8½
1912	13	8½	13	18	8½	13	9	14	8½
1913	13	8½	13	15	8½	14	9	14	8½
1914	13	8½	14	15	8½	16	11	14	8½
1915	14	8½	14½	15	9½	16	10	15½	8½
1916	15	10	14½	16	9½	15	10½	15½	10½
1917	15	10½	15	30	10	15	11	16	10½
1918	16	11	16	30½	10½	16	21½	27	11
1919	27	21½	27	37	21½	27	26	30½	21½
1920	30½	26	30½	33½	26	30½	36	37	26
1921	37	33	37	32½	—	42	26	32½	33
1922	32½	26	32½	—	33	32½	19½	26	26
1923	26	19½	26	—	26	26	19½	25½	19½
1924	25½	19½	25½	—	—	25½	19¼	25½	19½
1925	28	21½	28	—	—	28	21½	28	21½
Base	34	12½	7¾	25	45½	4½	32	14	17·0
1845	39	12	5¾	31½	45	2	31	11	19·55
1846	—	—	—	—	—	—	—	—	—
1847	—	—	—	—	—	—	—	—	—
1848	38	12	5¾	31½	45	2	28	10·1	21·15
1849	38	12	5¾	31½	45	2	28	10·1	17·4
1850	—	—	—	—	—	—	—	—	—
1851	30	11	5¾	31½	40	2	28	8·9	18·6

A. LAXTON'S PRICES—*continued*

Date (Base year 1910)	Stock bricks (shillings per 1000) (19)	Chalk lime (delivery and profit) (shillings per cu. yd.) (20)	Thames sand (delivery and profit) (shillings per cu. yd.) (21)	Portland cement (pence per bushel) (22)	Tiles (delivery and profit) (shillings per 1000) (23)	Countess slates (delivery and profit) (shillings per doz.) (24)	Portland stone (delivery and profit) (pence per cu. ft.) (25)	Deals (£ per Petrograd standard) (26)	Milled lead in sheets (£ per ton) (27)
Base	34	12½	7¾	25	45½	4½	32	14	17·0
1852	28	11	5¾	36	40	2	28	7·45	18·6
1853	38	12	5½	30	46	2	24	7·45	23·7
1854	38	14½	5½	30	46	2	24	10·1	23·7
1855	36	14½	5½	30	46	3	28	10·1	23·7
1856	36	14½	5½	30	46	3	28	10·1	25·4
1857	36	14½	5½	30	46	3	28	10·1	25·4
1858	36	14	5½	30	46	3	28	10·1	25·4
1859	36	12	5½	30	46	3	28	10·1	25·4
1860	36	12	5½	28	46	3	30	10·1	25·4
1861	40	12	5½	28	40	3	30	9·2	25·4
1862	40	12	5½	28	40	3	30	9·2	25·4
1863	40	12	5½	27	40	3	30	10·1	25·4
1864	40	12	5½	27	40	3	30	10·1	23·7
1865	40	12	6	27	42½	3	30	10·1	23·7
1866	40	12	6	27	42½	3	32	10·1	23·7
1867	45	12½	6½	30	42½	3	35	11	23·7
1868	45	12½	6½	30	42½	3	35	11	23·7
1869	45	11½	6½	30	42½	3	35	11	23·7
1870	45	11½	6½	30	42½	3	35	11	23·7
1871	45	11½	6½	30	42½	3	35	11	23·7
1872	45	11½	6½	30	42½	3	35	11	23·7
1873	45	13	6½	33	42½	3	37	11	23·7
1874	45	14	6½	39	42½	3	39	11	23·7
1875	38	14	8	36	42½	3	32	11	23·7
1876	42	14	8	33	42½	3¾	32	11	24·1
1877	42	14	8	32	42½	4½	32	11	23·7
1878	45	14	8	32	42½	4½	32	11	21·15
1879	45	15	8	30	45½	4½	32	11	17·8

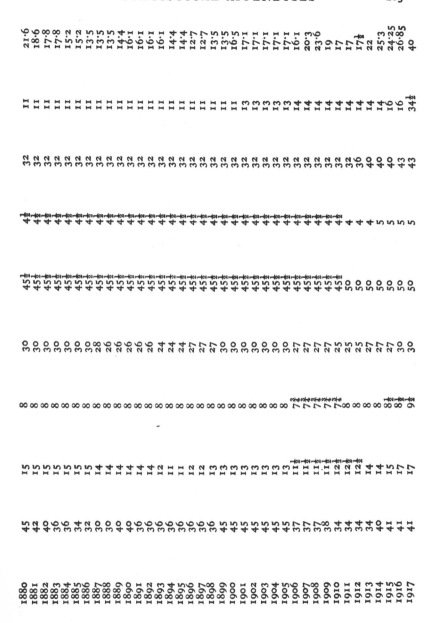

A. LAXTON'S PRICES—*continued*

Date (Base year 1910)	Stock bricks (shillings per 1000) (19)	Chalk lime (delivery and profit) (shillings per cu. yd.) (20)	Thames sand (delivery and profit) (shillings per cu. yd.) (21)	Portland cement (pence per bushel) (22)	Tiles (delivery and profit) (shillings per 1000) (23)	Countess slates (delivery and profit) (shillings per doz.) (24)	Portland stone (delivery and profit) (pence per cu. ft.) (25)	Deals (£ per Petrograd standard) (26)	Milled lead in sheets (£ per ton) (27)
Base	34	12½	7¾	25	45½	4½	32	14	17·0
1918	57½	17	13½	36	50	5	43	48	40
1919	115	31½	20	54	136	6	43	48	40
1920	130	31¾	23	69	130	9	48	48	43
1921	130	42⅓	23	78	200	14	60	48	47
1922	85	42⅓	23	78	200	14	69	36	38
1923	96	42⅓	19½	—	171½	10	—	25	35·8
1924	96	31½	18	—	146½	10	—	26	42·5
1925	96	31½	18	—	153½	10	—	26	54

Labour costs

Date (Base year 1910)	Brickwork (shillings per rod super reduced) (28)	Plain tile-work + Bangor slating (shillings per square) (29)	Rendering one coat plaster rough on brick (pence per yd. super) (30)	Masonry ordinary moulded work (pence per ft. super) (31)	Carpentry ceiling floor (joists only) + lean-to roof (shillings per square) (32)	Plumbing milled lead laid in flats (shillings per cwt.) (33)
Base	89	16	5	36	9·9	—
1845	40	11½	2	20	6	—
1846	—	—	—	—	—	—
1847	—	—	—	—	—	—
1848	40	11½	2	20	6	—
1849	40	11½	2	20	6	—
1850	—	—	—	—	—	—
1851	40	11½	2	20	6	—
1852	40	11½	2	20	6	—
1853	40	11½	2	20	6	—

Date (Base year 1910)	Brickwork (shillings per rod super reduced) (28)	Plain tile-work + Bangor slating (shillings per square) (29)	Rendering one coat plaster rough on brick (pence per yd. super) (30)	Masonry ordinary moulded work (pence per ft. super) (31)	Carpentry ceiling floor (joists only) + lean-to roof (shillings per square) (32)	Plumbing milled lead laid in flats (shillings per cwt.) (33)
Base	89	16	5	36	9·9	—
1886	56¼	16	3½	35	9	—
1887	56¼	16	3½	35	9	—
1888	55	16	3½	35	9	—
1889	55	16	3½	35	9	—
1890	55	16	3½	35	9	—
1891	55	16	3½	35	9	—
1892	55	16	3½	35	8·5	—
1893	55	15¾	3½	35	8·75	—
1894	60	15¾	3½	35	8·75	—

			6·5	6·5	6·5	6·5	6·5	6·5	6·5	6·5	6·5	6·5	6·5	6·5	5·5	5·5	5·5	5·5	5·5	5·5	6	8·5	9·5	11·9	15	10	11
8·75	8·75	9·25	9·25	9·25	9·5	9·5	9·5	9·5	9·25	9·9	9·9	9·9	9·4	9·7	9·7	10·3	10·3	11·75	13	16·5	22	27·5	22	17·25	17·25	19
35	35	35	35	35	36	36	36	36	36	36	36	36	36	30	30	30	30	30	30	30	69	86	96			
3½	3	3¼	3¼	3¼	6	6	6	6	6	7	7	7	7	7	5	5	5	5	7	7	7	7	11	13	16	14
15¾	15¾	16	16	16	16¼	15¾	15¾	15¾	16	16	16	16	16	16	16	16	16¾	16¼	16¾	23	28	37	41	37	37	37
70	70	75	85	85	85	85	85	85	89	89	89	89	89	89	89	89	89	94	94	105	120	155	200	260	270	194
1895	1896	1897	1898	1899	1900	1901	1902	1903	1904	1905	1906	1907	1908	1909	1910	1911	1912	1913	1914	1915	1916	1917	1918	1919	1920	1921

6	6	6	6	6	6·4	6·4	6·4	6·5	6·5	7	7	8	8	8	8	8	8·5	8·5	9	9	9	9	9	9	9	9	9	9	9
20	20	20	20	20	28	28	28	28	28	32	33	33	33	33	33	35	35	35	35	35	35	35	35	35	35	35	35
2	2	2	2	2	2	2	2½	2½	2½	3	3	3	3	3½	3½	3½	3½	3½	3½	3½	3½	3½	3½	3½	3½
11½	11½	11½	11½	12	12	12	14	14	14	15¼	15¼	15¼	15¼	15¼	15½	16	16	16	16	16	16	16	16	16	16
40	40	40	40	40	36½	36½	41	41	41	41	45	50	50	50	50	50	53	56½	56½	56½	56½	56½	56½	56½	56½
1854	1855	1856	1857	1858	1859	1860	1861	1862	1863	1864	1865	1866	1867	1868	1869	1870	1871	1872	1873	1874	1875	1876	1877	1878	1879	1880	1881	1882	1883	1884	1885

B. INDEX NUMBERS

The combined trades, i.e. the building industry

Date (Base year 1910)	Selling price of building			Trend of general prices*	Price of materials in the building industry	Efficiency wages in the building industry	Average weekly Summer wages in the London building industry
	Uncorrected	Corrected for labour and materials	Corrected for labour and materials and other expenses				
	(B 1)	(B 2)	(B 3)	(B 4)	(B 5)	(B 6)	(B 7)
Base	100	100	100	16·5	44·7	38·8	38·8
1845	103	124	122	18·3	44	20·5	26·4
1846	(102)	(124)	(122)	17·9	—	—	26·4
1847	(103)	(123)	(122)	17·3	—	—	26·4
1848	101	123	122	17·1	43	20·5	26·4
1849	99	122	121	17·3	41	20·5	26·4
1850	(96)	(121)	(120)	17·7	—	—	26·4
1851	92	120	118	17·9	37	20·5	26·4
1852	89	118	116	18·3	35	20·5	26·4
1853	93	117	115	18·5	40·8	20·5	27·1
1854	100	121	119	18·7	43·4	20·5	27·9
1855	100	120	117	19·2	43·2	20·5	28·7
1856	101	121	118	19·6	44·1	20·5	29·1
1857	100	121	117	20·0	44·1	20·5	29·1
1858	101	121	117	20·6	44·0	20·5	29·1
1859	101	121	117	20·8	43·8	20·7	29·1
1860	100	120	115	20·8	44·2	22·1	29·1
1861	94	112	107	20·8	44·7	22·1	29·1
1862	94	112	108	20·8	44·7	22·1	29·1
1863	99	116	111	20·6	45·4	22·7	29·1
1864	99	116	112	20·8	44·6	22·7	29·1
1865	100	117	113	21·0	44·8	23·7	29·5
1866	104	119	115	20·8	45·0	24·5	32·2
1867	103	121	117	20·8	48·7	27·6	32·6
1868	113	119	114	21·0	48·7	27·6	32·6
1869	104	112	107	21·3	48·5	27·6	32·6
1870	103	110	106	21·3	48·5	27·6	32·6
1871	103	111	106	21·0	48·5	27·6	32·9
1872	103	110	106	21·0	48·5	27·6	34·5
1873	109	114	109	20·8	49·0	29·2	34·5
1874	111	114	110	20·6	49·6	29·9	34·5
1875	108	114	110	20·2	49·6	30·8	34·5
1876	112	114	110	20·0	49·0	30·8	34·5
1877	110	114	111	19·8	48·6	30·9	34·5
1878	110	114	111	19·4	49·0	30·9	34·5
1879	109	114	112	18·7	47·7	30·9	34·5
1880	110	113	112	18·0	49·2	30·9	34·5
1881	107	113	112	17·7	46·8	30·9	34·5
1882	105	112	111	17·1	45·6	30·9	34·5
1883	101	110	110	16·5	43·9	30·9	34·9
1884	101	110	110	16·3	42·8	30·9	34·9
1885	100	110	111	15·8	45·6	30·9	34·9

* 1845–1910 Sauerbeck ten years' moving average, 1910–22 Ministry of Labour cost of living index.

Figures in brackets are estimated.

B. INDEX NUMBERS—*continued*

Date (Base year 1910)	Selling price of building			Trend of general prices	Price of materials in the building industry	Efficiency wages in the building industry	Average weekly Summer wages in the London building industry
	Uncorrected	Corrected for labour and materials	Corrected for labour and materials and other expenses				
	(B 1)	(B 2)	(B 3)	(B 4)	(B 5)	(B 6)	(B 7)
Base	100	100	100	16·5	44·7	38·8	38·8
1886	98	110	111	15·6	40·0	30·9	34·9
1887	97	110	111	15·4	39·3	30·9	34·9
1888	96	110	111	15·0	39·2	30·7	34·9
1889	101	110	112	14·8	43·9	30·7	34·9
1890	98	106	108	14·4	44·5	30·7	34·9
1891	95	105	107	14·2	42·8	30·7	34·9
1892	95	106	108	14·2	42·8	29·8	34·9
1893	90	100	103	14·0	42·5	30·3	34·9
1894	90	101	104	13·8	42·0	32·6	34·9
1895	91	101	103	13·8	42·0	32·6	35·3
1896	91	101	104	13·8	41·3	32·6	36·8
1897	93	101	104	13·8	41·3	34·5	37·2
1898	93	99	102	13·8	41·7	36·1	37·2
1899	97	98	101	13·8	45·7	37·4	37·2
1900	100	100	102	14·0	46·9	37·4	38·8
1901	103	99	101	14·2	48·9	38·0	38·8
1902	103	99	101	14·6	48·9	37·9	38·8
1903	103	99	101	14·8	48·9	37·9	38·8
1904	107	102	104	15·0	48·9	39·2	38·8
1905	107	103	104	15·2	48·9	39·2	38·8
1906	106	105	106	15·2	45·6	38·7	38·8
1907	107	104	105	15·4	47·3	38·7	38·8
1908	109	103	104	15·8	48·6	39·9	38·8
1909	107	103	103	16·0	52·6	39·9	38·8
1910	100	100	100	16·5	44·7	38·8	38·8
1911	100	102	101	16·9	44·7	37·2	—
1912	101	102	101	17·3	45·2	37·2	—
1913	106	104	103	17·5	47·6	37·7	—
1914	115	107	106	17·9	51·8	38·9	—
1915	116	104	99	21·7	53·9	40·9	—
1916	118	105	96	25·0	55·7	40·9	—
1917	140	103	89	30·2	76·2	45·2	—
1918	166	104	85	34·8	97·7	49·8	—
1919	273	161	141	36·9	129·2	64·2	—
1920	321	174	148	42·7	142·0	86·3	—
1921	388	213·5	191	38·7	147·9	109·3	—
1922	317	183·8	169	31·5	115·1	100·9	—

C. CENSUS RETURNS

Returns showing the numbers employed in the building industry by trades 1841–1921. Returns being grouped so as to give figures as nearly comparable as possible.

England and Wales, all ages in both sexes
(Figures in thousands)

Date	Bricklayer (including labourer)	Mason (including labourer)	Slater and tiler	Carpenter and joiner (including boys)	Plumber, painter, glazier, plasterer, paper-hanger and white-washer	Total engaged in building
1841	39	63	4	136	56	—
1851	67	77	4	156	72	390
1861	79	86	5	177	95	462
1871	99	97	6	205	131	567
1881	125	97	7	235	170	690
1891	130	84	6	221	200	706
1901	213	96	9	270	270	953
1911	172	63	8	214	284	887
1921	(173)	(42)	(6)	(246)	(281)	—

N.B. Brackets indicate estimates of doubtful value.

Notes on the construction of table of numbers employed in certain trades in the building industry from census returns

Figures are taken in:

1841. From the Preface to the Occupations Abstract of the Census of Great Britain 1841, Alphabetical Table, pp. 31–44, England and Wales.

1851. From the Census of Great Britain 1851, Population Tables II, Vol. I, Summary Table XXV, pp. ccxxiii, ccxxvi.

1861. From the Census of England and Wales 1861, Vol. II (C. 5597), Summary Tables XIX and XX, pp. xlviii, lx. Total in Table XVIII, p. xli.

1871. From the Census of England and Wales 1871, Vol. III (C. 872), Summary Tables XVII, XVIII, XIX, pp. xxxvi, xl, xlvi.

1881. From the Census of England and Wales 1881, Vol. III (C. 3722), Summary Tables IV, V, VI, pp. vii, xiii, xviii.

1891. From the Census of England and Wales 1891, Vol. III (C. 7058), Tables IV, V, VI, pp. viii, xvi, xvii, xxvi.

1901. From the Census of England and Wales 1901, Summary Tables (C. 1523), Tables XXX, XXXVI, pp. 194, 202.

1911. From the Census of England and Wales 1911, Vol. x, Occupations and Industries, Pt ii (C. 7019), Table xiii, p. 4.

1921. From the Census of England and Wales 1921, Occupations, and from the Classifications of Occupations and Industries.

No attempt was made in 1841 to group occupations by industries, but in 1851 a group "Persons engaged in Houses" (Class XI, Sub-class 15) starts, and this remains substantially the same under different names up to the 1911 Census:

1861. Class V, Order 10, Sub-order 14.

1871. Class V, Order 10, Sub-order 14: "Persons engaged in Houses and Buildings".

1881. Class V, Order 11, Sub-order 1: "Persons working and dealing in Houses".

1891. Class V, Order 11, Sub-order 1.

1901. Order XII, Sub-order 1: "House Building, etc."

1911. Order XII, Sub-order 1.

Even for 1841 and 1921 figures can be abstracted from the occupational groupings for the principal crafts which are fairly comparable with the other years, but these should be used with great caution.

A return to an Order of the House of Commons (1895) (408, Sess. 2) attempts to group the returns from the Census 1871, 1881, 1891, so as to be comparable where possible, while the 17th Abstract of Labour Statistics gives comparable figures for the Carpenters and Joiners, Bricklayers, Plasterers, Painters, Glaziers and others in the years 1891, 1901, 1911. My table is in agreement with these official returns.

1841–71. I A. Previous to 1881 Paviors are included under Masons, after 1881 they are grouped with the Road Labourers, being separately distinguished in 1881. The figures under Mason previous to 1881 have therefore been reduced 41 % to eliminate Paviors: the 41 % being based on the ratio of Paviors to Masons.

      I B. The figures for Carpenter and Joiner are probably slightly too low previous to 1871 owing to the omission of Packing-case Makers, etc.

1851. II. 727 female "Builders and House Decorators" have been distributed among the various trades in the proportions indicated by the 1841 Census.

     III. 2773 Surveyors have been transferred from the total Class XI, Sub-class 15, 1851, to secure comparable figures.

1861. IV. The numbers under House Proprietor, Rent Collector, Architect and Surveyor, have been deducted from the total under Class V, Order 10, Sub-order 14, to obtain results comparable with the earlier census figures (i.e. deduct 43,590).

1871. V. Items House Proprietor, Surveyor, Architect (namely 25,875 persons) have been deducted from the total under Class V, Order 10, Sub-order 14.

VI. The Items Locksmith and Bellhanger, Gas Fitter, House and Shop-Fitting Maker (23,282 persons) have been transferred from Class V, Order 11, Sub-order 2, to Sub-order 1 (houses) to get comparable figures.

1891. VII. The same items as in VI have been similarly transferred, namely 25,159 persons.

1901. VIII. Labourers are distinguished from Craftsmen in this Census; they have been added together. House and Shop-Fitting Makers have been transferred from Order XIII, Sub-order 1, to Order XII, Sub-order 1, to obtain comparable results.

1911. IX. 14,411 House and Shop-Fitting Makers have been transferred as in VIII.

1921. X. These figures are to be regarded as estimates pure and simple since employers, labourers, foremen and gangers, etc., are not sub-divided according to the craft with which they are associated. The figures given for Carpenter and Joiner, Bricklayer and Mason, are probably not very far from the truth.

APPENDIX II
THE LANCASHIRE COTTON INDUSTRY 1845–1913
INDEX NUMBERS, ETC.

Table I

Index numbers of prices and costs of grey cotton cloth 1845–1925

| | Selling price of grey cotton cloth | | | | |
Date (Base year 1910)	Uncorrected (1)	Corrected for labour, materials, and other expenses (2)	Price of raw cotton (3)	Efficiency wages (4)	Trend of general prices (5)
Base	100·0	100	61·0	22·0	17·0
1845	102·9	139	34·3	11·2	18·9
1846	92·4	126	37·2	11·2	18·5
1847	94·6	116	49·6	(10·9)*	17·9
1848	81·1	121	31·5	(10·6)*	17·6
1849	89·4	119	41·9	10·3	17·9
1850	104·2	122	53·4	10·3	18·3
1851	99·0	128	41·9	10·5	18·5
1852	95·4	125	40·5	10·7	18·9
1853	100·5	126	43·9	11·2	19·1
1854	93·8	122	41·0	11·1	19·4
1855	89·5	116	43·0	11·2	19·8
1856	93·2	113	48·1	11·8	20·2
1857	107·3	116	59·1	11·9	20·6
1858	103·2	118	52·4	12·0	21·3
1859	110·1	125	51·5	12·3	21·5
1860	113·2	131	47·7	13·1	21·5
1861	110·2	110	66·1	13·1	21·5
1862	158·2	92	131·6	12·8	21·5
1863	218·1	107	177·4	12·7	21·3
1864	240·6	97	209·8	12·7	21·5
1865	193·6	113	145·0	13·6	21·7
1866	179·1	125	118·3	14·7	21·5
1867	142·0	123	82·9	14·9	21·5
1868	123·5	107	80·1	15·2	21·7
1869	131·0	102	92·5	14·9	21·9
1870	124·6	111	75·8	15·5	21·9
1871	110·0	107	65·3	16·2	21·7
1872	125·2	106	80·6	16·7	21·7
1873	114·8	108	68·7	17·0	21·5
1874	110·8	111	61·0	17·3	21·3
1875	106·6	112	56·2	17·3	20·8
1876	96·4	111	47·7	17·6	20·6
1877	99·4	113	48·1	18·1	20·4

* Estimated.

Table I—*continued*

Date (Base year 1910)	Selling price of grey cotton cloth		Price of raw cotton	Efficiency wages	Trend of general prices
	Uncorrected	Corrected for labour, materials, and other expenses			
	(1)	(2)	(3)	(4)	(5)
Base	100·0	100	61·0	22·0	17·0
1878	89·0	106	46·7	16·8	20·0
1879	83·6	100	48·1	16·1	19·4
1880	91·4	103	53·0	16·7	18·7
1881	92·1	108	49·1	17·2	18·3
1882	90·2	105	50·5	17·3	17·6
1883	84·6	106	43·9	17·5	17·0
1884	83·2	103	45·8	17·5	16·8
1885	80·1	104	42·9	17·3	16·3
1886	78·4	106	39·1	17·1	16·1
1887	80·0	105	42·0	17·4	15·9
1888	82·0	106	42·4	18·0	15·5
1889	84·8	106	45·3	18·2	15·3
1890	85·2	106	45·8	18·6	14·8
1891	81·1	112	35·7	19·1	14·6
1892	74·3	108	32·0	19·4	14·6
1893	76·1	107	35·3	19·3	14·4
1894	68·6	106	92·1	19·3	14·2
1895	66·8	104	29·3	19·4	14·2
1896	68·2	98	33·1	19·4	14·2
1897	62·3	99	29·8	19·5	14·2
1898	62·4	103	25·3	19·8	14·2
1899	69·2	108	27·2	20·1	14·2
1900	78·4	102	41·7	20·5	14·4
1901	75·6	104	36·2	20·7	14·6
1902	73·3	101	36·4	20·5	15·1
1903	81·4	100	46·0	20·4	15·3
1904	90·7	104	50·4	20·7	15·5
1905	88·3	113	38·8	21·3	15·7
1906	94·0	111	45·4	22·0	15·7
1907	97·4	109	50·0	22·5	15·9
1908	87·6	105	43·6	22·5	16·3
1909	87·4	90	48·5	22·0	16·6
1910	100·0	100	61·0	22·0	17·0
1911	108·1	115	53·7	22·0	17·4
1912	101·4	111	49·4	22·7	17·9
1913	102·1	108	53·4	22·7	18·1
1914	95·4	105	48·9	22·7	18·5
1915	86·1	96	44·9	23·2	22·4
1916	115·5	96	68·9	24·2	26·4
1917	171·2	83	126·1	30·4	31·2
1918	368·8	216	170·8	46·4	35·9
1919	329·4	186	151·8	53·0	38·3
1920	514·5	327	176·3	68·2	43·1
1921	222·8	158	71·6	53·0	40·0
1922	184·0	115	94·2	42·1	32·5
1923	209·4	111	126·0	42·1	30·8
1924	238·4	141	124·4	42·1	31·2
1925	209·4	140	96·7	42·1	31·2

Table II

Size of the cotton industry

Date	Net imports of cotton to U.K. (million lbs.)	Net exports of yarn from U.K. (million lbs.)	Yarn produced in Great Britain (million lbs.)	Yarn consumed in Great Britain (million lbs.)	Yarn produced and yarn consumed (1000 lbs.)	Ten years' moving average of yarn produced and yarn consumed in Great Britain (1000 lbs.)
	(1)	(2)	(3)	(4)	(5)	(6)
1845	679	135	570	435	1006	—
1846	402	161	577	416	994	—
1847	400	120	415	295	710	—
1848	639	135	542	407	949	—
1849	657	149	592	443	1035	—
1850	561	130	553	422	975	1061
1851	645	143	619	476	1096	1101
1852	818	145	695	550	1246	1152
1853	747	146	715	569	1284	1218
1854	764	146	729	589	1313	1274
1855	767	164	789	624	1413	1315
1856	877	180	838	658	1495	1421
1857	837	176	776	601	1377	1483
1858	885	199	851	652	1503	1435
1859	1051	191	918	727	1645	1394
1860	1141	196	1019	822	1841	1360
1861	959	177	947	770	1717	1344
1862	309	92	425	333	757	1346
1863	428	74	478	404	882	1374
1864	649	75	520	446	966	1393
1865	675	103	680	577	1257	1388
1866	988	138	828	690	1519	1387
1867	912	168	909	740	1649	1423
1868	1005	171	932	761	1693	1548
1869	948	167	883	716	1598	1572
1870	1101	184	1010	826	1836	1792
1871	1416	192	1134	942	2077	1876
1872	1136	210	1105	894	1999	1941
1873	1308	214	1171	958	2129	1986
1874	1308	219	1190	971	2161	2014
1875	1229	214	1157	943	2100	2052
1876	1285	231	1198	967	2165	2105
1877	1186	224	1163	940	2103	2143
1878	1193	243	1106	863	1968	2195
1879	1281	229	1103	874	1977	2238
1880	1404	207	1290	1084	2374	2273
1881	1471	247	1353	1106	2459	2294
1882	1519	230	1374	1143	2517	2335
1883	1487	257	1408	1151	2559	2394
1884	1498	263	1387	1124	2511	2453
1885	1219	237	1273	1035	2308	2521
1886	1517	246	1410	1164	2574	2570
1887	1499	243	1420	1177	2597	2610
1888	1457	247	1452	1205	2657	2625
1889	1660	244	1449	1206	2655	2630
1890	1579	250	1558	1308	2867	2661
1891	1813	236	1543	1307	2850	2714

18-2

Table II—continued

Date	Net imports of cotton to U.K. (million lbs.)	Net exports of yarn from U.K. (million lbs.)	Yarn produced in Great Britain (million lbs.)	Yarn consumed in Great Britain (million lbs.)	Yarn produced and yarn consumed (1000 lbs.)	Ten years' moving average of yarn produced and yarn consumed in Great Britain (1000 lbs.)
	(1)	(2)	(3)	(4)	(5)	(6)
1892	1542	224	1446	1222	2668	2745
1893	1192	199	1408	1209	2616	2765
1894	1548	229	1525	1296	2821	2801
1895	1554	235	1542	1308	2850	2845
1896	1571	241	1554	1314	2868	2848
1897	1499	248	1524	1276	2800	2856
1898	1925	243	1630	1388	3018	2881
1899	1342	208	1648	1439	3087	2897
1900	1544	152	1526	1373	2899	2896
1901	1623	165	1549	1384	2934	2942
1902	1542	161	1539	1377	2916	2993
1903	1488	146	1463	1316	2779	3060
1904	1701	159	1485	1326	2810	3059
1905	1920	200	1752	1552	3303	3079
1906	1717	201	1790	1589	3379	3079
1907	2057	231	1854	1623	3477	3133
1908	1770	206	1603	1398	3001	3222
1909	1920	209	1749	1540	3290	3327
1910	1717	183	1541	1358	2898	3358
1911	1916	216	1845	1629	3474	3418
1912	2482	235	2023	1787	3810	3429
1913	1917	199	2015	1817	3832	3383
1914	1648	169	1645	1476	3121	3340
1915	2304	187	2044	1857	3901	3307
1916	1934	167	1828	1661	3489	3282
1917	152	132	1573	1441	3015	3117
1918	1489	101	1337	1236	2573	2997
1919	1837	161	1560	1399	2959	2849
1920	1693	145	1395	1251	2646	—
1921	1047	143	981	839	1820	—
1922	1402	198	1407	1209	2616	—
1923	1245	—	1241	1109	2345	—
1924	1489	—	—	—	—	—

Table III
Details of firms employed in Lancashire district
(C. S. M. Directory)

Date	Firms	Spindles	Looms	Index No. of size of firms*
1882	1874	38,410,067	485,264	(70)
1884	1709	40,533,882	534,403	82
1885	1755	41,298,110	546,048	82
1886–7	1708	40,993,386	550,077	84
1887–8	1778	40,946,709	582,504	83
1889	1795	41,284,088	597,287	83
1890	1801	41,417,379	606,585	84
1891	1793	42,401,701	610,934	85
1892	1818	43,054,227	615,719	85
1893–4	1777	42,970,528	602,627	86
1894–5	1785	43,186,657	627,585	88
1896	1771	42,681,081	638,469	88
1897	1760	42,061,287	641,547	89
1898	1735	41,795,731	629,942	89
1899	1760	42,190,910	638,972	89
1900	1787	42,640,201	648,820	88
1901	1775	43,119,580	651,023	90
1902	1774	44,594,385	647,599	91
1903	1764	44,620,950	647,372	92
1904	1764	45,195,641	653,120	92
1905	1769	45,972,951	652,166	93
1906	1824	48,322,684	684,811	95
1907	1900	52,585,362	725,221	98
1908	1976	55,218,024	736,325	97
1909	1977	57,026,422	739,382	99
1910	1977	57,731,829	741,197	100
1911	1966	58,002,435	741,260	101
1912	1968	58,140,220	758,712	102
1913	1999	58,481,031	786,205	102
1914	2011	59,317,187	805,452	103
1915	2009	59,904,873	808,145	104
1916	2008	59,811,222	808,796	104
1917	2004	60,973,381	807,543	106
1918	1951	59,522,833	787,679	106
1919	1968	59,182,683	790,936	105
1920	1974	60,079,394	798,083	106
1921	1959	60,053,246	790,399	106
1922	1960	59,812,303	799,000	106
1923	1943	59,818,670	795,244	107
1924	1942	59,510,867	791,674	107
1925	1917	59,902,954	788,197	108

* Size is to be measured by the number of spindles and looms in place. One loom is reckoned the equivalent of sixty spindles.

APPENDIX III

THE CLEVELAND PIG IRON INDUSTRY 1883–1925

A. INDEX NUMBERS, ETC.

Table I

Index numbers of price and costs of Cleveland pig iron 1883–1925

Date (Base year 1910)	Selling price of pig iron		Pig iron produced in Cleveland district (thousands of tons)
	Uncorrected	Corrected for labour, material and other expenses	
	(1)	(2)	(3)
Base	100·0	100·0	3679
1883	78·9	106·7	2779
1884	71·9	101·6	2504
1885	66·3	97·2	2477
1886	60·7	96·6	2436
1887	65·3	99·7	2524
1888	64·2	99·3	2631
1889	75·6	105·0	2782
1890	94·4	109·6	2837
1891	80·0	99·5	2631
1892	76·1	101·7	1944
1893	68·3	98·0	2713
1894	40·1	71·1	2973
1895	39·9	70·5	2926
1896	59·4	91·5	3211
1897	79·2	108·5	3197
1898	80·9	103·0	3198
1899	105·0	114·8	3251
1900	134·8	122·0	3109
1901	93·4	96·2	2820
1902	92·7	103·0	2960
1903	92·1	103·0	3108
1904	84·8	100·1	3123
1905	92·1	105·2	3485
1906	101·5	108·8	3628
1907	110·6	104·7	3681
1908	99·2	96·2	3389
1909	96·0	99·2	3550
1910	100·0	100·0	3679
1911	95·7	97·8	3542
1912	105·4	100·6	3258
1913	118·8	101·3	3869
1914	101·2	89·8	3306

Table I—*continued*

Date (Base year 1910)	Selling price of pig iron		Pig iron produced in Cleveland district (thousands of tons)
	Uncorrected	Corrected for labour, material and other expenses	
	(1)	(2)	(3)
1915	120·1	91·8	3006
1916	164·0	102·8	3097
1917	192·7 + 6·6	108·2 + 6·6	3230
1918	224·6 + 22·8	103·5 + 22·8	2991
*1919	287·1 + 7·6	105·2 + 7·6	2506
1920	407·9	143·0	2638
1921	281·1	90·8	1054
1922	173·5	76·1	1495
1923	197·9	97·2	2127
1924	175·3	86·9	2240
1925	144·6	—	1887

* The maximum prices of pig iron, ore and coal were fixed by Government from October 31, 1915, and a subsidy granted where necessary to April 30, 1919. The equivalent of the subsidy is indicated in the plusage.

Table II

Details of firms operating in Cleveland district and index numbers

Date (Base year 1910)	No. operating		No. of furnaces built	No. of furnaces in blast		Cost of ore	Cost of coal	Efficiency wages	General prices
	Works	Owners		Iron-masters' figures	Home Office records				
	(1)	(2)	(3)	(4)	(5)	(6)	(7)	(8)	(9)
Base	26	20	115	83	83	31·0	36·0	15·0	18·0
1883	31	26	163	118	123	22·8	22·3	9·1	18·0
1884	30	24	162	101	102	22·8	21·2	8·5	17·8
1885	29	24	159	96	97	22·8	20·7	8·2	17·4
1886	29	24	159	92	94	19·3	20·0	7·7	17·1
1887	27	24	158	93	94	20·5	20·1	8·1	16·9
1888	28	25	158	97	98	20·5	20·1	7·9	16·4
1889	28	25	153	101	102	22·8	23·3	8·3	16·2
1890	28	24	153	104	103	26·3	33·0	9·7	15·8
1891	28	24	149	91	92	24·6	31·3	9·1	15·5
1892	25	22	139	67	72	22·2	28·1	8·6	15·5
1893	25	22	139	87	86	21·6	25·1	8·3	15·3
1894	25	22	133	93	92	21·0	24·7	8·2	15·1
1895	25	22	134	90	91	22·8	23·2	8·3	15·1
1896	25	22	129	96	96	21·3	23·1	8·4	15·1
1897	24	21	123	94	95	22·8	24·1	8·7	15·1
1898	27	21	122	95	95	23·4	26·3	13·3	15·1
1899	27	21	123	96	99	29·2	31·3	14·6	15·1
1900	26	19	121	93	95	34·5	46·7	16·3	15·3
1901	26	20	121	78	79	27·5	38·8	15·4	15·5
1902	25	20	115	79	79	26·3	33·1	14·3	16·0
1903	25	20	114	80	81	26·3	32·0	14·6	16·2

Table II—*continued*

Date (Base year 1910)	No. operating Works (1)	Owners (2)	No. of furnaces built (3)	No. of furnaces in blast Ironmasters' figures (4)	Home Office records (5)	Cost of ore (6)	Cost of coal (7)	Efficiency wages (8)	General prices (9)
Base	26	20	115	83	83	31·0	36·0	15·0	18·0
1904	26	20	114	76	77	25·1	29·4	13·8	16·4
1905	26	20	116	84	83	26·9	29·2	14·3	16·7
1906	26	20	115	87	87	30·4	31·5	14·3	16·7
1907	26	20	116	87	90	32·9	39·4	16·7	16·9
1908	26	20	117	78	78	31·0	39·4	15·2	17·4
1909	26	20	116	79	80	30·4	34·1	14·7	17·6
1910	26	20	115	83	83	31·0	36·0	15·0	18·0
1911	26	20	116	79	79	30·4	34·2	14·8	18·5
1912	25	20	115	73	78	32·9	38·2	14·9	19·0
1913	26	20	115	83	85	35·7	45·9	16·7	19·2
1914	25	20	112	74	75	33·3	43·2	15·3	19·6
1915	26	20	113	68	70	37·4	50·0	(17·1)	23·8
1916	24	19	113	72	71	45·0	68·6	(20·2)	27·4
1917	25	19	113	76	76	53·8	74·0	(23·7)	33·0
1918	25	19	113	74	74	67·3	87·8	(28·0)	38·0
1919	25	19	115	69	68	86·5	120·2	(34·8)	40·4
1920	25	19	114	69	69	111·7	156·8	49·6	46·8
1921	24	19	114	20	24	102·9	99·5	45·4	42·5
1922	23	18	114	31	33	59·7	75·9	27·3	34·5
1923	24	12	111	43	44	53·2	86·2	28·7	32·6
1924	20	10	108	43	—	48·5	80·9	26·0	33·0
1925	20	10	107	37	—	—	64·6	23·3	33·0

N.B. In 1924 six works in the district were idle for the whole year. Figures in brackets estimated.

Table III

Pig iron produced in the Cleveland district and materials used (thousands of tons per annum)

Date	Pig iron produced (1)	Coal consumed (2)*	Ore used (3)	Cleveland ore raised (4)	Imports of foreign ore (5)	Home ore† brought from other districts (6)
1883	2779	5603	8018	6756	987	274
1884	2504	5017	7201	6052	794	355
1885	2477	4874	7074	5932	822	318
1886	2436	4745	6957	5370	1013	574
1887	2524	4887	7153	4980	1466	706
1888	2631	5188	7227	5395	1417	414

* Includes cinder, etc., up to 1920.
† Column (6) is simply the difference between columns (3), (4) and (5). It therefore includes ore taken from or added to stocks.

Table III—*continued*

Date	Pig iron produced (1)	Coal consumed (2)	Ore used (3)	Cleveland ore raised (4)	Imports of foreign ore (5)	Home ore brought from other districts (6)
1889	2782	5422	7581	5657	1655	268
1890	2837	5581	7740	5617	1865	257
1891	2631	5172	7199	5128	1569	502
1892	1944	3771	5124	3411	1521	191
1893	2713	5064	7072	4625	2061	386
1894	2973	5547	7782	5048	2410	323
1895	2926	5438	7655	5285	2038	331
1896	3211	6051	8407	5678	2357	371
1897	3197	6124	8422	5679	2335	408
1898	3198	6161	8446	5730	2278	438
1899	3251	6396	8496	5612	2455	428
1900	3109	6313	8288	5493	2238	556
1901	2820	5555	7480	5100	1873	506
1902	2960	5864	7859	5396	2131	331
1903	3108	6188	8274	5668	2145	461
1904	3123	6079	8342	5719	2279	343
1905	3485	6768	9040	5934	2833	273
1906	3628	7125	9499	6102	2974	422
1907	3681	7247	9746	6240	3067	439
1908	3389	6618	9098	6072	2589	436
1909	3550	6743	9367	6191	2717	458
1910	3679	6936	9684	6152	3137	394
1911	3542	6652	9373	6049	2806	516
1912	3258	6164	8410	5158	3047	204
1913	3869	7357	10016	6010	3356	648
1914	3306	6310	8724	5574	—	—
1915	3006	228 **3661**	7592	4746	—	—
1916	3097	222 **3735**	7630	4315	—	—
1917	3230	275 **3985**	8076	4821	—	—
1918	2991	280 **3789**	7674	4544	—	—
1919	2506	248 **3326**	6579	3712	—	—
1920	2638	48 **3474**	6499	3717	—	—
1921	1054	— **1292**	2147	1003	—	—
1922	1495	3 **1754**	2749	1169	—	—
1923	2127	— **2608**	4509	2079	—	—
1924	2240	—	4056	2234	—	—
1925	1887	—	3769	2300	—	—

N.B. After 1914 coke and coal are given separately. Black figures are tons of coke.

Table IV

Average output of pig iron in the Cleveland district

Date	Per works (1000 tons) (1)	Per firm (1000 tons) (2)	Ten years' moving average (previous column) (3)	Per furnace built (1000 tons) (4)	Per furnace in blast (1000 tons) (5)	Ten years' moving average (previous column) (6)	Ten years' moving average of pig iron produced (1000 tons) (7)
1883	90	107	—	17·0	23·5	—	—
1884	84	104	—	15·5	24·8	—	—
1885	85	103	—	15·5	24·7	—	—
1886	84	101	—	15·3	26·5	—	—
1887	94	105	—	16·0	27·2	—	—
1888	94	105	105	16·6	27·3	26·7	2555
1889	99	111	107	18·2	27·6	27·4	2548
1890	101	118	110	18·5	27·2	28·2	2595
1891	94	110	113	17·6	28·9	28·9	2640
1892	78	88	117	14·0	29·0	29·7	2718
1893	108	123	122	19·5	31·2	30·4	2785
1894	119	135	127	22·3	32·0	31·0	2842
1895	117	133	131	21·8	32·5	31·7	2889
1896	128	146	136	24·9	33·4	32·3	2916
1897	133	152	139	26·0	34·7	33·0	2935
1898	118	152	145	26·2	33·7	33·9	3036
1899	120	155	148	26·4	33·9	34·6	3076
1900	120	164	150	25·5	33·4	35·5	3090
1901	108	141	154	23·3	36·2	36·4	3147
1902	118	148	158	25·7	37·5	37·3	3188
1903	124	155	161	27·3	38·9	38·0	3237
1904	120	156	163	27·4	41·2	39·0	3256
1905	134	174	165	30·1	41·5	40·1	3286
1906	139	181	167	31·5	41·7	41·2	3343
1907	143	184	171	31·7	42·3	42·1	3415
1908	130	169	172	29·0	43·5	42·8	3445
1909	136	177	176	30·6	45·0	43·6	3521
1910	141	184	177	32·0	44·3	43·9	3539
1911	136	177	174	30·5	44·9	44·2	3491
1912	130	163	173	28·3	44·7	44·3	3438
1913	149	193	171	33·6	46·6	44·3	3393
1914	134	165	170	29·5	44·7	44·0	3353
1915	115	150	165	26·6	44·2	43·2	3249
1916	129	163	161	27·4	43·0	42·6	3145
1917	129	170	149	28·6	42·5	43·3	2896
1918	120	157	141	26·4	40·4	43·7	2720
1919	100	132	139	21·8	36·3	44·0	2545
1920	111	139	145	23·1	38·2	44·7	2439
1921	42	56	149	9·3	52·8	45·4	2327
1922	65	83	—	13·1	48·2	—	—
1923	89	177	—	19·2	49·5	—	—
1924	112	224	—	20·8	52·1	—	—
1925	94	189	—	17·6	51·0	—	—

B. RECORD OF FIRMS OPERATING IN THE CLEVELAND DISTRICT

Tabular statement of pig iron works operating on the north-east coast together with a record of the changes which have occurred in their ownership since 1883.

List of pig iron works in Cleveland (north-east coast) district 1883–1926

Works and situation: Durham, Yorkshire and Northumberland	Furnaces built 1883	Furnaces blowing 1883	Proprietors 1883	Remarks upon changes in ownership, etc., during the period 1883–1926	Furnaces built 1913	Proprietors 1926	Furnaces built 1926
(1)	(2)	(3)	(4)	(5)	(6)	(7)	(8)
Clarence, Middlesbrough	12	11	Bell Bros. Ltd.	Taken over by Dorman Long & Co. Ltd. in 1923	11	Dorman Long & Co. Ltd.	11
Newport, Middlesbrough	8	7	B. Samuelson & Co.	Taken over by Dorman Long & Co. Ltd. in 1923	8	,,	5
Acklom, Middlesbrough	4	3	Stevenson Jacques	Taken over by North Eastern Steel Co. in 1897, then by Dorman Long & Co. Ltd. in 1923	4	,,	4
Redcar, Middlesbrough	4	4	Walker, Maynard & Co.	Taken over by Dorman Long & Co. Ltd. in 1915	4	,,	4
Carlton, Stockton-on-Tees	3	2	Carlton Iron Co. Ltd.	Taken over by Dorman Long & Co. Ltd. in 1923	3	,,	3
Coatham, Redcar	2	2	Downey & Co.	Ceased to work 1887, was taken over by the N. P. Bank in 1893; by J. M. Lennard and Wm. Whitwell in 1896; by Walker, Maynard & Co. Ltd. in 1900 and by Dorman Long & Co. Ltd. in 1915	2	,,	2
South Bank, Middlesbrough	8	8	Bolckow, Vaughan & Cp. Ltd.	No change	7	Bolckow, Vaughan & Co. Ltd.	4
Tees Bridge, Stockton-on-Tees	3	3	Tees Bridge Iron Co. Ltd.	Taken over by Pease and Partners, Ltd. in 1916	3	Pease and Partners, Ltd.	3
Tees, Middlesbrough	5	5	Wilsons, Pease & Co.	Taken over by Pease and Partners, Ltd. in 1912	3	,,	3

B. RECORD OF FIRMS OPERATING IN THE CLEVELAND DISTRICT—continued

Works and situation: Durham, Yorkshire and Northumberland (1)	Furnaces built 1883 (2)	Furnaces blowing 1883 (3)	Proprietors 1883 (4)	Remarks upon changes in ownership, etc., during the period 1883–1926 (5)	Furnaces built 1913 (6)	Proprietors 1926 (7)	Furnaces built 1926 (8)
Lackenby, Middlesbrough	3	3	Downey & Co.	Taken over by Bolckow, Vaughan & Co. Ltd. in 1892; transferred to Tees Furnace Co. Ltd. in 1902; then to Pease and Partners, Ltd. in 1924	2	Pease and Partners, Ltd.	3
Linthorpe, Middlesbrough	6	5	Edward Williams	Taken over by Executors in 1891; then by Linthorpe and Dinsdale Smelting Co. Ltd. in 1903	6	Linthorpe and Dinsdale Smelting Co. Ltd.	6
Middleton, Darlington	4	4	Executors George Wythes	Ceased to work 1884, was taken over by Joseph Tobock 1892 but not worked; passed to Dinsdale Smelting Co. Ltd. in 1902 and was worked by them	4	,,	4
Consett, Durham	7	6	Consett Iron Co. Ltd.	No change	8	Consett Iron Co. Ltd.	8
Jarrow, Jarrow-on-Tyne	3	3	Palmer's Iron Co. Ltd.	No change	5	Palmer's Iron Co. Ltd.	5
Seaton Carew, West Hartlepool	3	2	Seaton Carew Iron Co. Ltd.	No change	4	Seaton Carew Iron Co. Ltd.	4
Clay Lane, Eston Junction (Clay Lane, South Bank, Middlesbrough)	6	6	Clay Lane Iron Co. Ltd.	Taken over by Bolckow, Vaughan & Co. Ltd. in 1900	6	Bolckow, Vaughan & Co. Ltd.	4
Grangetown, Yorks	—	—	—	Built by Bolckow, Vaughan & Co. Ltd. in 1905–6	2	,,	2
Cleveland Iron and Steel, Middlesbrough (Cleveland, South ...)	11	11	Bolckow, Vaughan & Co. Ltd.	No change	5	,,	5

... Bank, Middlesbrough	—	—	Three furnaces built in 1884 by Bolckow, Vaughan & Co. Ltd. Known as Bessemer Works from 1919	2	,,	2
Middlesbrough, Middlesbrough	2	Bolckow, Vaughan & Co. Ltd.	No change	2	,,	2
Skinningrove, Carlin How	2	Skinningrove Iron Co. Ltd.	Taken over for working purposes by Pease and Partners, Ltd. in 1922	5	Pease and Partners, Ltd.	5
Normanby, Middlesbrough (Normanby Cargo Fleet, Middlesbrough)	3	Jones Dunning & Co.	Became Jones, Pease and Crewdson in 1888, was returned to Jones, Dunning & Co. in 1889; became Normanby Iron Works Co. in 1890; A. A. F. and H. P. Pease in 1893; was returned to Normanby Iron Works Co. in 1897; and finally became Pease and Partners, Ltd. in 1911	4	,,	3
Ayresome, Middlesbrough	4	Gjers, Mills & Co.	No change	4	Gjers, Mills & Co.	5
Ormesby, Middlesbrough	5	Cochrane & Co.	No change	4	Cochrane & Co Ltd.	4
Thornaby, Stockton-on-Tees	3	William Whitwell & Co.	No change	3	William Whitwell & Co.	3
Cargo Fleet, Middlesbrough	5	Cargo Fleet Iron Co. Ltd.	No change	2	Cargo Fleet Iron Co. Ltd.	3
Tudhoe, Spennymoor	2	Weardale Iron and Coal Co. Ltd.	Became Weardale Steel, Coal and Coke Co. Ltd. in 1900. Dismantled 1924–1925	2	—	—
Stockton, North Shore	0	Stockton Iron Furnace Co.	Was not worked; was unoccupied in 1887 until taken over in 1892 by Joseph Tobock. Dismantled 1900	—	—	—
Elswick, Newcastle-on-Tyne	2	Sir W. G. Armstrong, Mitchell & Co. Ltd.	Ceased to work and was dismantled in 1900	—	—	—

B. RECORD OF FIRMS OPERATING IN THE CLEVELAND DISTRICT—continued

Works and situation: Durham, Yorkshire and Northumberland (1)	Furnaces built 1883 (2)	Furnaces blowing 1883 (3)	Proprietors 1883 (4)	Remarks upon changes in ownership, etc., during the period 1883–1926 (5)	Furnaces built 1913 (6)	Proprietors 1926 (7)	Furnaces built 1926 (8)
Walker, Walker-on-Tyne	2	2	Bell Bros. Ltd.	Not used after 1884 until taken over by Magnetic Iron Mountains Smelting Co, 1888, it was returned to Bell Bros. 1890, worked, and finally dismantled in 1898	—	—	—
Witton Park, Bishop Auckland	2	2	Bolckow, Vaughan & Co. Ltd.	Ceased to work in 1884 and was dismantled in 1897	—	—	—
Tees Side, Middlesbrough	4	4	Tees Side Iron and Engine Works Co. Ltd.	Dismantled 1897	—	—	—
Towlaw, Darlington	4	1	Weardale Iron and Coal Co. Ltd.	Did not work after 1888, and was dismantled in 1896	—	—	—
Ferry Hill, West Carnforth	8	0	John Rogerson	Did not work again; was taken over by the executors in 1894 and dismantled in 1895	—	—	—
Norton, Stockton-on-Tees	6	0	Norton Iron Co. Ltd.	Was not worked; taken over by Wm. Slater & Sons in 1889. Dismantled in 1894	—	—	—
Vane and Seaham, Seaham	2	0	Watson, Kipling & Co. Ltd.	Was not worked, taken over by Marquis Londonderry in 1893. Dismantled 1894	—	—	—
Grosmont, Whitby	3	2	C. and T. Bagnall, Jnr.	Taken over by Trustees in 1891 and was dismantled 1892	—	—	—
Glaisdale, Grosmont	3	0	S. Cleveland Iron Works Co. Ltd.	Did not work and was dismantled in 1891	—	—	—
Royal Creek, Wallsend-on-Tyne	2	0	Credit General Ottoman, Constantinople	Did not work and was dismantled in 1890	—	—	—
South Durham,	3	0	S. Durham Iron Co. Ltd	Was not worked. Dismantled 1884	—	—	—

APPENDIX IV

THE MASSACHUSETTS COTTON INDUSTRY 1845–1920

A. INDEX NUMBERS, ETC.

Table I

Data upon which Table II is based

Distribution of expenses of manufacture

Date (Base year 1913)	Selling price index (1 print cloth, 1 sheeting) (1)	Raw cotton (2)	Labour at current wage rates (3)	Labour at 1913 wage rates (4)	Margin (5)	Value of margin at 1913 prices (6)	Index of general prices (7)
Base	100	55·0*	24·0	24·0	21·0	21·0	100
1847	129	48·2	31·0	77·8	49·8	72·4	69
1848	98	34·5	30·7	76·3	32·8	49·8	66
1849	102	32·5	30·1	74·8	39·4	61·6	64
1850	116	53·1	29·5	73·3	33·4	49·8	67
1851	104	51·7	28·9	71·8	23·4	33·9	69
1852	104	40·8	27·4	70·3	35·8	53·5	67
1853	129	47·4	27·4	68·8	54·2	76·4	71
1854	125	47·1	26·6	67·3	51·3	71·4	73
1855	114	44·7	27·0	65·8	42·3	57·2	74
1856	116	44·3	27·5	64·3	44·2	59·8	74
1857	133	58·1	26·9	62·8	48·0	65·8	73
1858	124	52·7	26·5	61·3	44·8	68·0	66
1859	126	51·9	**25·6**	**59·8**	48·5	74·7	65
1860	125	47·3	25·6	60·3	52·1	80·2	65
1861	131	56·0	26·0	60·8	49·0	77·8	63
1862	244	134·5	26·5	61·2	83·0	110·8	75
1863	421	289·0	28·2	61·7	103·8	107·0	97
1864	627	437·0	31·6	62·2	158·4	117·0	135
1865	502	358·0	37·7	62·6	106·3	79·4	134
1866	334	185·7	44·8	63·2	103·5	85·6	121
1867	231	135·8	46·9	63·6	48·3	43·5	111
1868	210	106·9	46·1	64·0	57·0	52·8	108
1869	208	124·7	**47·5**	**64·5**	35·8	35·1	102
1870	183	103·0	44·7	60·2	35·3	37·6	94
1871	189	72·9	44·5	55·9	71·6	80·5	89
1872	191	95·4	42·7	51·6	52·9	58·8	90
1873	169	86·6	37·7	47·3	44·7	49·7	90
1874	143	77·2	**32·9**	**43·0**	32·9	36·6	90
1875	134	66·5	29·1	41·4	38·4	45·7	84
1876	108	55·8	26·2	39·8	26·0	32·5	80
1877	109	50·8	24·4	38·1	33·8	43·9	77
1878	93	48·3	23·7	36·5	21·0	29·6	71

* = $12.80 per yd.

Table I—*continued*

Distribution of expenses of manufacture

Date (Base year 1913)	Selling price index (1 print cloth, 1 sheeting)	Raw cotton	Labour at current wage rates	Labour at 1913 wage rates	Other expenses		Index of general prices
					Margin	Value of margin at 1913 prices	
	(1)	(2)	(3)	(4)	(5)	(6)	(7)
Base	100	55·0	24·0	24·0	21·0	21·0	100
1879	100	46·2	21·9	34·9	31·9	45·0	71
1880	111	49·5	23·3	35·4	38·2	50·3	76
1881	104	51·7	22·7	35·9	29·6	37·5	79
1882	101	49·7	24·2	36·4	27·1	33·5	81
1883	98	51·1	24·7	36·9	22·2	28·1	79
1884	89	46·8	24·6	37·4	17·6	23·2	76
1885	82	45·0	23·3	36·7	13·7	18·8	73
1886	85	39·9	23·4	36·1	21·7	30·2	72
1887	88	43·9	24·0	35·4	20·1	27·5	73
1888	94	43·2	24·2	34·8	26·6	35·5	75
1889	93	45·8	24·4	34·1	22·8	30·8	74
1890	87	47·6	24·5	33·8	14·9	19·9	75
1891	81	37·0	24·5	33·6	19·5	21·5	76
1892	84	33·2	24·3	33·3	26·5	35·8	74
1893	79	36·8	25·4	33·1	16·8	22·4	75
1894	67	29·8	22·9	32·8	14·3	19·9	72
1895	73	32·0	22·2	32·0	18·8	26·1	72
1896	68	34·0	23·0	31·2	11·0	15·5	71
1897	61	30·1	22·2	30·4	8·7	12·3	71
1898	52	25·5	21·5	29·6	5·0	7·1	71
1899	68	29·6	20·0	28·8	18·4	24·9	74
1900	79	39·8	22·9	29·5	16·3	21·5	76
1901	71	37·6	22·6	28·1	10·8	14·1	77
1902	74	38·7	22·4	27·8	12·9	16·3	79
1903	81	48·0	22·8	27·4	10·2	12·8	80
1904	89	50·5	22·3	27·0	16·2	20·0	81
1905	84	42·2	22·6	26·7	19·2	23·4	82
1906	92	49·4	24·2	26·3	18·4	21·7	85
1907	107	52·0	26·4	25·8	28·6	32·2	89
1908	87	45·7	25·0	25·4	16·3	18·3	89
1909	93	54·5	22·5	25·0	16·0	17·2	93
1910	99	65·0	21·8	24·7	12·2	12·7	96
1911	95	56·0	21·6	24·5	17·4	18·1	96
1912	98	49·5	23·8	24·2	24·7	25·0	99
1913	100	55·0	24·0	24·0	21·0	21·0	100
1914	93	47·8	23·9	23·7	21·3	21·1	101
1915	84	43·6	23·1	22·7	17·3	16·8	103
1916	117	44·9	26·6	21·6	45·5	39·2	116
1917	184	101·0	30·5	20·6	52·5	37·5	140
1918	306	136·2	35·7	19·6	134·1	81·8	164
1919	279	138·7	52·6	18·6	87·7	47·2	186
1920	292	145·7	67·4	(20)	78·9	37·0	213

N.B. The distribution of expenses shown by black figures was calculated from census returns and a figure was also obtained for labour at 1913 wage rates in 1838. The estimates for intermediate years were computed by interpolation.

Table II

Index numbers of prices and costs of grey cotton cloth

Date (Base year 1913)	Selling price		Selling price corrected for labour, materials, and other expenses		Selling price corrected for labour, materials and other expenses weighted according to their values in 1860	
	Annual average (1)	Seven years' moving average, i.e. money costs (2)	Annual average (3)	Seven years' moving average, i.e. real costs (4)	Annual average (5)	Seven years' moving average (6)
Base	100	—	100	—	100	—
1847	129	—	206	—	179	—
1848	98	—	181	—	158	—
1849	102	—	191	—	168	—
1850	116	112	178	185	152	162
1851	104	111	161	183	141	161
1852	104	113	178	182	158	161
1853	129	116	200	181	177	159
1854	125	118	193	181	171	161
1855	114	121	178	185	158	165
1856	116	124	179	186	159	167
1857	133	123	184	186	165	166
1858	124	124	184	186	165	167
1859	126	143	189	193	171	173
1860	125	186	195	200	176	179
1861	131	257	194	207	173	186
1862	244	311	227	209	204	188
1863	421	341	223	211	202	189
1864	627	356	235	206	212	185
1865	502	367	197	203	176	183
1866	334	362	204	192	182	173
1867	231	328	162	183	144	164
1868	210	265	172	175	161	159
1869	208	221	154	170	137	155
1870	183	197	152	163	138	149
1871	189	185	181	159	172	146
1872	191	174	165	154	151	142
1873	169	160	152	150	139	140
1874	143	149	135	148	125	139
1875	134	135	141	139	134	131
1876	108	122	127	135	120	127
1877	109	114	137	134	130	127
1878	93	108	122	133	115	126
1879	100	104	135	131	128	124
1880	111	102	141	130	134	123
1881	104	99	129	127	123	122
1882	101	98	125	125	120	120
1883	98	96	120	123	114	118
1884	89	93	116	120	111	115
1885	82	91	110	119	106	115
1886	85	90	122	119	115	114
1887	88	88	118	117	113	113
1888	94	87	125	117	120	112

Table II—*continued*

Date (Base year 1913)	Selling price		Selling price corrected for labour, materials, and other expenses		Selling price corrected for labour, materials and other expenses weighted according to their values in 1860	
	Annual average (1)	Seven years' moving average, i.e. money costs (2)	Annual average (3)	Seven years' moving average, i.e. real costs (4)	Annual average (5)	Seven years' moving average (6)
Base	100	—	100	—	100	—
1889	93	87	120	119	115	114
1890	87	87	109	117	104	113
1891	81	84	114	116	110	111
1892	84	87	124	114	120	110
1893	79	77	111	112	107	108
1894	67	73	108	110	103	107
1895	73	69	113	107	110	104
1896	68	67	102	105	100	102
1897	61	67	98	104	96	102
1898	52	67	91	102	92	101
1899	68	68	109	101	107	99
1900	79	69	105	99	103	98
1901	71	73	97	100	97	99
1902	74	78	99	102	99	101
1903	81	81	96	101	94	100
1904	89	85	102	102	101	101
1905	84	88	105	102	104	102
1906	92	90	103	102	103	101
1907	107	93	113	101	111	101
1908	87	94	99	101	99	101
1909	93	96	97	101	97	101
1910	99	97	93	101	93	100
1911	95	—	98	—	97	—
1912	98	—	104	—	104	—
1913	100	—	100	—	100	—
1914	93	—	100	—	96	—
1915	84	—	94	—	115	—
1916	117	—	116	—	113	—
1917	184	—	113	—	154	—
1918	306	—	157	—	121	—
1919	279	—	120	—	113	—
1920	292	—	112	—		

Table III

Summary of returns taken from federal and state censuses relating to cotton manufacture in Massachusetts

Date	Number of establishments (1)	Average number of wage earners (2)	Amount paid in wages ($1000) (3)	Value of product ($1000) (4)	Raw cotton consumed (1000 lbs.) (5)	Active spindles in cotton mills (1000) (6)	Looms in operation in cotton mills (7)	Average number of wage earners per establishment (8)	Wages as % of product (9)
1831	256	13,343	—	—	24,872	340	8,981	52	—
1839	278	20,928	—	16,553	—	665	—	75	—
1844	302	20,710	—	12,193	—	817	—	69	—
1849	213	28,730	—	19,712	100,623	—	—	135	—
1854	294	34,787	—	26,141	—	1,520	42,779	118	—
1859	217	38,451	7,798	38,004	134,013	1,673	—	177	20·3
1864	237	24,151	—	35,356	—	1,914	—	102	—
1869	191	43,512	10,844	47,475	130,654	2,620	55,343	228	22·8
1874	220	60,176	16,712	69,585	—	3,859	—	281	23·0
1879	175	61,844	15,829	72,292	273,719	4,236	95,321	353	21·9
1884	165	60,132	16,916	61,425	—	5,133	—	365	27·6
1889	187	76,213	26,231	100,203	386,767	5,825	133,227˙	408	26·2
1894	188	83,113	27,447	93,916	—	—	—	442	34·2
1899	177	92,515	32,479	111,125	560,984	7,785	179,280	523	29·2
1904	161	88,640	32,555	130,069	489,990	8,411	194,686	550	25·0
1909	182	108,914	45,117	186,462	622,368	9,372	—	598	24·2
1914	189	113,559	50,706	197,322	624,728	10,557	228,127	601	25·7
1919	231	124,150	111,141	604,938	662,726	11,207	225,379	538	18·8
1921	224	107,488	97,474	317,602	—	—	—	480	32·6
1923	245	116,751	118,045	429,326	—	—	—	477	27·5
1925	—	—	—	—	—	—	—	—	—

Note. (1) Statistics for 1831 taken from C. D. Wright's *Factory System*, Tenth Census.

(2) The statistics refer to "cotton goods including small wares" or the grouping most nearly comparable.

(3) Values for 1864, 1869, 1874 are expressed in gold.

(4) Up to 1919 the federal census returns cover all establishments whose product was greater than $500.00. For 1921, 1923, the minimum is $5000.00. The state census returns, 1844, 1854, 1864, 1874, 1884, 1894, profess to cover cotton factories of all sizes.

(5) Spindles and looms engaged in cotton small wares are not included after 1889.

Table IV

Size of establishments—United States cotton manufactures 1879–1919

Date	Establishments (1)	Wage earners (2)	Active-producing spindles (1000) (3)	Wage earners per establishment		Active-producing spindles per establishment		Index number of output per establishment (8)
				Actual number (4)	Index number (5)	Actual number (6)	Index number (7)	
1879	756	172,544	10,652	228	100	14,091	100	—
1889	905	218,876	14,188	242	106·1	15,677	111·2	—
1899	1055	302,861	19,051	287	125·8	18,058	128·1	—
1904	1154	315,874	23,195	274	120·1	20,100	142·6	—
1909	1324	375,880	27,426	286	125·4	20,715	147·0	—
1914	1328	393,404	30,915	296	129·8	23,279	165·0	—
1919	1496	446,852	33,796	299	131·1	22,591	160·3	—

Note. Part Table XVI, p. 55, of United States Census Monograph III.

Size of establishments in Massachusetts cotton manufactures 1830–1920

Date	Establishments (1)	Wage earners (2)	Active-producing spindles (1000) (3)	Wage earners per establishment		Active-producing spindles per establishment		Index number of output per establishment (8)
				Actual number (4)	Index number (5)	Actual number (6)	Index number (7)	
1831	256	13,343	340	52	15	1,330	6	—
1839	278	20,928	665	75	21	2,390	10	8
1844	302	20,710	817	69	(20)	2,710	(11)	(8)
1849	213	28,730	—	135	38	—	—	18
1854	294	34,787	1,520	118	(33)	5,170	(21)	18
1859	217	38,451	1,673	177	50	7,720	32	(17)
1864	237	24,151	1,914	102	(29)	8,090	(33)	29
1869	191	43,512	2,620	228	65	13,700	57	(16)
1874	220	60,176	3,859	281	80	17,500	72	35
1879	175	61,844	4,236	353	100	24,200	100	65
1884	165	60,132	5,133	365	103	31,100	125	100
1889	187	76,213	5,825	408	116	31,200	126	97
1894	188	83,113	—	442	125	—	—	118
1899	177	92,515	7,785	523	148	44,000	182	133
1904	161	88,640	8,411	550	156	52,300	216	173
1909	182	108,914	9,372	598	170	51,500	213	201
1914	189	113,559	10,557	601	170	55,906	231	236
1919	231	124,150	11,207	538	153	48,500	200	286

N.B. Bracketed figures are based upon state census returns at a time when the state classification differed materially

APPENDIX V

THE AMERICAN PIG IRON INDUSTRY 1883–1925
INDEX NUMBERS, ETC.

Table I. Price series relating to the American pig iron industry

Date	Selling price of composite pig iron		Selling price of Connellsville coke		Selling price of Lake Superior iron ore			Relative hourly wages of blast furnace men	Index of general prices
	Average price, $ per ton (2240 lb.)	Index number	Average price, $ per short ton (2000 lb.)	Index number	Average price, $ per ton (2240 lb.)		Index number		
					Bessemer	Non-Bessemer			
	(1)	(2)	(3)	(4)	(5)	(6)	(7)	(8)	(9)
1883	20·00	130	1·14	39	—	4·75	110	77	79
1884	18·14	118	1·13	38	—	4·50	104	77	76
1885	16·26	105	1·22	41	4·00	4·00	93	74	73
1886	17·31	112	1·36	46	5·00	4·50	110	70	72
1887	19·39	126	1·79	61	6·00	5·00	127	74	73
1888	16·53	107	1·19	40	4·75	4·00	101	77	75
1889	16·28	106	1·34	45	5·00	3·75	101	77	74
1890	16·82	109	1·94	66	6·00	4·50	122	77*	75
1891	14·83*	96	1·87	63	4·75	3·75	98	77	76
1892	13·48	87	1·83	62	4·50	3·75	96	79	74
1893	12·20	79	1·49	51	4·00	3·25	84	77	75
1894	10·39	67	1·00	34	{2·75, 2·50}	{2·00, 1·75}	55*	67	72
1895	11·71	76	1·23	42	2·25	1·90	54	71	72
1896	11·14	72	1·90	64	3·25	2·40	73	74	71
1897	9·98	65	1·65	56	2·10	1·80	50	69	71
1898	10·41	68	1·55	53	2·15	1·70	50	69	71
1899	17·34	112	2·00	68	2·25	1·90	54	76	74
1900	17·82	116	2·70	92	4·40	4·00	108	79	76
1901	14·35	93	1·95	66	2·75	2·35	66	80	77
1902	19·89	129	2·37	80	3·00	2·60	72	82	79
1903	17·75	115	3·00	102	4·00	3·20	93	84	80
1904	13·34	87	1·75	59	2·75	2·35	66	81	81
1905	15·96	103	2·26	77	3·50	3·00	84	83	82
1906	18·84	122	2·75	93	4·00	3·50	97	84	85
1907	22·49	146	2·90	98	{4·90, 4·75}	{4·10, 4·00}	116*	88*	89

Table I—continued

Date	Selling price of composite pig iron		Selling price of Connellsville coke		Selling price of Lake Superior iron ore			Relative hourly wages of blast furnace men	Index of general prices
	Average price, $ per ton (2240 lb.)	Index number	Average price, $ per short ton (2000 lb.)	Index number	Average price, $ per ton (2240 lb.)		Index number		
					Bessemer	Non-Bessemer			
	(1)	(2)	(3)	(4)	(5)	(6)	(7)	(8)	(9)
1908	16·02	104	1·80	61	4·25	3·50	103	85	89
1909	16·23	105	2·00	68	4·25	3·50	103	83	93
1910	15·55	101	2·10	71	4·75	4·00	116	87	97
1911	14·00	91	1·72	58	4·25	3·50	103	89	96
1912	14·82	96	1·92	65	3·50	2·85	84	92	99
1913	15·42	100	2·95	100	4·15	3·40	100	100	100
1914	13·52	88	2·00	68	3·50	2·85	84	101	101
1915	14·15	92	1·80	61	3·45	2·80	83	101	103
1916	20·31	132	2·58	88	4·20	3·55	103	—	116
1917	39·99	259	6·25	212	5·70	5·05	142	156	140
1918	34·38	223	7·25	246	5·99	5·44	151	—	164
1919	29·91	194	4·70	159	6·20	5·55	156	250	186
1920	43·80	284	8·30	281	7·20	6·55	182	283	213
1921	24·05	156	4·07	138	6·20	5·55	156	—	178
1922	25·00	162	7·15	242	5·70	5·05	142	191	170
1923	27·15	177	5·90	200	6·20	5·55	156	—	181
1924	—	—	3·85	131	5·40	4·75	134	254	—
1925	—	—	3·67	125	(4·40)	4·25	120	—	—
1926	—	—	—	—	(4·40)	4·25	120	—	—

N.B. Index numbers are all to the base 1913 = 100. Figures in brackets estimated.

Note. In the years marked by an asterisk * splices were effected between different series of prices.

(1) The composite product is made up as follows:

1883–91: 1 ton Bessemer pig at Pittsburgh.
1 ton Gray Forge (Lake Ore) at Pittsburgh.
1 ton Gray Forge at Philadelphia.

1891: The standard composite of the American metal market.

(2) The ore prices are quoted "delivered at Lake Erie Dock"; from 1883 to 1894 they refer to "Old Range", since 1894 to Mesabi ores. In 1907 there was a change in the natural iron content of the ore quoted as base and the Bessemer was again changed in 1925.

(3) The wage index is taken from the bulletins of the United States Bureau of Labour Statistics, the early series being spliced with the later in 1907. From 1883 to 1890, however, the index has been extended by means of the Pitts-

Table II
Distribution of the expenses of the manufacture of pig iron

Date	Selling price index (1)	Cost of ore at current prices (2)	Cost of coke		Cost of labour		Margin for other expenses	
			At current prices (3)	At 1913 prices (4)	At current prices (5)	At 1913 prices (6)	At current prices (7)	At 1913 prices (8)
1883	130	55	—	76·9	15·4	20·0	29·6	37·5
1884	118	52	28·2	74·3	14·8	19·2	23·0	30·3
1885	105	47	29·4	71·7	**(13·7)**	**(18·5)**	14·9	20·4
1886	112	55	31·8	69·1	12·4	17·7	12·8	17·8
1887	126	64	40·6	66·5	12·6	17·0	8·8	12·1
1888	107	51	25·5	63·9	12·5	16·2	18·0	24·0
1889	106	51	**27·6**	**61·3**	**11·9**	**15·4**	15·5	21·0
1890	109	61	38·7	58·7	11·8	15·3	− 2·5	− 3·3
1891	96	49	35·4	56·1	11·8	15·3	− 0·2	− 0·3
1892	87	48	33·2	53·5	12·0	15·2	− 6·2	− 8·4
1893	79	43	26·0	50·9	11·6	15·1	− 0·6	− 0·8
1894	67	28	16·4	48·3	10·0	15·0	12·6	17·5
1895	76	27	19·2	45·7	10·6	15·0	19·2	26·7
1896	72	37	26·7	43·1	11·0	14·9	− 2·7	− 3·8
1897	65	25	22·7	40·5	10·2	14·8	7·1	10·0
1898	68	25	20·1	37·9	10·2	14·8	12·7	17·9
1899	112	27	**24·0**	**35·3**	**11·2**	**14·7**	49·8	67·3
1900	116	54	33·3	36·2	10·9	13·8	17·8	23·4
1901	93	33	24·5	37·1	10·3	12·9	25·2	32·7
1902	129	36	30·4	38·0	9·8	12·0	52·8	66·8
1903	115	47	39·7	38·9	9·3	11·1	19·0	23·8
1904	87	33	**23·5**	**39·8**	**8·3**	**10·2**	22·2	27·4
1905	103	42	31·0	40·3	8·5	10·2	21·5	26·2
1906	122	49	38·0	40·9	8·6	10·2	26·4	31·1
1907	146	58	40·7	41·5	8·9	10·1	38·4	43·2
1908	104	52	25·7	42·1	8·6	10·1	17·7	19·9
1909	105	52	**29·0**	**42·7**	**8·4**	**10·1**	15·6	16·8
1910	101	58	29·5	41·6	8·4	9·7	5·1	5·3
1911	91	52	28·5	40·6	8·2	9·2	2·3	2·4
1912	96	42	25·7	39·6	8·1	8·8	20·2	20·4
1913	100	50	38·4	38·4	8·3	8·3	3·3	3·3
1914	88	42	**25·4**	**37·4**	**8·0**	**7·9**	12·6	12·5
1915	92	42	22·7	37·2	8·1	8·0	19·2	18·6
1916	132	52	32·4	36·9	—	8·1	—	—
1917	259	71	77·8	36·7	13·0	8·3	97·2	69·4
1918	223	76	89·5	36·4	—	8·4	—	—
1919	194	78	**57·6**	**36·2**	**21·4**	**8·5**	37·0	19·9
1920	284	91	—	—	—	—	—	—
1921	156	78	—	—	—	—	—	—
1922	162	71	—	—	—	—	—	—
1923	177	78	—	—	—	—	—	—
1924	—	67	—	—	—	—	—	—
1925	—	60	—	—	—	—	—	—
1926	—	60	—	—	—	—	—	—

Note. (a) The weights assigned to coke and labour shown by black figures have been computed from the federal census returns except in 1885 when labour is weighted according to the reports of 121 establishments in Pennsylvania. The weights for intermediate years have been obtained by interpolation.

(b) Ore is assigned a constant weight corresponding to a cost at 1913 prices of 50 units, i.e. equivalent to 7 tons of Lake Ore for the 6½ tons of pig iron in the selling price index.

Figures in brackets estimated.

Table III

Index numbers of prices and costs of pig iron

Date	Selling price of composite iron		Selling price corrected for labour, materials, and general prices		Pig iron produced in the United States (1000 tons)	
	Annual average	Five years' moving average	Annual average	Five years' moving average	Annually	Five years' moving average
	(1)	(2)	(3)	(4)	(5)	(6)
1883	130	—	184	—	4,596	4,301
1884	118	—	174	—	4,098	4,608
1885	105	118	161	164	4,045	4,967
1886	112	114	155	158	5,683	5,346
1887	126	111	146	153	6,417	6,047
1888	107	112	154	145	6,490	7,079
1889	106	109	148	138	7,604	7,598
1890	109	101	121	131	9,203	8,146
1891	96	95	121	123	8,280	8,273
1892	87	88	110	120	9,157	8,084
1893	79	81	115	123	7,125	8,133
1894	67	76	131	119	6,657	8,201
1895	76	72	137	120	9,446	8,300
1896	72	70	104	124	8,623	9,230
1897	65	79	115	131	9,653	10,623
1898	68	87	131	128	11,774	11,491
1899	112	91	167	133	13,621	12,942
1900	116	104	123	144	13,789	14,576
1901	93	113	130	142	15,878	15,823
1902	129	108	167	134	17,821	16,399
1903	115	105	124	135	18,009	18,239
1904	87	111	127	135	16,497	20,125
1905	103	115	127	131	22,992	21,717
1906	122	112	132	131	25,304	21,303
1907	146	116	145	129	25,781	23,162
1908	104	116	122	125	15,936	24,025
1909	105	109	120	119	25,795	23,693
1910	101	99	107	114	27,304	24,482
1911	91	99	102	110	23,650	27,488
1912	96	95	119	107	29,727	26,996
1913	100	93	100	109	30,966	27,518
1914	88	102	108	—	23,332	30,675
1915	92	134	114	—	29,916	32,454
1916	132	159	—	—	39,435	34,072
1917	259	180	164	—	38,621	35,608
1918	223	218	—	—	39,055	37,010
1919	194	—	115	—	31,015	32,461
1920	284	—	—	—	36,926	30,181
1921	—	—	—	—	16,688	—
1922	—	—	—	—	27,220	—
1923	—	—	—	—	40,361	—
1924	—	—	—	—	31,406	—
1925	—	—	—	—	36,701	—

Table IV

Active and idle blast furnaces in the United States, 1880–1925

(From the *Annual Reports* of the Iron and Steel Institute and its predecessor)

Date Dec. 31	Active	Idle	Total	Per cent active
1880	446	170	616	72
1881	445	176	621	72
1882	417	185	602	69
1883	307	291	598	51
1884	236	348	584	40
1885	276	315	591	47
1886	331	246	577	57
1887	339	244	583	58
1888	332	257	589	56
1889	344	226	570	60
1890	311	251	562	54
1891	313	256	569	53
1892	253	311	564	45
1893	137	381	518	26
1894	185	326	511	36
1895	242	226	468	52
1896	159	311	470	34
1897	191	232	423	45
1898	202	212	414	49
1899	289	125	414	70
1900	232	174	406	57
1901	266	140	406	66
1902	307	105	412	75
1903	182	243	425	43
1904	261	168	429	61
1905	313	111	424	70
1906	340	89	429	79
1907	167	276	443	38
1908	236	222	458	52
1909	338	130	468	72
1910	206	267	473	44
1911	231	234	465	50
1912	313	153	466	67
1913	205	257	462	44
1914	164	287	451	36
1915	310	135	445	70
1916	333	115	448	75
1917	339	116	455	75
1918	360	99	459	77
1919	280	173	453	62
1920	216	236	452	48
1921	125	325	450	28
1922	263	186	449	59
1923	239	193	432	55
1924	235	190	425	55
1925	238	157	395	60
1926	—	—	—	—

Note. (a) Prior to 1908 the totals refer to furnaces completed on December 31 of each year, since 1908 furnaces in process of rebuilding are included. (b) "Abandoned" furnaces are not counted: in 1885 the list of furnaces was revised and eighty-five furnaces which had been "wholly unproductive for many years" dropped. I have, therefore, deducted eighty-five from the original returns for 1880–4 to obtain comparable figures.

Table V

Size of blast furnace establishments, 1869–1923

Census year	Establishments		Wage earners		Physical product		Wage earners per establishment		Physical product per establishment	
	Number	Percent. of increase	Total (average number)	Percent. of increase	Amount (thousands of tons)	Percent. of increase	Actual number	Index number	Actual amount (tons)	Index number
1869	386	—	27,554	—	1,833	—	71	100·0	4,749	100·0
1879	341	− 11·7	41,695	51·3	3,376	84·2	122	171·8	9,900	208·4
1889	304	− 10·9	33,415	− 19·9	8,845	162·0	110	154·9	29,095	612·6
1899	223	− 26·6	39,241	17·4	14,448	63·3	176	247·9	64,789	1,364·2
1904	190	− 14·8	35,078	− 10·6	16,624	15·1	185	260·5	87,495	1,842·3
1909	208	9·5	38,429	9·6	25,652	54·3	185	260·5	123,327	2,596·9
1914	160	− 23·1	29,356	− 23·6	23,270	− 9·3	183	257·7	145,438	3,062·4
1919	195	21·9	41,660	41·9	30,543	31·3	214	301·4	156,631	3,298·1
1921	134	− 31·3	18,698	− 55·1	16,618	− 45·6	139	195·8	124,018	2,611·5
1923	169	26·1	36,712	96·3	40,163	141·7	217	305·6	237,650	5,004·2

Note. The table has been taken from *United States Census Monograph*, III, p. 59, and brought up to date from the biennial census returns.

INDEX